Screening Divinity

Titles available in the series
Rome *Season Two: Trial and Triumph*
Edited by Monica S. Cyrino
Ben-Hur: *The Original Blockbuster*
Jon Solomon
Cowboy Classics: The Roots of the American Western in the Epic Tradition
Kirsten Day
STARZ Spartacus: *Reimagining an Icon on Screen*
Edited by Antony Augoustakis and Monica S. Cyrino
Ancient Greece on British Television
Edited by Fiona Hobden and Amanda Wrigley
Epic Heroes on Screen
Edited by Antony Augoustakis and Stacie Raucci
Designs on the Past: How Hollywood Created the Ancient World
Lloyd Llewellyn-Jones
Screening the Golden Ages of the Classical Tradition
Edited by Meredith E. Safran
Screening Divinity
Lisa Maurice

Forthcoming Titles
Pontius Pilate on Screen: Soldier, Sinner, Superstar
Christopher M. McDonough
Screening Antiquity in the War on Terror
Alex McAuley
Battlestar Galactica: *An American* Aeneid *for the Twenty-First Century*
Meredith E. Safran

Visit the series website at: https://edinburghuniversitypress.com/series-screening-antiquity.html

Screening Divinity

Lisa Maurice

EDINBURGH
University Press

Edinburgh University Press is one of the leading university presses in the UK. We publish academic books and journals in our selected subject areas across the humanities and social sciences, combining cutting-edge scholarship with high editorial and production values to produce academic works of lasting importance. For more information visit our website: edinburghuniversitypress.com

© Lisa Maurice, 2019, 2021

First published in hardback by Edinburgh University Press 2019

Edinburgh University Press Ltd
The Tun – Holyrood Road
12(2f) Jackson's Entry
Edinburgh EH8 8PJ

Typeset in 11/13 Sabon by
Servis Filmsetting Ltd, Stockport, Cheshire

A CIP record for this book is available from the British Library

ISBN 978 1 4744 2573 5 (hardback)
ISBN 978 1 4744 2574 2 (paperback)
ISBN 978 1 4744 2575 9 (webready PDF)
ISBN 978 1 4744 2576 6 (epub)

The right of Lisa Maurice to be identified as the author of this work has been asserted in accordance with the Copyright, Designs and Patents Act 1988, and the Copyright and Related Rights Regulations 2003 (SI No. 2498).

Contents

List of Illustrations

Series Editors' Preface

Screening Antiquity is a new series of cutting-edge academic monographs and edited volumes that present exciting and original research on the reception of the ancient world in film and television. It provides an important synergy of the latest international scholarly ideas about the onscreen conception of antiquity in popular culture and is the only book series to focus exclusively on screened representations of the ancient world.

The interaction between cinema, television, and historical representation is a growing field of scholarship and student engagement; many Classics and Ancient History departments in universities worldwide teach cinematic representations of the past as part of their programmes in Reception Studies. Scholars are now questioning how historical films and television series reflect the societies in which they were made, and speculate on how attitudes towards the past have been moulded in the popular imagination by their depiction in the movies. Screening Antiquity explores how these constructions came about and offers scope to analyse how and why the ancient past is filtered through onscreen representations in specific ways. The series highlights exciting and original publications that explore the representation of antiquity onscreen, and that employ modern theoretical and cultural perspectives to examine screened antiquity, including: stars and star text, directors and *auteurs*, cinematography, design and art direction, marketing, fans, and the online presence of the ancient world.

The series aims to present original research focused exclusively on the reception of the ancient world in film and television. In itself this is an exciting and original approach. There is no other book series that engages head-on with both big screen and small screen recreations of the past, yet their integral interactivity is clear to see: film popularity has a major impact on television productions and, for its part, television regularly influences cinema (including film spin-offs of popular television series). This is the first academic series to identify and encourage the holistic interactivity of these two major media institutions, and the first to promote interdisciplinary research in all the fields of Cinema Studies, Media Studies, Classics, and Ancient History.

Screening Antiquity explores the various facets of onscreen creations of the past, exploring the theme from multiple angles. Some volumes will foreground a Classics 'reading' of the subject, analysing the nuances of film and television productions against a background of ancient literature, art, history, or culture; others will focus more on Media 'readings', by privileging the onscreen creation of the past or positioning the film or television representation within the context of modern popular culture. A third 'reading' will allow for a more fluid interaction between both the Classics and Media approaches. All three methods are valuable, since Reception Studies demands a flexible approach whereby individual scholars, or groups of researchers, foster a reading of an onscreen 'text' particular to their angle of viewing.

Screening Antiquity represents a major turning point in that it signals a better appreciation and understanding of the rich and complex interaction between the past and contemporary culture, and also of the lasting significance of antiquity in today's world.

Monica S. Cyrino and Lloyd Llewellyn-Jones
Series Editors

Acknowledgements

For me, as for many people, screen divinities were a part of my cinematic experience, albeit one to which I was not particularly sensitive at the time. But as a child I remember going to Universal Studios in California and squealing with excitement as the tour bus drove through the parting of the Red Sea, while Christmas and Easter holidays were marked by the screening of ancient and Biblical epics on television. When Charlton Heston received the Ten Commandments, and Ben-Hur saw the light – although I was Jewish, I recognised the trope – all was right with the world. Then in 2014 I went to the cinema with my husband and youngest daughter to see *Exodus: Gods and Kings*. When we came out, I knew that I had just witnessed something radically different from the epic films with which I had grown up, and I knew that I wanted to find out more about what had happened to the world and the movies.

Since I am lucky enough to be working within the field of Classical Reception, I had a head start, and the project grew, fuelled by the enthusiasm of those with whom I discussed it. My colleagues at Bar-Ilan University are a pleasure and an honour to work with, and I am grateful for their support at all times. From the start Monica Cyrino and Lloyd Llewellyn-Jones were inspiring and supportive, encouraging me to work on the project further. Others at the Film and History conferences in Milwaukee, and the Celtic Classics Conference in St Andrews, responded to the idea with excitement, and provided helpful feedback on the material presented in two of the chapters of this book. Various people read and edited the work with an eagle eye, and a devoted attention to detail, that were second to none. Finally, the wonderful staff at Edinburgh University Press have been a delight, and I am eternally grateful for their professionalism and their patience with me and with this project.

On a more personal level, there are a few other people I must thank: this book is dedicated to my parents, who never wavered in their support and encouragement of my strange fascination with people who died two thousand years ago. My mother passed away fifteen years ago, aged 56, but her influence lives on. During the course of writing this book, my father became terminally ill, emigrated in order to move in and live with us, and passed away, all within six months. The time spent caring for him slowed down the pace of writing, but ultimately also inspired it; when faced with death, and in hospitals and hospices, one spends more time contemplating God than is usually the case, making the subject matter that I was pondering more poignant than it had been. The incredible support I received from my family and friends at this time was also a reminder of the strength of human bonds, for which I am deeply grateful.

Thoughts of the Almighty are not – or should not be – confined to moments of sadness, however. It is in happiness that we also give thanks for our blessings, of which I have many; a devoted husband, four amazing children, all married to wonderful life-partners who are as beloved to me as their spouses. Finally, there are the two most perfect grandsons in the world, the elder of which was born, three weeks early, in October 2016, as I touched down in the USA on my way to the Film and History Conference, and who provide me with the greatest joy imaginable.

To all the above, who remain innocent of all faults in this work: *bene fecisti; gratiam habeo maximam.*

To my parents
Anne Lebetkin (1946–2003) David Lebetkin (1945–2018)
who both left school at the age of fifteen, but who ensured that I
was able to take advantage of things of which they were deprived
and to receive the best education available.

1 Screening Divinity: Introduction

BIBLE FILMS AND FANTASY MOVIES: TWO SIDES OF ONE COIN

Two kinds of film, fantasy films and religious/Biblical epics and biopics, are considered in this work. At first glance, these are two very different kinds of production, seemingly with little in common, other than the fact that both often fall into the category of epic movies. Each, indeed, has been the subject of considerable independent scholarship. Film and theology has in fact developed as a branch of research in its own right in recent decades. John Lyden has even argued that popular films perform a religious function in our culture, providing values and ways in which to view the world. He illustrates how films provide collective myths that answer the challenge of cultural anxieties and hopes, and catharsis in the form of rewarded heroes and punished villains.[1] With the development of film and theology as an area of research, theoretical foundations are gradually being established.[2]

The focus of this field was originally on Christianity and, to a lesser extent, Judaism. Concentrating on Biblical epics and biopics, such research centred on the intersection between the Bible, theology and cinema, studying retellings of Biblical stories on film in their social contexts, according to the understanding that these films reflect the issues and trends that are important to the film makers who created them. Such studies apply a range of theoretical approaches, including formalism, expressionism, realism, textual analysis, contextual analysis, postmodern eclecticism, narrative criticism and cultural studies. They focus on the movies that depict events from the Old Testament, with their heroic figures such as Moses, David, Esther and Solomon, or on the retellings of Jesus and early Christianity, as well as how elements of the Bible epic have permeated a far wider range of movies that are unrelated in subject matter to the genre.[3] More recent years have seen an expansion of the field to include other world religions as well, as is reflected by works such as *The Routledge Companion to Religion and Film*, which includes chapters on Islam, Buddhism, Hinduism, postcolonial religious syncretism and new religious movements.[4]

Examinations of pagan gods have not so far been included in this research, and studies of fantasy films, in which Greek gods and heroes feature, have fallen into a different category, usually that of classical reception studies, although they may feature as well in more general works on epic movies and in film studies. Such investigations place emphasis on the continued importance of the Graeco-Roman tradition in the modern world, considering how modern screen texts interact with the cultural heritage of classical antiquity, and try to examine reasons for the tradition's continued popularity. In particular, the importance of classical myth as a medium for critiquing Western narratives is stressed by Monica Cyrino and Meredith Safran, who point out that 'the authority of classical antiquity is still mobilized as a medium for working out contemporary preoccupations' on the modern mythic screen.[5]

Biblical films and fantasy movies are rarely considered together in film studies or in classical reception, unless as subsets of general works on epic movies. The connection between the two genres was touched upon by Cyrino and Safran in the third section of *Classical Myth on Screen*, 'Negotiating the Cosmic Divide', which looks at 'the problematic gap between mortals and immortals and the modern conceptualization of ancient divinities from mortal perspectives'.[6] The papers in this section present case studies in which the traditional divisions between mythology and scripture start to be breached.

This is just a beginning, however, and aims only to consider some individual presentations of ancient religious figures, within the context of cinematic mythmaking. The present work elaborates on these ideas and expands and develops them more fully.[7] In particular, it places an emphasis upon both audience reception and directorial intent, and draws on structuralist and anthropological theory, as well as recent work done on theology and film. For there is, in fact, far more connecting Bible films and mythological movies than the epic genre; no matter what the name of the deity on screen, the film makers are all presenting the divine, and we are all 'god-watching', when viewing these films, which I would suggest are a genre all of their own, which might be termed 'divinity movies'.

Mythologies and belief systems underpin all societies, and these underlying ideologies show up most clearly in the depiction of other mythological and theological systems. In presenting a deity on screen, certain assumptions underlie the depiction, whether it is of a god whose authority and divinity are accepted by some or all of the audience, or one who is regarded as no more than a pagan fantasy. Those assumptions alter according to time, place, personal bias, societal trends and much more. Yet the questions of what makes gods divine, in the eyes of film maker and audience, and how their interaction in the world is to be viewed, may be considered more clearly through a comparison of the portrayals in the two different genres. Moreover, modern Western society is built on two main foundations, the Graeco-Roman and the Judaeo-Christian, which have combined and intertwined to produce the cultural heritage that underpins our world. An investigation of the two kinds of films is an opportunity to examine the complex relationship between them, and untangle the threads of ideology at various points throughout the twentieth and twenty-first centuries.

In addition, the overlap of central subject matter, namely the interaction between humankind and a deity, allows for some interesting comparisons with regard to genre, by investigating how far genre and subject matter are related, and what elements actually define a particular genre. An example of such an issue is the question of whether a Biblical epic, containing representations of features such as miracles, is, in the eyes of a non-believer, a fantasy movie. Explorations such as this provide insight into the whole nature of genre.

In order to focus the work and keep it to a manageable length, some limitations have been necessary. First of all, this book only includes silent movies in the most minimal way, with the project focusing on the mid-twentieth century onwards.[8] Further, the focus is almost entirely on English-language works, the only exceptions being those in other languages that were widely released in the UK and USA over this period. Another regrettable but necessary limitation is the exclusion of Islamic movies, on which there is also a considerable amount of academic writing;[9] nevertheless, the less central role of Islam in Western civilisation, at least until recent years, drove the decision to leave this fascinating area for future research. Even with the narrower focus on Judaeo-Christianity, the depiction of divinity in both films on classical mythology and those on religious themes communicates ideas about how the West thinks of, and presents, deities and the human relationship with the divine, with the portrayal in movies that deal with overtly religious themes colouring that in depictions of the pagan gods, and vice versa.

THE ANCIENT MYTHOLOGICAL AND BIBLICAL WORLDS ON SCREEN

Since the very beginning of the cinematic age, the ancient world has provided an attractive source of material for film makers, in the form of both the Graeco-Roman traditions and texts, and those sacred to Judaism or Christianity. The pull of 'colourful costumes, classical architecture, and military heroics – the vaguely familiar trappings of our past'[10] was strong, and productions based on ancient history, classical mythology and the Bible have appeared in vast numbers at various periods in cinematic history, including the silent era, the Hollywood golden age of epic and the present century, periods in which epics were produced as 'self-conscious demonstrations of film's capabilities in cinematic virtuosity'.[11] As scholars have outlined, there are multiple reasons for the appeal of the ancient world to the modern screen – the larger-than-life spectacle, the powerful figures, the elements of fantasy, the exotic yet familiar nature of the characters, as well as the identification with those societies that were the root of our own.[12]

From the beginning, Graeco-Roman antiquity was regarded as brimming with sex, violence and grand narrative, with the added bonus that, in the words of Sam Leith, it offered film makers 'a giant, out-of-copyright, myth kitty'.[13] Where this world overlapped with the Bible, an even greater pool of material became available. Not only was this materially unproblematic from a copyright point of view, it was also familiar, and, in the Production Code era, a permissible way to include more explicit material than could be used in a modern setting.

The first movies set in the ancient world, in the silent era, were influenced not only by performing arts such as drama and opera, but also by art and literature. The written word in particular was an important source, including most prominently the best-selling book of all time, namely the Bible.[14] Early epic films were also often based on popular historical novels; books such as *Quo Vadis*, *The Life and Passion of Jesus Christ* and *Ben-Hur* provided fertile soil in which to plant cinematic seed.[15] Even these were usually tales of early Christianity, coated in the titillating guise of ancient Rome in all its wicked and decadent glory, and beyond these novels the ancient world was a treasury of mythic plots, Bible stories and tales that, as the staples of education in the nineteenth and early twentieth centuries, were easily recognisable to viewers.

Later adaptations inevitably looked back not only to the written fictional sources but also to these earlier screen productions,[16] which set the tone for the 'ancient' movie. This included those set in ancient Rome, both Christian and pagan, those based on mythology and even Biblical epics, and those set in other ancient cultures such as Egypt, so that often the typical *mise en scène* is a mixed picture, composed of motley elements including pillars, gold, pools, elaborate palaces, cloaks and, of course, swords and sandals.[17]

In making these movies, film makers searched for a vehicle with which to parade the latest technical advances, whether widescreen projection and Technicolor in the 1950s or computer-generated imagery in the twenty-first century. Epic films set in the ancient world have come and gone over the past century in a recurring cycle[18] under the impetus of such technology, but also in response to the ideas and needs of current society, as movies both consciously and unconsciously reacted to and critiqued contemporary issues through the lens of the past, reflecting social and cultural trends and currents. Winkler describes this phenomenon, as he talks of cinema's role as a 'cultural seismograph', in which different kinds of films reveal tensions and issues that resonate with the society producing the movie, rather than that of past times represented on screen.[19] There are many examples of this kind of cultural projection onto films; Winkler mentions expressionist films reflecting the instability in Germany after the First World War, and montage cinema as an expression of feelings in post-revolutionary Russia, amongst other examples.

Such projections are not confined to movies featuring the pagan world; those dealing with tales from the Old Testament or Jesus, as reflections of faiths still followed by people today, display the attitudes and beliefs of their creators just as strongly. Indeed, any portrayal of the events central to Judaism or Christianity has to take into account a myriad of issues. As W. Barnes Tatum stresses, with regard to movies about Jesus, a cinematic version must be 'not only *cinematically* interesting, but *literarily* sensitive to the gospel sources, *historically* probable, and *theologically* satisfying'.[20] By this is meant that the production is complicated by the fact that the Gospels themselves, the main source of evidence for the existence and life of Jesus, are literary documents, whose historical accuracy is a matter for debate. The same of course can be said of productions centring on the Old Testament; in both cases the theological aspect of the issue makes any portrayal a potential minefield for commercial film makers, whose aim is generally to entertain and, of course, make money. As products of contemporary culture, film portrayals must conform to the cinematic conventions of their era and genre,[21] but also reflect and influence wider societal issues and perceptions, not only of religion but also of contemporaneous ideals, heroism, virtues, vices and more.[22] In particular, Jesus in Hollywood cinema is 'the American icon', so that such films are projections of American mythology and self-identity.[23] As hagiopics, such movies deal with the intersection of the divine figure himself, the world in which he lived and the Christian (or other) tradition in the receiving society producing the picture. Thus both Biblical and mythological movies that feature divinities will, by their very nature, provide insight into the place and status of religion in society, and therefore give a fascinating window onto the changing values and ideas of modern society.

PERCEIVING DIVINITIES, PAST AND PRESENT

The question of how gods are, and have been, perceived by the different societies of the ancient classical world and those following them, right up to the present day, is, of course, one that has troubled philosophers and thinkers for millennia. Discussion of the topic here aims to do no more than present a whistle-stop tour of some of the major issues and ideas that have evolved in the Graeco-Roman, Jewish and Christian traditions throughout history, each of which not only is the subject of a vast body of scholarship of its own, but has also influenced film makers at various junctures.

The Graeco-Roman Gods

GODS IN THE GRAECO-ROMAN TRADITION
Any movie dealing with ancient Greece and Rome must decide how to portray the polytheism that was such a part of those societies; movies based on mythological themes often portray gods and their interaction with mankind, and such depictions reveal a great deal about the contemporary beliefs and relationship with the divine. So who were these gods? What role did they play in ancient societies? And how were they received from ancient times until our own day?

To the modern eye, the Greek gods seem remarkably ungodlike. They behave in capricious and even immoral ways, they have petty quarrels and torrid love affairs with other gods and with mortals, and their behaviour seems frivolous in the extreme. These anthropomorphic gods:

> look and act like humans. . . . Their beauty is beyond that of ordinary mortals, their passions more grand and intense, their sentiments more praiseworthy and touching; and they can embody and impose the loftiest moral values in the universe. Yet these same gods can mirror the physical and spiritual weaknesses of human counterparts: they can be lame and deformed or vain, petty, and insincere; they can steal, lie, and cheat, sometimes with a finesse that is exquisitely divine.
>
> The gods usually live in houses on Mt. Olympus or in heaven. . . . They eat and drink, but their food is ambrosia and their wine nectar. Ichor (a substance clearer than blood) flows in their veins. Just as they can feel the gamut of human emotion, so too they can suffer physical pain and torment.[24]

Mighty and larger than life, they are not, however, omnipotent or omniscient, or even all-virtuous. Their defining characteristic is, as Bowra stresses, power.[25] According to Vernant's reading, this power was what defined them as gods, and each god represented a different kind of force or power.[26] Thus, for example, Zeus is the power of the thunderbolt and of the rule of law, Ares is the power of battle-frenzy and Aphrodite is the force of sexual love. What set the gods apart from humanity was not their wisdom, perfection, benevolence or goodness, but their might. The gods were the powerful lords of this earth, who controlled the forces of nature, bringing or withholding rain, sending and curing illness, bringing about victory or defeat in war. Much of ancient Greek religion is centred on communal attempts to appease the gods, with the emphasis not on individual salvation but on communal survival, not in a world to come, but in this world.

Although the gods may look and act like humans, however, there is a fundamental difference between mankind and these deities, namely that the gods are immortal and never ageing, eternally beautiful. This is in contrast to humans, who can never achieve everlasting life, a fact which in itself lends gravity and indeed, meaning, to mortal life, in a way that cannot be experienced by divine existence. Greek myth places great emphasis on the inevitability of human suffering, making the mortal perspective on life far removed from that of the gods, and, in Greek eyes, fascinating to the divine beings themselves. As Harris and Platzner summarise:

> The gods possess everything that the Greek male desires or admires – eternal youth, good looks, honor, reputation, power and the uninhibited assertion of individual selfhood. For all their superiority to mortals, however, the gods are

driven by the same kind of competitive ambition and jealous regard for their prerogatives that ruin the mental peace of human leaders. Worshipping divine beings who were largely projections of their own idealized (and fallible) selves, the Greeks created myths in which the gods are almost as fascinated by human activities as their mortal subjects are intrigued by gods. [27]

Despite these myths, in which the gods often play less than virtu-ous roles, it should not be assumed that the Greeks did not honour, fear and worship their deities. The connection and interplay between myth and religion are complicated and seem foreign to contemporary eyes. In the Greek mind, there was a wide gap between human and divine, with mankind far below the gods in the world view and struc-ture. There was an understanding that just as gods could transform their appearance into that of other creatures or objects – a bull, a swan, a shower – so their appearance in human form was just that, an appearance and no more. As Harris and Platzner comment:

> For all their anthropomorphism, the Greeks realised that the gods belonged to the *Other*, a dimension of reality profoundly different from the material realm to which humans are bound. Mysterious and unpredictable, the gods represent forces beyond human ability to control or comprehend ... They belong to an unknowable mode of existence intrinsically different from that of humanity.[28]

Despite this remoteness, the Greek gods are very present in the mortal world, interacting with humans in practical ways, even to the extent of intervening on the battlefield to protect favourites or harm their enemies. This is not a sign of weakness however; it is only the truly deserving – in classical terms, the heroic – who receive such blessings and aid from the gods. Assistance from a deity indeed marks a man out as a hero and shows him to be a great man, for to whom else would such powerful and mighty being show favour?

THE RECEPTION OF THE GODS IN WESTERN TRADITION

The Graeco-Roman concept of divinity is obviously at great variance with that of Christianity, a point that is reflective of the fact that their value systems also differed greatly. With the fall of Rome, and the decline in literacy as a result of political and social upheaval, the clas-sical texts which so centred on mythology were less widely known, while the Christian opposition to paganism weakened the position still further.[29] Nevertheless, classical myth did not disappear entirely, and in fact the attacks of the early Church Fathers such as Jerome and Augustine actually helped preserve the tales in the end.[30]

Classical mythology, therefore, continued to be a feature of life throughout the medieval and Renaissance periods, albeit in modified form. One approach to the difficulties of dealing with the figures of classical myth was to treat them as allegorical, or as broad archetypes, thus allowing them to be utilised and reinterpreted despite the altered philosophies and world view of the later age. Ovid's works in particular were recast and adapted as they were retold in a moralising mode that fitted in with Christian theology and beliefs, while Virgil's allusion to a child redeemer was understood as a prediction of the coming of Christ, allowing his works to be interpreted in an acceptable manner.

One method of interpretation was what was called 'fourfold allegory', which comprised simultaneous readings at different allegorical levels. Dante of course exemplifies this approach, but as David Brumble stresses, 'fourfold allegory is just one expression of the Medieval and Renaissance inclination to multiple interpretation',[31] which is found throughout the period in countless authors and works. From late antiquity onwards classical myths were taken as allegories of the resurrection of the soul, the triumph of virtue over evil, and ways to achieve everlasting life. These motifs appear in funerary art and manuscript illuminations, as well as on a wide range of objects, including mosaics, ivory plaques, boxes, silver work, pottery, and textiles, evidence that reflects the fact that the classical gods and heroes were everywhere to be found, even in the post-classical societies of the medieval period. Mythical handbooks, important for astrology and for magic, also abounded in the late Middle Ages.

Although the classical gods continued to feature in medieval society, it was Renaissance artists who restored their classical forms. Inspired by the ideas and forms of the classical past, artists attempted to create a universal and noble form of art, in keeping with the new and confident mood of the time. With the rebirth of Greek, artists such as Botticelli, Bellini, Titian, Michelangelo and Correggio found inspiration in classical mythology, and began to depict (often scandalous) stories from classical mythology, or contemporary rulers in the guise of pagan deities. Driven by the ideals of humanism, which placed emphasis on the individual, works of art now displayed a renewed interest in the human body, which had been excluded from art for a long time thanks to religious prudery, and which now found a new expression in the portrayal of the gods, goddesses and heroes of classical myth. The merging of the different strands allowed mythology, Christianity and humanism to co-exist peacefully, as reflected by Raphael's *Stanza della Segnatura* in the Vatican, where Apollo, surrounded by the Muses and the ancient classical poets, is presented in tandem with contemporary humanists, reflecting the perfect synthesis between classical mythology and Renaissance humanism.[32]

From the sixteenth to the nineteenth centuries, classical myth remained central to art, literature, drama and other expressions of culture in England, France, Germany and indeed throughout Europe, providing material for Dryden, Spenser, Rubens, Milton, Moreau and Goethe among others. The enduring centrality of classical poetry to education at this time meant that familiarity with classical myth continued, while it also featured strongly in drama, pageants and progresses, as well as in art and literature.[33] Mythology provided a common cultural language, appearing sometimes even in the light-hearted frivolity of works of Rococo art. In these cases, artists found 'the pink bodies of lovely young goddesses and plump cupids well suited to the pastel colors they preferred', while 'their pleasure-seeking sensibilities were piqued by the amorous pursuits of gods and goddesses, nymphs and satyrs'.[34]

The main attraction to classical myth, however, was in Neoclassicism. With the discovery and excavation of Herculaneum and Pompeii in the mid-eighteenth century, a great enthusiasm for all things classical arose. People were able to look directly not at Renaissance interpretations of the ancient world but at original art, statuary and buildings, and a wide passion grew for everything Graeco-Roman. Travel to Italy and Greece became fashionable, and a classical fervour swept Western Europe and North America. People wanted classical-style dishes, wallpaper, dresses and hairstyles, furniture, architecture and art.[35] Contemporary figures were depicted in art as Greek gods and heroes, one of the most famous examples being Horatio Greenough's statue of George Washington, clad and enthroned in the manner of Pheidias' statue of Zeus (see Figure 3.2 below). Thus classical myth retained its dominant position. This has continued through to the present day, in what Geoffrey Miles calls 'a continuous line of inheritance and influence' that connects the myths of ancient Greece with our own societies.[36]

Although classical mythology remained a constant feature, understandings and reactions to ancient myth varied over time. In the nineteenth and twentieth centuries, a number of approaches to understanding the classical gods emerged in scholarship, with debates as to the origins of these deities and the beliefs in them, the role they played in society, and the nature of their portrayals in the ancient world. The gods were no longer seen as true deities or allegories, but as projections of ideas and emotions. Research into the origin of myth produced a range of methodologies and ways of understanding them and their role in society.[37] Graeco-Roman gods in the Western tradition continued to exert philosophical influence, and to be regarded as having value; as one of Peter Shaffer's characters in *Amadeus* says to Mozart, when he attempts to write the gods out of opera: 'They go on forever – at least what they represent. The eternal in us, not the ephemeral.'[38] Such understandings ensured the gods' continuing presence, and ever-changing interpretations of their nature, for different purposes in literature, art and, of course, on screen as well. It is this last that is the focus of the present study, along with the screen depictions of the Judaeo-Christian God, to which we now turn.

The Monotheistic God in Western Civilisation

GRAECO-ROMAN PHILOSOPHICAL APPROACHES TO GOD

Western concepts of God have covered a wide range throughout history, from Aristotle to Spinoza and beyond. Despite this fact, for most of their history, the vast majority of members of Western societies have accepted some form of theism, i.e. the belief in a deity who is the creator and sustainer of the universe. This god, referred to in the masculine, although ostensibly sexless, is generally regarded as omniscient, omnipotent, omnipresent and morally flawless.

The question of the nature of God is one pertinent to both philosophers and religious thinkers, and both have grappled with it. Some philosophers have attempted to use philosophy, especially in the early Christian period, to strengthen their religion while others, in particular as rationality and secularism rose, have used it to reject belief in the divine. In the ancient world, as philosophy and science began to emerge, both Plato and Aristotle examined the concept of divinity, considering the role of gods in the creation of the world and its contents. Unlike earlier Greek philosophers, who regarded the world as eternal, Plato argued that the world was created, in which case there must also have been a creator who formed the world and everything in it from matter (although this matter was in itself pre-existing).[39] His theory is most clearly outlined in the *Timaeus*, where he presents

an elaborately wrought account of the formation of the universe. Plato is deeply impressed with the order and beauty he observes in the universe, and his project in the dialogue is to explain that order and beauty. The universe, he proposes, is the product of rational, purposive, and beneficent agency. It is the handiwork of a divine Craftsman ('Demiurge', *dêmiourgos*, 28a6), who, imitating an unchanging and eternal model, imposes mathematical order on a preexistent chaos to generate the ordered universe (*kosmos*). The governing explanatory principle of the account is teleological: the universe as a whole as well as its various parts are so arranged as to produce a vast array of good

effects. It strikes Plato strongly that this arrangement is not fortuitous, but
the outcome of the deliberate intent of Intellect (*nous*), anthropomorphically
represented by the figure of the Craftsman who plans and constructs a world
that is as excellent as its nature permits it to be.[40]

This creator of Plato's universe is not a divine intelligence or a personal ruler, but a craftsman. As such, he is not really compatible with
the Judaeo-Christian view of God. Plato's 'The Form of the Good',
which was the ultimate form from which every other form derived its
goodness, is perhaps closer to the idea of such a deity, but this force
was also impersonal, and without the paternalistic aspects seen in
both Judaism and Christianity's beliefs.

Aristotle's ideas concerning an ultimate being and creator differed
from those of Plato. With regard to the origin of the world, he postulated three kinds of substances, two of them being physical and one
being the unmovable. This last substance is metaphysical (the other
two being the 'sensible perishable' (matter) and the 'sensible eternal'
(potential)), and is the force that turns the potential into the actual.
This substance is the closest equivalent in Aristotle's thought to God.

Neither Plato nor Aristotle, despite these theories, was anything
close to being a monotheist in the sense that we understand the word.
Philo, however, a first-century CE Hellenistic Jew from Alexandria,
the centre of philosophy and learning, and a follower of the middle-Platonist school, did believe in one God as modern Jews and
Christians do. Influenced by the ideas of Plato and Pythagorean
scholars, as well as by Stoicism, the middle-Platonists conceived of a
three-level pattern to the world, with God as the supreme transcendent being. This being was the source for the *logos*, the image of God,
and the container of all ideas (inspired by Platonic Forms), which in
turn was the basis for the visible, corporeal level of the world.[41]

The transcendent being was called various names by different philosophers of the middle-Platonist school (e.g. God, the Monad, the
One), but all agreed that such a being existed, an element that explains
the attraction for a Jew such as Philo. He, therefore, attempted to
combine Jewish exegesis and Stoic philosophy through the use of
philosophical allegory. Philo's understanding of God, however, places
God even higher than other philosophers of the same school, for
Philo sees him as 'better than virtue, better than knowledge, better
than the Good itself, and the Beautiful itself'.[42] Such a transcendent
and perfect being could not have been involved directly in creating
the world, formed from limitless chaos; the world was therefore created by God's incorporeal powers. This depiction of God sees him as
omnipotent, omniscient and perfect, so much so that he is actually

unknowable, for he cannot be understood or named; he can only be comprehended by what he is not, rather than for what he is. His goodness is such that it is only his graciousness that enables humans to find favour, for He cares for the world and for humanity.

The thoughts of Philo and others from his school also influenced the Neo-Platonic philosophers, such as Plotinus (204/5–270 CE), who conceived of God as a being he calls 'the One', who is the source of the universe. Plotinus was unable to accept the idea of creation, since this would have entailed a conscious decision on the part of God, who would therefore be limited in some way. Thus, the world itself is the inevitable overflow of divinity, in a timeless process. As with Philo, to Plotinus, God can only be described negatively, in terms of what he is not. Despite this fact, Plotinus made a number of claims about the nature of God, identifying the 'One' with the concept of 'Good' and the principle of 'Beauty'.[43] Since, in Plotinus' eyes, it is not possible to connect with God intellectually, union with the divine is ecstatic and mystical. In this way, this philosophy also influenced a number of Christian mystics.

CHRISTIAN PERCEPTIONS OF GOD

As an offshoot of Judaism, Christianity was unequivocally mon-otheistic (despite its depiction of the Trinity, which it considered as multiplicity within unity) and regarded the world as a creation by God *ex nihilo*. Nevertheless, some early Christian thinkers had respect for philosophy, believing that the discipline contributed to an understanding of God. Clement of Alexandria, for example, saw philosophy as the covenant given to the Greeks, and as a stepping stone on the way to the true beliefs of Christianity.[44] Others, such as Justin Martyr (c. 100–c. 165 CE), saw compatibility between the ideas of Greek philosophy and those of Christianity, although others, like Tertullian (c. 160–c. 225 CE) rejected philosophy, believing that there could be no common ground between Jerusalem and Athens.

Augustine (354–430 CE) was one of the most important figures who merged Greek philosophy with Judaeo-Christian belief. According to Augustine, God is omniscient, omnipotent, omnipresent and morally perfect. He created the world as an act of love, *ex nihilo*, and sus-tains it still. Since God is good and God created the world, it follows that the world, and everything in it, is good; evil is merely the lack of good, and was not created as a separate force. It is not without purpose, however, but exists in order to show what is good, by way of contrast.

With the fusion of Platonic and Aristotelian theology with

Christianity, the perception of God as omnipotent, omniscient and benevolent became commonplace and central from that time on. In the medieval period, Anselm of Canterbury raised the perfect-being concept to new heights when he used it as the basis for his famous ontological argument, which asserts that God is the highest level of being and therefore perfect goodness.[45] Thomas Aquinas (c. 1225–74) laid down his Five Ways as proofs for the existence of God, and for his nature as perfection and as the guide of all purpose in the world.

William of Ockham (c. 1280–c. 1349), however, sharply opposed such ideas, arguing instead for fideism, i.e. that belief in God is a matter of faith alone, and his existence cannot be proved. Ockham also held that being omnipotent, there were no limits to what God could do, and therefore a person could perceive something by sheer act of divine will, even if it did not exist. Accordingly, faith and reason can be contradictory. Ockham's 'razor' sought to shave off unverifiable elements from explanations, and while Ockham himself was no atheist, this approach was later developed to remove ideas such as divine intention, and even, eventually, belief in God itself.

In the Renaissance, the connection between reason and faith grew weaker yet. With the rise of humanism, and its return to the texts of ancient Greece and Rome, and with the spread of the Reformation in Europe, there arose new ideas about divinity, in which the question of man's centrality and the role of free will were prominent. This is not to say that atheism became acceptable; even though the Renaissance and Reformation opened up new religious possibilities for believers, religious and political authorities nevertheless firmly controlled what they deemed to be heretical. Calvin, for example, emphasised the absolute sovereignty of God and the innate depravity of man, who is predestined for salvation or damnation and therefore lacking in free will.

Some philosophers, following in Occam's wake, emphasised fideism, that God could not be understood, or his existence proven, by reason, but only by faith. Others emphasised God's role in the world in light of the developing knowledge of the time. As interest in science developed, the mathematical regularity of the natural world was understood, as ideas such as Kepler's laws of planetary motion and Newton's laws were formulated. These discoveries, seeming to imply the exist of a supreme engineer, led to the idea of divine purpose taking a central role, for the world suddenly seemed far from random.

Ideas developed further with the discoveries of Galileo and

Copernicus, who introduced a separation between religion and science with their theories about the nature of the universe, which radically affected conceptions of the place of humans within this cosmos. In the infinitely large universe that Galileo postulated, the world, and mankind, were no longer at the centre of things and therefore the focal point of God's creative activity. With the physical universe regarded as potentially self-sustaining, a mechanistic explanation of the cosmos' operation, which did not rely on God's continual oversight and control, now became possible.

As reason came to the fore as the main source of knowledge, philosophy began to split from religion. René Descartes (1596–1650) famously sought to ground all knowledge on a foundation he could not doubt: that he was a thinking being. Seeking to prove that God exists and that he is the cause of our clear and distinct perception, by which we understand the world, Descartes argued that since we have an idea of God, as a necessary, perfect being, that idea must have been caused by God, since only he has the properties of perfection. Since God is the cause of the idea we have of him, he must, therefore, exist. God is omnipotent, perfect and, in some manner that is not entirely clear, the cause of all, including of himself.

Baruch Spinoza (1632–77) agreed with Descartes that clear and distinct ideas indeed reflect reality, but he asserted that for a concept of God to make any sense at all, God must simply be nature. God, he argued, cannot be something outside nature that controls it, but must necessarily be part of it. Although he was condemned as an atheist by both Jews and Christians (he was actually excommunicated by his Amsterdam Jewish community), Spinoza himself was very devoutly religious, and regarded any idea of anthropomorphism as an abomination, believing that nature is instead the true expression of God. These ideas continued to be refined in the early modern period by other philosophers of the Enlightenment. Kant, Hume and Hegel all addressed this issue as the philosophy of religion began to develop. Both sceptics, Hume critiqued the idea of miracles, and Kant the 'ontological argument' for God.[46] Hegel's philosophy, meanwhile, objected to traditional concepts of God, seeing the deity as the fullest reality, achieved through the self-determination of all things.

Until the nineteenth century, religion and science were generally seen to be compatible, with the Bible and nature both understood to be aspects of the same truth (God's word and God's works). From the 1860s onwards, however, as scientific discoveries, particularly those of geology, seemed to be at odds with the story of creation told in Genesis, the ways began to part.[47] It was in the nineteenth century that attempts were first made to construct a humanism that was separate from God. This atheist humanism was the source of contemporary atheism, which purports to have 'moved beyond God'.[48]

JEWISH UNDERSTANDINGS OF GOD

According to Jewish understanding, God is one, absolute, an indivisible and superlative being.[49] As well as the universal creator of the world, he is also specifically the god of Abraham, Isaac and Jacob and of their descendants, who delivered the children of Israel from the Egyptian slavery, gave them the Torah at Mount Sinai, and brought them safely to the land he had decreed was to be theirs. In addition to these universal and national aspects, God is also traditionally regarded as a personal deity, a father figure to the individual.

As a result of this personal element, Judaism holds that man and God can have a bi-directional relationship, whereby he has knowledge of and influence over individuals, by whom he may be directly addressed and accessed, making him unambiguously involved in the world.[50] As the contemporary thinker Rabbi Jonathan Sacks expresses it,

> Unlike the god of the philosophers, the God of Abraham is a *personal* God. He is not an abstract concept: the first cause, force of forces, the prime mover, the pure Being. He is a God who relates to us as persons, sensing our suffering, hearing our prayers, a presence in our lives.[51]

Edward Kessler summarises Sacks' position as arguing that God 'is not distant in time or detached, but passionately engaged and portrays an encounter with a God who cares passionately and who addresses humanity in the quiet moments of its existence'.[52] Jewish prayer, therefore, includes phrases such as 'our Father, our King' and whole verses acknowledging this special and personal connection, as in the Adon Olam ('Master of the Universe') prayer, which has been a regular part of the daily and Sabbath liturgy since the fifteenth century:

> He is my God, my living redeemer
> Rock of my affliction in hard times.
> He is my banner and protection,
> The measurement of my cup on the day I call.
> Into his hand I deposit my spirit
> At the time of sleep, and of wakefulness.
> And with my spirit, and with my body;
> The Lord is with me, I will not fear.[53]

As a strongly monotheistic religion, God's unity is central to Judaism, and held to be a tenet of faith; ideas such as the Trinity are antithetical and regarded as heretical by Orthodox Judaism, and have been for centuries, as reflected in Maimonides'*13 Principles of Faith*, the second of which runs:

> God, the Cause of all, is one. This does not mean one as in one of series, nor one like a species (which encompasses many individuals), nor one as in an object that is made up of many elements, nor as a single simple object that is infinitely divisible. Rather, God is a unity unlike any other possible unity.[54]

Because of this unity of God, there is little, according to the philosophy of Maimonides, that can be predicated of him, except his existence. This rationalist approach was followed by many Jewish thinkers, but other philosophies do exist, particularly in the realm of kabbalah, where there is a concept of the ten *sephirot*, often translated as 'attributes' or 'emanations' of God, through which he reveals himself and continuously creates both the physical realm and the chain of higher metaphysical realms ("Seder Hishtalshelut'). God himself is described as the 'Ein Sof ' meaning 'Infinite', and in this aspect represents a facet that lies beyond the *sephirot*. Thus, even according to this philosophy, God is no more able to be understood than he is held to be by the rationalist thinkers.[55] Within Judaism the idea that God may be experienced, but not understood, is a not uncommon position. This is based on the fact that God is utterly unlike man, who, as a corporeal being, cannot even truly conceive of or comprehend a creation without body or anything parallel to the human material experience of the world. The only way in which humans can think about such a god is in physical terms, through anthropomorphisation of the deity. How and why this occurs are the subject, therefore, to which we will now turn.

NOTES

1 Lyden (2003).
2 See e.g. Johnston (2000).
3 See e.g. Reinhartz (2013).
4 Lyden (2009).
5 Cyrino and Safran (2015: 6).
6 Ibid. 8.
7 The whole topic of the semi-divine figure of the hero, or demi-god, to which a whole book could easily be devoted, has, however, with considerable regret, been excluded, other than where it pertains directly to the question of divinity itself, for example in human–divine relationships, where the god interacts with his mortal offspring.
8 There is a growing body of research on silent moves. See in particular Wyke and Michelakis (2013).

9   Ramji (2003); (2009); Yorulmaz and Blizek (2014); Pak-Shiraz (2011).
10 Solomon (2001: xvii).
11 Llewellyn-Jones (2009: 564).
12 See e.g. Solomon (2001: 1–4).
13 Leith (2010), also quoted by Elliott (2014: 8).
14 Solomon (2001: 133).
15 Versions of *Quo Vadis* appeared in 1913 and 1925, of *Ben-Hur* in 1907 and 1925 and of *The Last Days of Pompeii* in 1900, 1908, 1913 and 1926.
16 See Elliott (2014: 6–7).
17 These last two are so ubiquitous they gave rise to the term 'sword-and-sandal movies' to describe them. Another popular term is 'peplum movies', derived from the short skirts worn by the characters in the films.
18 Ibid. 5–6.
19 See Winkler (2001: 15).
20 Tatum (1997: 12).
21 Reinhartz (2010: 521).
22 See e.g. Walsh (2003); Humphries-Brooks (2006).
23 Walsh (2003: 173–85).
24 Morford and Lenardon (2003: 128).
25 Bowra (1988: 58).
26 Vernant (1991: 273).
27 Harris and Platzner (2007: 22).
28 Ibid. 11.
29 Ibid. 997.
30 See Morford and Lenardon (2003: 673–4).
31 Brumble (1998: 416).
32 See Joost-Gaugier (2002).
33 Vine (2016: 103–18).
34 Brenner and Warnement (1996: 12).
35 See Bietoletti (2009: 8–12).
36 Miles (1999: 3).
37 For an overview of these approaches see Graf (1993: 9–56).
38 I am indebted to Lloyd Llewellyn-Jones for this point.
39 For a detailed examination of Plato's views see Van Riel (2013).
40 Zeyl (2014).
41 Schenck (2005: 56–8).
42 Philo, *De Opificio Mundi* 8.
43 Plotinus, *Enneads* 1.6.9.
44 Clement, *Miscellanies* 6.8.
45 For Anselm's ontological argument see Davies (2004: 157–78).
46 For Spinoza and Hume, see Hedley and Ryan (2013: 2–3); for Kant see ibid. 3–4.
47 See Fyfe (2004), esp. introduction.

48 For humanism see Law (2011).

49 Many modern scholars maintain that the non-corporeality of God dates only from the post-exilic era, and was a concept influenced by Proto-Zoroastrianism. Whatever the origins of the invisible God, his non-corporeal essence was what was accepted by Orthodox mainstream Judaism, and has for centuries formed a central tenet of the Jewish belief system.

50 See Kessler (2007: 43–4).

51 Sacks (2009: 9).

52 Kessler (2007: 44).

53 Translation is my own.

54 Maimonides, *13 Principles of Faith*, Second Principle. It should be noted, however, that Maimonides' perception of God was not as a personal deity, but as one further removed from mankind.

55 Fine (1984: 6).

2 Anthropomorphism

THE CONCEPT OF ANTHROPOMORPHISM

'I don't like to brag, but if I appeared to you just as God – how I really am, *what* I really am – , your mind couldn't grasp it', explains George Burns in *Oh, God* (1977) as God appearing in human form. Many theologians argue that it is impossible to eradicate anthropomorphism from religion, since human beings can only relate to an object of devotion through features with which they can identify. Despite the fact that philosophers from each of the three Mosaic faiths have traditionally sought to minimise anthropomorphism in their religions, attributing alternative interpretations to Biblical phrases that seem to suggest God's corporeality, a certain amount of anthropomorphism must be employed, so human minds can, indeed, grasp it. At the very least, deities must possess the human character-istics of speech and language, for instance, in order for prayer to be possible.[1]

Explanations as to why humans anthropomorphise have long been suggested by philosophers. Francis Bacon, with his emphasis on the scientific, rejected the idea of teleology in nature, asserting that to claim nature had aims and purpose was to attribute human reactions where they did not belong.[2] Spinoza also held that gods and other transcendental beings are the mere creation of human imagination, invented only in order to provide reasons for natural events by mor-tals unable to countenance other possibilities. David Hume attrib-uted anthropomorphism to intellectual causes, arguing that humans used what was a familiar model, namely themselves, in order to explain a strange and inexplicable world. The German philosopher, anthropologist and atheist Ludwig Feuerbach (1804–72) argued that mankind cannot transcend human nature, and therefore attributes human characteristics to higher powers, in order to provide hope of a better future. Extrapolating from this idea, he postulated that religion stems from 'man's cognitive confusion and not from a supra-terrestrial transcendent being called God' and concludes that 'man comes first and God ranks second'.[3] Stating that *homo homini Deus est* ('man's God is Man'), he saw this as both the highest law of ethics, and the turning point of world history.[4] Following Feuerbach, Marx argues along the same lines, seeing religion, and therefore God, as a manmade invention whose purpose was to soothe and comfort the suffering and oppressed. He substituted society and state for man as the ultimate principle, seeing religion, famously, as 'the opiate of the masses',[5] but the depiction of the Almighty as a being fashioned by man in man's image remains.

The work of Darwin and the theories of evolution served further to weaken belief in an ultimate power that created and is master of the world. As Shah points out:

> Biblical metaphysics is based on the concept of a loving God who created man in a unique fashion. The Christian worldview revolves around the concept of a fallen human nature, divine intervention through atoning sacrifice, and resultant redemption through the crucifixion and resurrection of Jesus Christ. Darwin's worldview and interpretation of nature as autonomous, self-directing, and evolutionary undermined the traditional Christian worldview more than the scientific revolutions of Copernicus, Galileo, and Newton.[6]

If Feuerbach replaced God with man, and Marx replaced God with society, Darwin replaced God with ever-evolving nature. Perhaps paradoxically, this resulted in greater anthropomorphism than before. For if previously the deity was conceived of as the creator of the universe located in the heavenly sphere, after Darwin people sought God in the human experience, attempting to understand the abstract by identifying points of contact with the physical and human world. Thus, despite the non-corporeal nature of this deity, anthropomorphic ideas of God continued to appear in monotheistic descriptions and conceptions, just as they do in connection with the genuinely anthropomorphic Greek gods; and such elements feature not only in philosophical discussions but also in popular culture, not least on the modern screen.

THE ANTHROPOMORPHIC GREEK GODS ON SCREEN

The Greeks suppose, says Xenophanes (570–c. 475 BCE), that:

> the gods have human shapes and feelings, and each paints their forms exactly like their own, as Xenophanes says. Ethiopians say their gods are snub-nosed and black; Thracians that theirs are blue-eyed and red-haired . . . But if horses or oxen or lions had hands or could draw with their hands and accomplish such works as men, horses would draw the figures of the gods as similar to horses and oxen as similar to oxen, and they would make the bodies of the sort that each of them had.[7]

In Xenophanes' view, the tendency of mankind to conceive of gods in human terms is a fault.[8] Yet since the dawn of time, people in all societies have attributed human characteristics to divine beings. The ancient Greeks in particular, influenced strongly by the Homeric depiction of the gods, thought of their deities as having much in common with mortals, although scholars have attempted to find other ways of interpreting this understanding. As Walter Burkert stresses,

> We may say that the experience of a storm is Zeus, or that the experience of sexuality is Aphrodite, but what the Greek says is that Zeus thunders and that Aphrodite bestows her gifts. . . . [The gods] are human almost to the last detail. . . . Vital elements of corporeality belong inalienably to their being.[9]

Such corporeality is an aspect that makes them both easier and harder to depict on screen. For, on the one hand, it is surely easier to cast and portray a god who has the appearance of a human in form than one who has no corporeality; but on the other, if the former appears like a human in form, what marks him or her out as divine and different from mortals?

The most traditional way of portraying the gods and indicating their divine status is by creating a visual look that is as close as possible to the manner in which they have most commonly been seen in the post-classical world, namely Greek sculpture. Statues of the gods, and their temples, are the best-known concrete extant remains that indicate their nature to the modern viewer, and bring home most clearly the perception of these divinities, for the similarity between human and god meant that relationships between the two could also function analogously. In Jennifer Larson's words:

> Gods and goddesses, heroines and heroes, were provided with houses and invited to attend gatherings in their honour. They enjoyed the same things humans found pleasing: gifts, music, perfumes and poetry. Through appro-

priate ritual methods, they were presented with food and drink. In turn they could indicate their acceptance of offerings by means of predetermined signs.[10]

Such a correspondence between human and divine, implicit in the human form of the gods, with the implied existence of a tangible physical presence also, as Albert Henrichs points out, enabled divine epiphanies, for the Greeks were able to 'see' and recognise their gods.[11] Equally they were able to depict them in art, through drawings, paintings, and of course statuary, particularly in the form of the cult statue that represented and was often revered as the god itself. The archaised elements of front-facing statues of gods invited the gaze and evoked reverence; when combined with their huge size, more naturalistic form and wealth of materials – ivory, glass, jewels, gold, richly woven cloth – in statues such as those of Pheidias' Zeus and Athena, the perception of the statue could become a true encounter with the god, in that 'their spectacular size, wealth and radiance did not invoke divinity by symbolic means, but actually sought to reproduce divine encounter'.[12]

It is these statues that are sometimes invoked to convey the impression of divinity on screen, when depicting the Olympians. Since the statues are white, their paint having long been lost, gods appear dressed in robes that echo the white marble of the statuary. Traditionally the deities are distinguishable from mortals, and from each other, by their individual iconography, including symbols, standardised characteristics and the presence of particular animals. Thus Poseidon has his trident and horse-drawn or hippocampi-drawn chariot, Zeus his lightning bolt and eagle, Athena her aegis and so on. Such iconography makes the immortals instantly recognisable to the contemporary audience, and also features in film as a symbolic shorthand conveying their identity.[13] Thus gods may appear dressed in the identifiably 'classical' garb of white robes and/or with their traditional symbols. Zeus often wears a crown, and carries or wields his thunderbolts; Hermes wears his distinctive hat and winged sandals and carries his caduceus staff.[14]

Some screen receptions show the animation of these cult statues in order to represent the gods themselves. Despite the fact that it is an animated movie, where the gods themselves are depicted without difficulty, in Disney's *Hercules* (1997) it is through the medium of the cult statue that Zeus speaks to his son Hercules, maintaining the conceit of the separation between mortal and divine, whereby humans cannot usually see the immortals. In this case, the statue is the means whereby a meeting between natural and supernatural can occur. Such a depiction has precedent; in Harryhausen's *Clash of the Titans* (1981), the face on the statue of Thetis comes to life with Maggie Smith's features projected onto the marble; in his *Jason and the Argonauts* (1963), the statue of Hera is shown with the goddess standing in its shadow, while the figurehead statue of Hera on the *Argo* is also partially animated.[15] This association with the statue, rather than pure animation of the stone, is also seen in *The Legend of Hercules* (2014); when Alcmene goes to pray at the statue of Hera, the goddess takes over the body of the priestess standing at the foot of the enormous statue. The girl's eyes roll and glaze over, with the pupils turning white, recalling the marble of the statue. With a synthetic echoing quality, the goddess' voice projects from her mouth, as Hera appears to the queen through this medium.

This film also uses another technique through which it depicts the presence of a god, namely by making him invisible, but showing the effect he has on the mortal world. With Hera's agreement, Zeus comes to impregnate Alcmene with Hercules (the infidelity condoned here 'for the sake of peace'), and the act is shown by means of the bedclothes lifting and moving, and Alcmene's reactions to sexual intercourse, as if the god has concrete yet invisible body and form. Such an episode in fact reflects the closest form of encounter, however, between god and mortal, namely the act of sexual intercourse, which fills the annals of Greek mythology. Despite the fact that the god (it is almost invariably the male god and the human female) sometimes takes on animal form in order to seduce the woman (a swan in the case of Leda, a bull in that of Europa), it is only because the gods themselves are in form similar to mortals that such acts can take place, and that the resultant offspring look human rather than monstrous. Human and divine, for all the differences between them, are in essence comparable, and the overlap between them is considerable.

The sexual exploits of the gods, and other examples of deviation from mainstream morality, were problematic even in the ancient world. Xenophanes, as mentioned above, scorns anthropomorphism; in his theology, divinities are, unlike the Homeric gods, morally perfect, and there is one particular god, the greatest of all mortals and immortals, who is completely different from mankind in both body and mind. Other ancient philosophers, from Parmenides to Plato and beyond, struggling with the imperfect behaviour of the deities, also described the gods less anthropomorphically, as perfect, absolute, impersonal properties, rather than human-like personalities.[16] In the Hellenistic period, there arose an idea that Homer's portrayal of the gods could be understood as not only metaphorical but even allegor-ical, as philosophers grappled with this issue.[17]

Even for the average citizen of ancient Greece, although they under-stood their deities to have human form, the assets of immortality and power radically altered the gods' natures. This difference means that humans can only approximately understand the gods in the form in which they reveal themselves to mankind. This form is, however, a long way from their true essence, and despite their human-seeming appearance, 'the anthropomorphism of the Greek gods is always a compromise between the visible and the invisible, the immanent and the transcendent'.[18]

In an attempt to convey such understanding of the gods cine-matically, their divinity is often highlighted through the utilisation of special effects, in particular making use of the association of the gods with light (and of Hades/Satan with the dark), by illuminating the figures of the deities in a particular manner. In *The Odyssey* (1997), the gods (Athena, played by Isabella Rossellini, and Hermes, played by Frederick Stuart) are depicted glowing with luminosity. The gods in Disney's *Hercules* from the same year are also illumi-nated with a supernatural radiance surrounding their bodies. The BBC's *Gory Greek Gods* (2004) uses another form of animation, namely rotoscoped animation, and here again, the faces of the actors are unnaturally highlighted and glowing. Similarly, in *Clash of the Titans* (2010), in which the gods are clad in armour rather than white robes,

> All the armor needed to be made to look as though it was made of different precious metals and to have the ability to be made almost 'light emitting' by the visual effects department. ... Zeus, played by Neeson, looked particu-larly regal and shone brightly, causing an awed silence to fall on set when he arrived in his 15-foot-long cloak.[19]

Other special effects are also implemented to create a 'divine' aspect. The importance of such techniques is discussed by Ray Harryhausen himself in his description of the choices he made in his mythological films:

> Both the Art Director and I discussed how we could depict the actors as gods. We didn't want to cut from the mortal world to the gods with barely anything to differentiate between them, so we decided to use a variety of images and designs to give the impression that the gods were truly omnipotent and dom-inated the world of humans.[20]

The first technique he mentions is to make the gods gigantic in size compared to humans, a technique also employed in Greek visual arts, whereby the gods are recognisably human in form,[21] but are also distinguished from humans by their size, being notably larger than the mortals. Thus, for example in the Harryhausen mythological movies, the humans are depicted as tiny figures in an arena or on a board, no more than toys in the hands of the enormous deities.[22] In *Percy Jackson and the Lightning Thief* (2010), at the end of the movie, when the gods are gathered at Olympus, they seem to be of normal size until Zeus approaches Percy, at which point it becomes apparent that the god is gigantic in comparison to the mortal. Similarly, Poseidon is seen as huge when emerging from the sea at Brighton Beach and then is shrunk to human size as he reaches land, thanks to the use of special effects.

Such onscreen transformations before the eyes of the cinema audience are another way in which divinity is conveyed. In Harryhausen's *Jason and the Argonauts*, an old seer is revealed to be the god Hermes as he changes appearance on screen, the face of the old man melting into that of the deity. The process is described on the storyboard sketches of the film as, 'The seer's face becomes watery and is transformed . . . into Hermes.'[23] Similarly in the 2010 version of the myth in *Clash of the Titans*, Hera appears disguised as an old woman, and then morphs into her divine form thanks to the miracles of the screen techniques.

Another way of implying immortality is by situating the gods in a recognisably divine location. Unlike in the Judaeo-Christian tradition, where the supreme deity is the creator of the universe, in Greek mythology, while Zeus is regarded as 'Father of Gods and Men', both gods and men are part of the world, born from Gaia, the earth. The Greek gods were born on earth, and live in their home on Mount Olympus in hierarchical and familial structures that resemble those of humans. On screen, this domain is often situated in the sky, with their home surrounded by white clouds, or a classically themed scenario with white marbled pillars and other traditional architectural elements. In the case of the latter settings, despite the fact that the scene is markedly similar to the human settings of ancient Greece, a clear differentiation is made between mortal and divine, as Lloyd Llewellyn-Jones emphasises:

> Even the casual reader of Homer will know that the gods frequently intervene in human affairs, to such an extent that they can alter human behaviour and thought processes – imbuing a hero with courage, or limiting his desire for a vengeful frenzy of slaughter. This premise forms the basis for the filmic use of the gods, as the storylines cut between heaven and earth, showing the gods viewing, deliberating on, or interfering in the lives of the on-screen heroes.[24]

It is an accepted fact, on screen, that the gods' abode is outside of human chronology or space, inaccessible and intangible, unable to be perceived by mortal eyes. The remoteness of this place is traditionally symbolised by the inclusion of elements associated with the sky. Thus as early as 1903, in Georges Méliès' *Le Tonnerre de Jupiter*, the throne of the king of the gods rises in an eagle-drawn chariot from a backdrop of stylised clouds.[25] In Harryhausen's *Jason and the Argonauts*, the audience is treated to the sight of 'the camera panning upwards from the earth to the sky (usually passing through the clouds) as the story cuts from earth to heaven'.[26] In the 2000 remake of this film, Zeus' and Hera's head and shoulders are seen in the sky, surrounded by clouds. Aerial photography and clouds again surround the Olympus of *Clash of the Titans* (1981), but in this case mixed with traditional conceptions of Paradise. Both the Harryhausen Olympus depictions were influenced by nineteenth-century paintings, in particular John Martin's *Joshua Commanding the Sun to Stand Still Upon Gibeon* (1816)[27] and Michael Gandy's *Jupiter Pluvius* (1819). Harryhausen himself emphasised the importance of the latter painting as a source of inspiration, saying:

> Gandy is a relatively unknown painter but for sheer spectacle there are few others who come anywhere near him. This painting is one of my most prized possessions and has been a huge inspiration to me throughout my career, teaching me to think big and give my inspiration free rein.

The painting was also recently featured in an exhibition at Tate Britain, where its centrality to Harryhausen was once again stressed:

> This spectacular work, completed in 1819, depicts a huge, sprawling, ancient city; vibrantly alive, showing the everyday life of the civilisation that dwelt there, as imagined by Gandy. The entire city is dominated by a colossal seated statue of the god Jupiter. The architectural scene depicted was a direct influence on Ray's vision of Hera's temple in 'Jason and the Argonauts' . . ., as well as the sprawling city of Argos in 'Clash of the Titans' (1981). This painting was one of Ray Harryhausen's prize possessions, and hung proudly in his London home.[28]

More recent depictions of Olympus continue this trend of association with the heavens, but give them a modern twist. The Olympus of *Immortals* (2011) is an even more innovative take on the usual home of the gods, which is here depicted as a stark and sparsely decorated white marble platform,[29] this material being the only real nod to traditional interpretations. It has a curved back wall, decorated with an eagle and classical-styled reliefs, with stairs going from a central section to an archway, presumably leading to further spaces. Perhaps inspired by *Hercules* (1983), which sets Zeus' abode on the moon, this Olympus is far out in space; sitting looking down, the gods can see events on earth, and influence them too, as when Poseidon dives from Olympus into the sea, causing a tsunami.

The remake of *Clash of the Titans* also has an Olympus set among clouds, which actually float around the gods' feet. Featuring high-backed marble thrones and bathed in a brilliant light, this is an airy palace, where the interior shots filmed were heavily augmented by the special effects team. Visual effects supervisor Tim Webber explains:

> After the set was filmed, it was decided to make the whole Olympus set much more grand and fantastical. We concepted it up, did some design work, and had some briefs from Nick Davis. . . . We created a semi-photoreal landscape, sea and clouds floating above it, to make it seem like they were walking on a miniaturised version of Earth. When we were creating that, there was some concern that the audience would think that actually was Earth they were walking on, and whether the Gods were actually stepping on villages and in the sea. So we had to slightly pull back from the photorealistic aspect of it and add a lot of atmosphere and clouds and make it quite almost surreal. We generated clouds to cover it which wisp around the Gods' feet. We created the walls all around them and replacing about 90 per cent of the set.[30]

The Percy Jackson movies, with their conceit that the gods move to wherever the centre of power in the world is at any period, situate Olympus in New York, but again, it floats in the clouds high up in the sky, and is accessed from the six-hundredth floor of the Empire State Building. The appearance of the throne room of this Olympus, however, is rather different from earlier portrayals. Although white marble still features, in the form of pillars, as do classical motifs such as the key floor border and the classically styled chairs for the gods, they are set in a hall that is inspired by the Art Deco style of the Empire State Building and architecture of other New York landmarks. Thus the white columns are set against a background of darker marble that recalls the dark pink and purplish Rose Famosa and Estrallante marbles of the lobby of the Empire State Building.[31] The huge round clock instrument in the centre of the hall of Olympus is reminiscent of several of the Art Deco elements of the Rockefeller Centre – the clock on the tower of the plaza, the armillary sphere held by Atlas in the famous statue, and the masonic compass on the relief on the GE building. In this way, Olympus here is a mixture of the traditional and the modern, attempting to place Greek mythology seamlessly in the contemporary world. This is a feature of both movies and the books from which they were adapted, and was a principal aim underlying the whole conception behind the look of the film, according to director/producer Christopher Columbus and producer Michael Barnathan.[32] Like the other depictions of the Greek gods on screen, it also reflects the attempt to represent these anthropomorphic gods as both like and unlike the humans with whom they share physical shape.

ANTHROPOMORPHISM IN CHRISTIANITY: THE PHYSICAL DEPICTION OF JESUS

Christianity centres on the figure of Jesus, who, as the earthly embodiment of God, can be portrayed corporeally and anthropomorphically. Moreover, moviegoers know what Jesus looks like; he has piercing blue eyes, shoulder-length brown hair, a calm and serene appearance; in other words, he is Robert Powell, or someone very like him. Despite these commonly held ideas, the very issue of portraying a figure who is regarded as both divine and human in form is not without complication, as one critic noted:

> I wonder if there is not instant diminution when we put a figure of Christ upon the screen. How to personify the mystery and divinity and, once personified, how to make the figure move among men? These are of the imagination, and our traditional film-makers leave nothing to the imagination. How then are they to 'visualize' the vision that has endured for centuries primarily within the human heart? . . . No, the great big screen and the great big names are too much for the survival of matters of the spirit. So many aspects of big movie-making intervene that the Passion cannot predominate.[33]

Nevertheless, the temptation to portray the living form of God is great, as Adele Reinhartz points out:

> By the late first century, when the gospels were written, Jesus had been absent from the world for more than four decades. At that time, and for the subsequent nineteen centuries, those with an interest in Jesus have not been able to see Jesus directly. . . . With the birth of the cinema in the late nineteenth century, however, a new and highly appealing medium for seeing Jesus became available to anyone who could afford the low price of admission. The ongoing desire to see Jesus, and the suitability of cinema to fulfill that desire, has spawned hundreds of Jesus movies in numerous countries, from the earliest years of the movie industry to the present.[34]

How then, given this desire to depict Jesus, does one go about doing so in a manner that conveys both his divinity and his humanity? Either or both of these elements may be proposed or challenged according to the approach and agenda of the individual production, for not all depictions are by any means supportive of religions or the Church. No matter what the intention or ideology behind the movie, however, the question of how to show Jesus on screen is one that must be dealt with by the film maker.

One approach is to highlight Jesus' effect on others. Since the human element of Jesus is easier to portray than his divine aspect, what Reinhartz calls 'high Christology' is more often shown thus, 'in the rapt responses of those around Jesus, both their facial expressions and their words'. Other techniques such as lighting and camera angles, along with grand backdrops and settings ('big sky') and stirring epic music, also help to convey the divine aspect of Jesus ' identity.[35] Similarly the performance of miracles contributes to the effect of supernatural power, as well as creating powerful dramatic episodes on screen if they take place before the eyes of the audience. In some instances, however, they are merely described, or treated as allegories for spiritual abilities, but the very fact of their inclusion contributes to the depiction of Jesus as divine.[36]

Another answer to the dilemma in productions that approached the subject reverently was not to portray the face of Christ at all, and in fact up until the 1930s, this was a policy insisted upon by British film censors. In *Ben-Hur* (1959), for example, this decision was famously taken, so that Jesus' features are never seen, while *The Redeemer*, a film produced in the same year by a priest, Father Patrick J. Peyton, head of the Family Rosary Crusade, took the same route. Others approach the issue by deliberately choosing an unknown actor to play the role, in order to avoid connotations or impressions caused by perceptions of the star or the roles he might have played. Thus George Stevens chose Max von Sydow, at that time little known in the USA, to play the lead in *The Greatest Story Ever Told* (1965), despite sprinkling the rest of the cast with famous movie stars.

Such approaches echo the discomfort felt by the early Church with regard to the pictorial representation of Jesus. As late as the fourth century, Canon 36 of the Synod of Elvira prohibited the use of images in churches. This was the first official statement on art by the Christian Church, and although it probably represents Church policy only within the limits of the synod's jurisdiction of Spain, it is likely also to reflect widespread suspicion of pictorial depictions of the divine in other areas too.[37] When images were used, symbolism was often employed, and since craftsmen were often pagans who did not understand the symbols, this led to sometimes startling mixes of imagery, with pagan and Christian elements side by side. In particular, Christians attached their own interpretation to pagan symbols, with Dionysian elements representing the God who died and was reborn, or Hermes, the ram carrier, signifying Jesus as the Good Shepherd.[38] The inclusion of Jesus and Mary in Old Testament scenes was also adopted as a means of conveying the message of secession and the rejection of the Jews. While the Jewish iconography of the Hand of God, often emerging from a cloud, continued to appear, the Ark of the Covenant is replaced by Jesus himself, whose sacrifice replaced the Temple sacrifices in Christian eyes.[39] Initially, Jesus himself was represented indirectly by pictogram symbols such as the Ichthus (fish), the peacock, or an anchor. Other early representations feature the baby Jesus, usually in his mother's arms.[40] During the fourth century, scenes depicting the Son of God as an adult became more popular,[41] although at this early stage, none of the later classic identifiers of Jesus, such as the beard or halo, had yet been developed.

In fact there were myriad differences of opinion among early Christians about what Jesus looked like. According to Gnostic belief, he could alter his appearance at will;[42] other early Christian figures, including Tertullian, thought that he had an unremarkable appearance, but this led to pagan mockery of the 'ugly' Christian God, and subsequent claims of beauty for Jesus by figures such as Jerome and Augustine. A striking aspect of the depiction of Jesus in the early Christian period is that he appears in dual imagery, as a glowing child or young man, and also as an older figure with shoulder-length hair and beard. Both depictions often appear in scenes of the same subject, sometimes even simultaneously on one monument. The portrayal as young, almost childlike, as Zanker suggests, is 'related to the type of the intellectual wunderkind, which ... was especially popular in Roman funerary art of the later third century', and which 'represents a definitive break with the traditions of Greece, where mental powers and wisdom were always associated with advancing age'. In contrast, according to Zanker, this 'new and miraculous kind of wisdom' is a the sign of the miracle worker, a gift with which one is born, as opposed to the result of hard work, and therefore adds a new dimension to the depiction of Christ, who as a divine youth 'stands for an all-encompassing hope for a new world'.[43]

Other depictions show Jesus as slightly older, but still a youth, in which case the inspiration is that of mythological or historical Greek heroes such as Achilles or Alexander. Thus, in many early portrayals, he is portrayed as beardless, as in the earliest extant portrait of Jesus (approximately 235 CE), from Syria, where he is depicted as a young man, dressed in tunic and pallium, and with the appearance of a philosopher, with short hair and no beard, a far cry from his historical Jewish origins.[44] Such a portrayal is not uncommon; with the official recognition of Christianity by Rome, a new Christian iconography replaced traditional mythological scenes, and the depiction of miracles took the place of bucolic symbolism of peace and happiness; in

this new framework, Christ, the teacher of wisdom, appears as a culti-
vated Roman citizen, in a forward-facing pose inspired by depictions
of magistrates in Roman state art, and thus giving an impression of
authority.[45] Thus many pictures from catacombs and sarcophagi of
this period show him as 'a healer, magician, teacher or philosopher',[46]
while in many depictions, 'Christ himself, the apostles, prophets, and
saints are all depicted like pagan intellectuals. As a rule they wear
the ... *pallium* ... with undergarment and hold a book roll in one
hand – even when this seems rather an impediment in certain scenes
of miracles.'[47]

With regard to the second common portrayal as an older, bearded
man, the beard may be an element stemming from the influence of
statues of Zeus.[48] It is also an element seen in portraits of philosophers in classical and Hellenistic art, and was a sign of the intellectual, featuring in depictions of the Hadrianic and Antonine emperors
as a mark of culture and learning.[49] Classical and Hellenistic portraits of intellectuals, however, almost invariably show them with
short hair, with Homer being a (still relatively rare) exception to
this rule.[50] The long hair in fact relates to the 'holy man' tradition
of pagan miracle workers. In many cultures, long hair is associated
with special powers or with authority; Samson's uncut hair gives
him his strength, according to popular culture, while kings and
rulers, such as David and Absalom, are also depicted with luxuriant
locks. Similarly prophets can be associated with such a style; Elijah
is described as a *baal sear* ('a hairy man'[51]), while John the Baptist is
described in the same way. Thus the combination of shoulder-length
hair and beard together is an innovation created uniquely for the
depiction of Jesus.

In 313 CE Christianity was legalised by the Edict of Milan. As a
result of imperial favour towards the religion, new elements appeared
in the depiction of Jesus, as his authority as 'Christ the King' was
accepted and adopted into art.[52] Thus the physical types outlined
above both remain, but with the imposition of the clothing and features of imperial iconography. As Syndicus describes:

> Title, throne, purple robe, halo, enthronement on the vault of heaven or the
> globe of earth, the stance on the clouds or the defeated dragon, the ruler's ges-
> ture of the raised hand, the acclamation and presentation of gifts by dignitar-
> ies, the reception of the gifts on veiled hands, the obliquely set throne room,
> the baldachin as a miniature copy of the heaven, the names aula and sacrar-
> ium (= palace and throne room, literally 'sanctuary') for church and altar
> space, the orientation of the building usual in sun worship, incense, candles,
> genuflection: all these things and many others pass over, partly in the fourth
> century, completely in the sixth, from the emperor to Christ the Lord.[53]

Despite these symbolic and iconic developments, there was still remarkable variety in the depiction of the actual physical character-istics of Jesus at this time, as well as differences of opinion as to how, if at all, he should be portrayed. As Bakker stresses:

> a great majority of Christians were strongly opposed to depicting Jesus, with the result that there has been a great variety in attitudes throughout the cen-turies . . . there was also great diversity in the images of Jesus, visually as well as ideologically or theologically.[54]

The point is made at more length by Mathews:

> The alarming truth is that, travelling from Rome to Constantinople in the fifth or sixth century, the Christian pilgrim would have encountered a dizzy-ing diversity of Christ types. From church to church the Lord would undergo the most radical metamorphoses. Now calmly conversing with a circle of disciples . . . now climbing rosy clouds into the empyrean . . . now sitting on rainbows and waving to the viewer from a great bubble of light above the landscape . . . Christ's face was alternately old and grave, youthful and vigor-ous, masculine and feminine. Staring at the glittering apse must have been like experiencing a series of volatile hallucinations. The Early Christian Church was truly polymorphous.[55]

This variety in depiction continued in some localised traditions, such as the Ethiopian Church, which showed him, along with other Biblical figures, as Ethiopian in appearance.[56]

Nevertheless, Christ did gradually develop into a more standard-ised figure, as an older, bearded, long-haired man, now with a cru-ciform halo, came to dominate, especially in the Eastern half of the Empire. Once this depiction became conventional, so too his facial features gradually were fixed as well, although this process took several hundred years, particularly in the West. By the sixteenth cen-tury, the beard was so accepted a feature that when Michelangelo painted Christ without facial hair in the Last Judgement fresco in the Sistine Chapel, he was attacked for the depiction, which was clearly based upon that of Apollo.[57] Along with a beard, Jesus is now shown with a long oval face, long, straight brown hair with a centre part-ing, and almond-shaped eyes, a portrayal influenced by items such as the Image of Edessa, the Veil of Veronica and the Turin Shroud. Renaissance images of Jesus also drew on classical sculpture in their poses, and presented an idealised, perfect Jesus. So consistent has this bearded, serene figure with shoulder-length hair become by this stage that although European depictions show some local ethnic elements, Jesus is consistently shown as demonstrating less of these features than the surrounding figures. In contrast to the Virgin Mary, for example, who often appears with blonde hair, Christ's is rarely paler than a light brown. This conventionalised appearance has carried through to the screen depictions, as discussed in detail in Chapter 4 of this book.

ANTHROPOMORPHISM AND THE JUDAEO-CHRISTIAN GOD

It is clear that the God of the Old Testament, whether in the Jewish or Christian traditions, is of a very different nature from either the pagan deities or Jesus.[58] Some aspects of his divine nature are universally accepted by both religions: all followers of these religions believe, for example, that he is omniscient, omnipotent and morally perfect. Beyond these points, however, there are multiple opinions and beliefs, both between the different religions and within each faith, as well as changing ideas over time and in different places. Within Judaism, the belief in the unity of the non-physical God is central; he is believed to be without physical form at all, although he is described throughout the Old Testament in human terms (God speaks, hears, grows angry etc.). This God is eternal, omnipotent, omniscient and omnibenevolent, points that were emphasised from the medieval period onwards. Most importantly, God is without body, and therefore without human form in any physical way; Maimonides' third principle is, indeed, belief in God's non-corporeality. Throughout history, Jewish philosophers and scholars have debated as to how far corporeal terminology can even be used to describe God, since he possesses no corporeality. Furthermore, according to the second of the Ten Commandments, he is not to be depicted in image, graven or otherwise.

Cinema itself is, of course, centred firmly on image, but this has not prevented film makers from showing God on screen, despite the difficulties in depicting a non-corporeal figure. Commonly film makers solved the problem by having a substitute for God, such as the heavenly administrator Mr Jordan in *Here Comes Mr Jordan* (1941) and its remake, *Heaven Can Wait* (1978), or Gabriel in *A Life Less Ordinary* (1997). Another approach to depicting God is to use a figure who, although named differently, represents the role of God, such as the Judge in *A Matter of Life and Death/Stairway to Heaven* (1946) or the Supreme Being in Terry Gilliam's fantasy, *Time Bandits* (1981). In the last case, the God character is an 'archetypal, utterly reasonable, besuited English civil servant of mature years, gently but firmly attempting to bring order and logic to a crazy universe'.[59]

Strangely, what is almost never seen is the portrayal of God along traditional lines, with beard, white robes and grey hair, a rare exception being Charlton Heston's role in *Almost An Angel* (1990). This is startling since, despite the accepted non-corporeality of God, there are clear conventions within art as to how he should appear. Although the symbols found in Jewish art were also adopted by Christians, as time passed, gradually portrayals of the head and later the whole figure were made, and by the time of the Renaissance artistic representations of God the Father were freely used in the Western Church.[60] In these, he is, almost without exception, an old, white-haired man with flowing white beard, often enthroned, frequently with a halo of light around his head, and sometimes surrounded by clouds. This depiction dates back as far as the early Venetian school, where it may be seen in Giovanni d'Alemagna and Antonio Vivarini's *Coronation of the Virgin* (1443), and is largely derived from, and justified by, the description of the Ancient of Days in the book of Daniel:[61]

> I beheld till the thrones were cast down, and the Ancient of Days did sit, whose garment was white as snow, and the hair of his head like the pure wool: his throne was like the fiery flame, and his wheels as burning fire.[62]

This portrayal remains constant, utilised by figures such as Michelangelo (the Creation images from the Sistine Chapel), Titian (the *Assumption of the Virgin*), Rubens (*The Last Judgement* and the *Coronation of the Virgin*), Velázquez and Murillo, and is the standard representation of God in popular media, and in particular children's books, until the present day.

In place of such depictions, in other Biblical epics and similar movies of the second half of the twentieth century, God's presence is indicated by phenomena such as the burning bush, and his voice is heard in tones that provide a sense of authority. According to Wikipedia, this voice is 'deep, resonant, and masculine, and usually the American English of Southern California (sometimes with a touch of British English)'.[63] Thus for example, director John Huston provided the voice of God in his 1966 epic *The Bible: In the Beginning . . .*, while in Cecil B. DeMille's *The Ten Commandments*, Charlton Heston took a similar role,[64] and in fact, in the words of Paul Schrader's commentary to the film, God who gives the stone tablets to Moses is 'off-screen to the right'.

Such depictions are rooted in traditional Jewish fear of divine representation and use of abstract symbolism. So strong was aversion to depicting God that not only were images of the deity himself banned, but also those of people or angels, or any images of heavenly bodies. Such aniconism was maintained or disregarded at varying levels throughout history, both with regard to religious iconography and more widely, but despite this attitude, throughout history Jews consistently utilised pictures, in texts, synagogue decoration and religious artefacts of all kinds.[65] The ancient world differentiated between *historiae*, narrative pictures, and *imagines* (portraits), and Judaism, like Christianity, found an acceptable accommodation in the use of the former, due to the belief in God's revelation to mankind through historical events, which could indeed be depicted. This accommodation was made easier by the fact that pictorial narratives were rarely accurate or simple depictions of events described in Biblical texts, but rather, 'through purposeful selection, references in costume and setting, and intertextual interpolations, they were constructed to make the ancient stories from distant lands relevant to the present viewers'.[66]

Nevertheless, Jews, unlike Christians, while depicting miraculous events, were more circumspect about portraying God pictorially. The closest they came to this was the use of the Hand of God, which symbolised the Voice of God. Another alternative was the symbolic use of the Ark of the Covenant, the place of interaction between man and deity as the locus of communication with the High Priest in the Holy of Holies. Both of these are, in Kessler's words '*anti-icons* that confirmed Jewish belief in Jehovah's essential immateriality and invisibility'.[67] Like the 'Voice of God', the absence of the physical revelation actually enhances the majesty and power of the deity.

In keeping with the reverential tone that such depictions evoke, there is no indication whatsoever that this God is anything other than a great and powerful, merciful saviour of his people, who are clearly the 'good guys', while those who oppose him are the 'bad guys'. There is no question in Judaism, no possibility even, of God behaving in a way that is not virtuous, or of any of his acts being less than perfect.[68] God's perfection is stressed by Maimonides, whose first *Principle of Faith* is:

> 1. Belief in the existence of the Creator, who is perfect in every manner of existence and is the Primary Cause of all that exists.

Film has until recent years maintained this stance; as late as 1997, in *Prince of Egypt*, where God is still heard as a voice (Val Kilmer) and seen as a blue flame on the burning bush, this non-corporeal voice is the benevolent revelation of the ultimate benefactor of mankind. It is striking that the most negative depiction of the Jewish God is also the most anthropomorphic of all, that of *Exodus: Gods and Kings* (2014), in which he is portrayed as a child, seen only by Moses. In the second millennium, not only has the non-corporeal divinity been made flesh, he has also been diminished and even demonised.

NOTES

1 See e.g. Jevons (1913: 573–4); Meynell (1977: 23–43); Duggan (1979: 195); Brown (1982).
2 Guthrie (1997: 51).
3 Shah (2012: 9).
4 Feuerbach (1841).
5 The quotation originates from the introduction of Marx's work *Zur Kritik der Hegelschen Rechtsphilosophie (A Contribution to the Critique of Hegel's Philosophy of Right)*, written in 1843 and published separately in 1844, in Marx's own journal *Deutsch–Französische Jahrbücher*. The work itself, however, was not published until after Marx's death.
6 Shah (2012: 10).
7 Xenophanes, fragments 16 and 15, translation by Lesher (1992: 89–90).
8 See Shah (2012: 3).
9 Burkert (1985: 183).
10 Larson (2015: 70).
11 Henrichs (2010: 34).
12 Platt (2011: 89).
13 Llewellyn-Jones (2007: 428–9).
14 These points are discussed in depth in the next chapter.
15 Llewellyn-Jones (2007: 431–2).
16 See e.g. Larson (2015: 69–70).
17 Kearns (2006: 71).
18 Kindt (2012:172).
19 <http://www.slashfilm.com/41-high-resolution-photos-from-clash-of-the-titans/> (accessed 13 December 2017).
20 Harryhausen and Dalton (2005: 154).
21 Even Pan, the only central god to retain animal features, walks uprights and seems more human with animal elements than animalistic.
22 See Llewellyn-Jones (2007: 430).
23 Harryhausen and Dalton (2005: 105), quoted in Llewellyn-Jones (2007: 430).
24 Ibid. 426.
25 Viewable at <https://www.youtube.com/watch?v=nIylL8ufx3Y> (accessed 11 December 2017).
26 Llewellyn-Jones (2007: 427).
27 Richards (2008: 140); <http://www.tate.org.uk/context-comment/video/tateshots-ray-harryhausen-on-john-martin> (accessed 6 December 2017).
28 <https://vimeo.com/171819503> (accessed 6 December 2017).

29 This look inspired one blogger to comment that 'The result is that Ancient Greece looks like it was furnished by IKEA', <https://flicker ingscreen.net/2011/12/12/its-all-about-the-hats-immortals/> (accessed 11 December 2017).

30 <https://www.fxguide.com/featured/clash_of_the_titans_cinesite_frame store_and_mpc/> (accessed 11 December 2017).

31 Tauranac (2014: 207, 233–4).

32 See e.g. Percy Jackson 'Behind the Scenes' featurette, <https://www.you-tube.com/watch?v=jiVh-1h7zRc> (accessed 6 December 2017).

33 Crist (1965: 271).

34 Reinhartz (2010: 519).

35 Ibid. 523.

36 Reinhartz (2007: 104–8).

37 See Rudolph (1993: 3–55); (2004: 1–7).

38 Hinson (1996) 175.

39 Bigham (1995: 6).

40 See e.g. depictions of the Adoration of the Magi from catacomb paintings and sarcophagus reliefs of the fourth century

41 Syndicus (1962: 94–5).

42 Every (1970: 65).

43 Zanker (1995: 299–300).

44 'The Healing of the Paralytic'. See Brandon (1975: 166–7).

45 Zanker (1995: 289).

46 Bakker (2009: 55).

47 Zanker (1995: 289).

48 Syndicus (1962: 93); Zanker (1995: 292).

49 Zanker (1995: 269).

50 Ibid. 262.

51 But see the discussions on this phrase in 2 Kings 1:8, often translated as 'wore a garment of hair'. See e.g. Hallpike (1969) as well as individual Bible commentaries.

52 Syndicus (1962: 96–7).

53 Ibid. 94.

54 Bakker (2009: 54).

55 Mathews (1993: 98).

56 Such depictions continued throughout history; the Ethiopian church in Jerusalem, built between 1874 and 1901, contains a picture of a black African-looking Jesus. Similarly, some Chinese portraits depict him with Asian features, as in the depiction of Jesus and the rich man produced in Beijing in 1879. Viewable at < https://en.wikipedia.org/ wiki/Jesus_and_the_rich_young_man#/media/File:ChineseJesus.jpg> (accessed 30 November 2018).

57 See Blunt (1995: 112–14, 118–19).

58 It is of course equally true that Allah in Islam is very different from both pagan gods and Jesus, but since Islam has been less influential on

Western film makers, at least until recent years, I do not include this
perspective in this study.

59 <https://www.theguardian.com/culture/2016/apr/01/10-best-representa
tions-god-culture-morgan-freeman-alanis-morissette> (accessed 21
May 2018)

60 Ferguson (1977: 92).

61 Bigham (1995: 73–6).

62 Daniel 7:9 (King James translation).

63 <https://en.wikipedia.org/wiki/Portrayals_of_God_in_popular_media>
(accessed 21 May 2018).

64 No onscreen credit is given for the voice of God, which was heavily
modified and mixed with other sound effects. Although various people
were said to have been responsible for the voice, Heston in an interview
on the 2004 DVD edition claimed that he was the Voice of God.

65 For a discussion of ancient synagogue mosaics and the destruction of
living creatures therein, possibly as a reaction against iconography, see
Barber (1997).

66 See Kessler (2000: 1).

67 Ibid. 4.

68 There is, however, also a strong tradition of protest against, and arguing
with, the Deity in Judaism. See Weiss (2017).

3 Physiology and the Physical Appearance of the Divine (1): The Patriarchal King Figure and the Devil

ZEUS

Dressed in angelic white robes, seated on a throne, head surrounded by halo-like rays, Laurence Olivier's commanding, paternalistic presence in *Clash of the Titans* (1981), his grey hair and beard attesting to his venerability, leaves us in no doubt of his identity (see Figure 3.1). He is Zeus, king of the gods, in all his majesty. The depiction in these films is strongly based on ancient epic,[1] with the gods living in an Olympus of white marble columns;[2] despite being gigantic in comparison to mortals, their appearance is typical of ancient Greece on screen, with white and gold garments and elaborate Grecian hairstyles.

He is also heavily involved in mankind's doings, with humans depicted as toy figures on a chessboard (*Jason and the Argonauts* (1963)) or in an arena (*Clash*), which the gods watch as entertainment or use as pawns in their own schemes, favouring particular worthy individuals. In Harryhausen's own words, 'Zeus would put the figures in the arena, where the gods would control their destinies. It was a vital tool in introducing the characters of our story.' Despite the similarity between the two movies with the use of gaming symbolism, there is also a difference, as Stephen Trzaskoma has pointed out, in that in the latter movie, Zeus is 'the sole owner and proper manipulator of the figurines. . .He stands in as the creator of our narrative.'[3] While Trzaskoma argues that Zeus in *Clash* becomes a Harryhausen animator figure, I would also suggest that this Zeus,

Figure 3.1 Zeus (Laurence Olivier) in *Clash of the Titans* (1981).
Charles H. Schneer Productions.

as sole ruler and controller of the world, introduces a monotheistic element into this pagan world.

In Olivier's Zeus there is also a strong element of Judaeo-Christian godliness, with the emphasis upon Zeus as a white-clad, angelic, bearded figure on a throne, head surrounded by halo-like rays. Nevertheless, as an ostensibly pagan god, Zeus, and the other Olympians, cannot completely rival God. While the deities of the Harryhausen movies are all–powerful, they are also flawed, treating human life with fickle casualness, and it is even hinted that their days may be numbered:

> **Thetis:** What if there were more heroes like him? What if courage and imagination became everyday mortal qualities? What will become of us?
> **Zeus:** We would no longer be needed. But, for the moment, there is sufficient cowardice, sloth and mendacity down there on Earth to last forever.

The implication seems to be that mankind will not need these gods if they have courage and imagination instead. It is also stated that the gods are best served by those who want their help least, a message with implications for a secular world in which humans do not ask help from the gods. If they do have need of such a god, it will be a traditional, all-powerful, bearded, male figure, as symbolised by Laurence Olivier's Zeus, who owes more to Judaeo-Christian tradition than to Homer. Such a link was made explicit in a review of a recent film concerning God, *The Brand New Testament* (2015), in which the reader is told that the 'traditional, vaguely Zeus-like notion of God as an old man with white beard and flowing robes' has now disappeared.[4]

Despite the connections with the God of the Bible, the pagan king of the gods also has his own identity and iconography, exploited by film makers as a short cut for a whole range of associations with the ancient world. Whether as Zeus or Jupiter (in which guise he was cast with the face of the emperor on coins, statues and reliefs, associating the physical ruler with divinity),[5] the ancient god is a recognisable figure portrayed as 'a seated, mature, bearded figure, with a naked torso, a mantle over one shoulder and legs draped, accompanied by one or more of his attributes, such as an eagle, thunderbolt or scepter'.[6] This depiction reached a pinnacle with, and was afterwards heavily influenced by, Pheidias' iconic statue of the god, described by Pausanias as follows:

> The god is sitting on a throne made of gold and ivory. A garland lies on his head, in the form of olive shoots. In his right hand he carries (a statuette of) Victory, itself too of gold and ivory, with a ribbon and a garland on the head. In the left hand of the god there is a sceptre, richly decorated with every sort of metal; and the bird sitting on the sceptre is the eagle. The god's sandals too are of gold and the robe likewise. On the robe there are embroidered animal figures and flowers, lilies. The throne is decorated with gods and precious stones, and also with ebony and ivory. And there are depictions of animals painted on it and figures worked in it. There are four Victories in the form of dancers at each foot of the throne, and two further at the base of each foot.[7]

In the words of Dowden:

> This then is Zeus when he is depicted on his own and when he is the exclusive focus of contemplation. The image projects his power: standing to wield the thunderbolt, or seated in majesty, this is the most powerful of all the gods. In an anthropomorphic religion he had been clearly envisaged as far back as Homer. This stabilises in the art, with its insistence on regular attributes – the lightning, the eagle. But since the statue of Pheidias gave new life to Homer's portrait, his iconography has changed for ever. Every later portrayal has Pheidias' Zeus in mind.[8]

These elements can be seen consistently at various periods in post-classical depictions, especially during the neoclassical period of the nineteenth century, as reflected by works such as Jean Auguste Dominique Ingres' *Jupiter and Thetis* (1811) and Horatio Greenough's *George Washington* (1840) (see Figure 3.2). It is also the case with film, where he is most commonly depicted as an elderly, white-haired, bearded king, complete with crown. As early as 1903, Georges Méliès' god in *Le Tonnerre de Jupiter* sported a bushy white beard and a crown. Jumping forward in time, *Hercules in New York* (1970) with Ernest Graves, then aged 51, as Zeus, features a grey, curly-haired, bearded god, crowned with a gold laurel wreath, and clad in a long white and gold tunic. Claudio Cassinelli's Zeus from the 1980s Hercules movies (*Hercules* (1983) and *The Adventures of Hercules* (1985)) has a Santa Claus appearance, with long, wavy, white hair and beard and large, mitre-style crown. He is dressed in white furry robes, decorated with a turquoise looping pattern on the skirt, the fur being necessary, presumably, since he lives on the moon. Hulk Hogan's Zeus from *Little Hercules in 3-D* (2009) also has a gold laurel-leaf crown upon his long, straight, white hair, but is rather more unclothed than other depictions of the god, wearing a gold-bordered, white chiton over a gold underskirt, leaving his left shoulder bare, presumably in order to show off his wrestler's muscles. Jason Sudeikis' gold-trimmed, white chiton is rather less revealing in a parodic sketch from *Saturday Night Live* in 2011, and again features the recurring iconic symbols of white hair, beard and gold laurel crown.

Other versions of Zeus will utilise only one or two of these symbols to indicate his role. Thus, in some productions his crown may appear, but not the beard. One such example is *Blasphemy, the Movie* (2001), where Zeus wears a concealing, full white robe, covered by a gold cloak, and a laurel wreath, but is clean shaven. Joe Estevez in *Hercules in Hollywood* (2005) appears more like a Roman emperor than the king of the gods, but again features the gold laurel crown along with his white and gold tunic and purple cloak. Amedeo Falgiatore's Zeus in *For the Love of Zeus* (2015) is once again in a white chiton and with gold laurel crown, but without the beard seen in other versions. All of these productions are comedies, where the rough impression of the character in his role as king (often undermined comically by his impotence on screen) is of importance.

Yet other productions place the emphasis upon Zeus as an aged, wise and venerable being, showing him with the stereotypical white hair and beard, but no crown. These tend to be versions for younger audiences, with the animated movies generally following this route, starting with Disney's *Hercules* (1997), but followed also by *Mythic Warriors: Guardians of the Legend* (1998–2000) and *Class of the Titans* (2006–8) (although his hair is perhaps more blond than white or grey in this version). Three of the four depictions of Zeus in *Hercules: The Legendary Journeys* (1994, 1995–9), those by Roy Dotrice, Peter Vere-Jones and Charles Keating, provide further examples. One recent comedy, *Man Seeking Woman* (2015), also features a Zeus with flowing white hair and beard, dressed in the traditional white flowing robes and golden decorated cloak.

Figure 3.2 *George Washington* (1840), statue by Horatio Greenough in the National Museum of American History, Smithsonian Institute, Washington, DC. Photograph taken by Wknight94 talk [GFDL (http://www.gnu.org/copyleft/fdl.html) or CC BY-SA 3.0 (https://creativecommons.org/licenses/by-sa/3.0)], from Wikimedia Commons, <https://commons.wikimedia.org/wiki/File:George_Washington_Greenough_statue.jpg>.

A few cases represent Zeus as a mature, but not elderly, figure, sometimes with a crown and/or a beard, but with dark hair. In contrast to his later portrayal of Zeus in *Clash of the Titans* (1981), Harryhausen's Zeus from *Jason and the Argonauts* falls into this category. Played by the 50-year-old Niall MacGinnis, this Zeus has brown curly hair and beard, and is dressed in long white and gold robes, but has no crown. Similarly, in the remake of *Jason and the Argonauts* from 2000, in many ways a tribute to the earlier movie, Angus Macfadyen, who was 37 at the time, took the role of Zeus. In this role, like his predecessor, he sported dark brown, shoulder-length hair and a luxuriant beard and moustache, and was of gigantic size, looking down upon the world from a mass of clouds. One of the youngest-looking Zeuses is that from the TV series *Once Upon a Time* (2011–18 (Season 5, 2016)), played by 36-year-old David Hoflin. The casting call for this part ran:

> Male. Late 30s–Late 40s. Looks and acts like he was born to be King. He is wise, handsome, and authoritative. A ruler who will deal harsh justice when it is necessary, but he also knows the power of kindness and forgiveness.

Dressed in a long, white, gold-trimmed, short-sleeved tunic, cinched at the waist with a gold belt and pteruges-style apron in the manner of a Roman soldier, he is clean-shaven and boyish looking, in strong contrast to most other productions.

There are in fact some more recent depictions that feature a somewhat younger Zeus. Such portrayals are not without historical precedent. After the classical period, with its paternalistic representations of the king of the gods, the Graeco-Roman divinities were replaced in art in the Byzantine and early medieval periods by Christian iconography. With the rediscovery of classical antiquity in the Renaissance, Greek mythology came to the fore again and remained there, with varying amounts of popularity, throughout the subsequent developments in art. From the early years of the Renaissance, artists portrayed subjects from Greek mythology alongside more conventional Christian themes. In particular, the rediscovery of Graeco-Roman culture also restored the nude to the heart of creative endeavour. Nude figures based on antique models appear in Italy as early as the mid-thirteenth century, and by the mid-fifteenth century, nudes had become symbols of antiquity and its reincarnation. Thus Zeus is now usually depicted as partially or entirely unclothed, and frequently within the context of one of his sexual exploits (Io, Pasiphae, Leda etc.). Since many of these affairs involved the god taking a non-human form, he does not often figure with the standard elements in these paintings and statues, but where he does, for example in depictions of Semele or Thetis, he is, again, usually bearded, mature but not elderly – his hair is usually dark rather than grey and he is a powerful, muscled figure.[9]

In many ways, recent depictions of Zeus echo this approach with regard to physical appearance, but with a modern twist, in that the god is now portrayed as a warrior. *Clash of the Titans* (2010) has a Zeus with long dark hair, moustache and beard, played by Liam Neeson, 58, wearing silver armour and shining with a bright white light evoking the thunderbolts that are his trademark weapon, and indicating his divine power (see Figure 3.3). This armour was specially constructed, according to Simon Brindle, the costume armour supervisor for the film:

> Zeus is in a woven, soft-bounded leather and a compressed linen, which is another Greek armor technique. They compressed dozens of layers of linen together under an awful lot of weight, and it actually became impervious to blades. So Zeus' armor was layers of linen and felt and woven leather with fine metal bounding running up and down the surface of the armor – just little bright details that catch the light every now and then.[10]

Sean Bean's Zeus in the Percy Jackson movies (2010, 2013) is also a powerful figure, clad in armour rather than flowing robes. The depiction of the gods in the two Percy Jackson movies, closely based upon the original books by Rick Riordan, somewhat unusually shows the ancient Greek gods interacting with the modern Western world. Like their Homeric models, they are a superhuman version of humanity, with both strengths and weaknesses writ large. Divided by rivalries and hatreds, such as that between Athena and Poseidon, they are presented as human in behaviour, creatures from whom very

Figure 3.3 Zeus (Liam Neeson) in *Clash of the Titans* (2010).
Warner Bros. Pictures.

few moral lessons can be learned, and in place of the wise and venerable father figure, we see a dysfunctional family, apparently in the prime of life, troubled by the relationship issues that concern mortals of a similar age.

Perhaps the most striking such depiction, however, was that of Tarsem Singh's *Immortals* (2011), in which 31-year-old Luke Evans played the part of Zeus (see Figures 3.4 and 3.5). The choice of such a young actor was a conscious move on the part of the director. With regard to the more youthful depiction of the gods in this movie, Henry Cavill, who plays Poseidon, commented 'It's funny when I have people asking me "isn't Poseidon supposed to be old? Isn't he supposed to have a grey beard?" Why? Because you guys watch movies like that?'[11] Similarly Luke Evans talks of Tarsem Singh's 'vision, his overall vision for the movie and the concept of the gods being young or at least looking young'. The interview continues:

> **We're more used to seeing someone like Liam Neeson as Zeus in 'Clash of the Titans', with the long beard.**
> Yes, exactly and Laurence Olivier, the traditional idea of what you think of as Zeus and obviously we're breaking all those clichés in this movie. Tarsem's argument is, if you're a god and you have all the power in the world, why would you want to be old? Why wouldn't you just keep yourself young, in great physical shape, being able to fight if you needed to? And I thought, 'I can do that, I can see that.' And my charge was just channeling all the other aspects of Zeus, being a king, being thousands of years old, and all of those aspects which, as an actor was a real challenge.
> **The gods in 'Immortals' are in great shape, but they're not as massively buff as you might expect. Is that part of Tarsem's vision, that they're more vulnerable and able to be killed?**
> Well, Henry was in insane shape. The thing about the gods is that they have these immense powers and I think that was something Tarsem wanted to use, that they were like superheroes, they can fly to earth and they can fight at immense speeds, there was that that was interesting. I don't think Tarsem was worried about the size of us being different, what was interesting, was that when the gods come to earth, they're human sized, which in a way I think as an audience member, you can relate much better to a 'god' in inverted commas.[12]

Similarly, Tom Belding's Zeus in *Prometheus: Retribution* (2014) is also a younger god, with short dark hair and short beard, again dressed as a fighter.

An even more extreme deviation from tradition is the depiction of Zeus without any classicising or superpower elements, presenting a modernised god instead. In such cases it is power that defines the god. In some cases, this creates a negative stereotype. The BBC's *Gory Greek Gods* (2004), for example, a two-part documentary

Figures 3.4 and 3.5 Zeus (Luke Evans) in *Immortals* (2011). Relativity Media.

series, presents Zeus as a Mafia boss, a stylishly cartoon-like, svelte, clean-shaven, dark-haired man in an evening suit. This is in keeping with the idea behind this production, as set out in the accompanying publicity blurb:

> The Olympians – the mythical Greek Gods – were almost like a fantasy family firm of mobsters. While not dealing directly in crime, these ancient-world Sopranos were certainly in the protection business. Divine protection was on offer. To their ancient worshippers, Greek religion was all about appeasing and honoring the Gods. However, these gods weren't like our God. They could be good, but very often they could be unfair, ungrateful, spoiled, and sometimes, downright nasty. In short they could be like Gangsters.
>
> In these BBC two one-hour episodes this is how we depict the Gods: – a Firm – not from New York, Chicago, or the East End – but somewhere in between – a place where archetypes exist.[13]

In *Prometheus and the Butcher*, a short piece from 2006, described as 'a modern retelling of Prometheus set in a butcher shop in the 70's. A dark, funny, tragicomedy', Zeus is again a mob boss figure. This time he is short and manic, with fur-trimmed cloak, purple satin shirt, gold-trimmed trousers, cowboy hat and flashy jewellery, and the number plate 'PIMP N'. In several recent versions (two recent film school projects, *Eric of the Gods* (2009) and *Cupid* (2011), and the internet webseries *A God Named Pablo* (2010–15)) he is presented as a businessman or corporate figure, with open-necked shirt and dark jacket, projecting an air of authority. Zeus also appears in an episode of *Supernatural* (2005–) (Season 8, Episode 16, 'Remember the Titans', from 2013), and here too the grey-haired, bearded figure is dressed in formal, modern garb, in this case a grey suit, paired with black shirt and tie. A similar approach was taken in the (in the end unreleased) comedy *Gods Behaving Badly* (2013), in which Zeus, like the other Olympians, appears in modern dress, apart from in flashback scenes to ancient Greece, in which case he is clothed in the traditional gold-trimmed, white robes and gold laurel-wreath-decorated crown.

The conveying of power is also central to the depiction that has caused the most controversy, namely the most recent one, that of *Troy: Fall of a City* (2018), in which Zeus is played by a 55-year-old black British-Nigerian actor, Hakeem Kae-Kazim. This king of the gods has none of the usual symbols (although an eagle does sometimes indicate his presence), and wears simple clothes, a rough brown tunic and long, hooded cloak in darker brown. The materials look homespun and unfinished, and the necklace he wears contains three beads on a thick cord. Yet Kae-Kazim plays the part with power, his digitally enhanced voice when he speaks sounding resonantly god-like, and he has a commanding presence as he sits broodingly watching the insignificant mortals whom he treats with remote aloofness. Despite his lofty and dignified performance, the casting caused a backlash, with some outraged viewers accusing the production of 'blackwashing' the story. Others pointed out the ridiculous nature of such an accusation, bearing in mind that the characters are played neither by Greeks nor by natives of Asia Minor, and dismissed the criticisms as racist nonsense.[14] In fact, Kae-Kazim's Zeus, with his quiet yet palpable strength, is, in essence, a suitable heir to the tradition handed down from Homer until the present day.

The Biblical God on Screen

- A hugely powerful, disembodied voice booms out over a low and suspenseful musical track. 'Mo..o...oses.... I am the God of thy father, the God of Abraham, the God of Isaac, and the God of Jacob.'
- An elderly man in sweatpants and baseball cap, speaking through an intercom, muses gently, 'Tobacco was one of my big mistakes. ... Ostriches were a mistake. Silly-looking things. Avocados, made the pit too big. Like I say, you try.'
- An 11-year-old boy perches on a rock and says malevolently 'Sometimes children have to die.'

All of the above are screen depictions of God, the God of the Old and New Testaments, of Judaism and Christianity, who is of course regarded in a wide and varied range of ways, both internally within each religion, and between the two traditions. 'God' is a multifaceted term that conveys multiple, and differing, concepts to individuals, and yet on screen, God must be instantly recognisable for who he is.

It is perhaps paradoxical that, despite the fact that Zeus is sometimes depicted as a variant of the paternalistic God of the Old Testament, God himself is rarely represented in such a way on screen. The issue is, of course, complicated by the thorny issue of faith. While Zeus is not generally a deity in whom the modern world believes, the same cannot be said of God. Any depiction of him must deal with the question of who the intended audience is and how it will react to the representation. In particular, the Hays Code of 1930 specified that movies were forbidden to 'throw ridicule on any religious faith'. The series *God, the Devil and Bob* (2000) was cancelled by NBC due to complaints and protests by conservative Christian groups. Even without these issues of control and pressure, however, any portrayal of God will inevitably be influenced in some way by how those making the film relate to the question of divinity and religion.

Nor is there only one interpretation or view on the subject of the nature of God or how he can or should be portrayed; Christians, Jews and Muslims of all denominations may have strong views on this issue, and movies on religious themes or depicting holy figures invariably provoke fierce reactions, even when done reverently. As one review of *Bruce Almighty* (2003) emphasised, 'Everyone has their own idea of God, and Hollywood is usually keen not to cause offence, especially when it's trying to sell the world an otherwise innocuous summer comedy.'[15]

While television and film makers may differ radically in their portrayals, all are grappling with the question of how to represent the all-powerful, all-loving, yet non-anthropomorphic deity. As already discussed, some film makers have reverently avoided showing God on screen, preferring to substitute representative figures or the Voice of God, particularly in the twentieth century when religion in the form of Christianity played a more prominent role in society than in the current climate. Not every representation of God has followed this route, however, for he also been depicted corporeally on screen, particularly within the comic genre, and such portrayals have no negative overtones with regard to the deity. In the second of the three examples mentioned above, George Burns famously took on the role in three movies in the 1970s and 1980s (*Oh, God* (1977), *Oh, God, Book II* (1980) and *Oh, God! You Devil* (1984)). These feel-good movies provide a gentle but comic speculation on what might happen if God attempted to appear once more to mankind, and did so in human form. Burns, as a grey-haired, clean-shaven, bespectacled God in clothes typical of a septuagenarian, has a gentle authority and an amusingly sardonic take on the world, explaining why he is appearing as he is ('because if I showed myself to you as I am, you wouldn't be able to comprehend me'), and including amongst his reminiscences not only the less successful inventions mentioned above, but also some unexpected miracles, a prime example of which, he says, is the 1969 Mets. Affectionate in tone, the movie depicts a kindly if not altogether efficient deity, who is gently disappointed with his children, at whose feet responsibility for evil is placed.

Despite this benign attitude towards the concept of God, even this gentle movie was not unequivocally accepted by believers, as reviews and debates at the time reflect. One website hosts a review in which two Christian ministers debate the merits of the film:

Pastor Peter Richard Hartford: Okay, you can stop right there! Can you seriously tell me that you would recommend this superficial movie to anyone? Any good Christian knows that no one has seen God at any time and that it is written in the Bible: 'My ways are not your ways.'

Pastor Harvey Boston: That's one of the valid points this little movie is making. We always expect God to fit into our limited ways of perceiving. We expect him to prove himself by miracles or playing the role of Mr. Fixit. Our attitude is – Let God Do It. This film says that God does care about how we handle our lives on earth, but also – and this is important – that we are responsible for what happens here. We can't just abdicate our task of ushering in the future because we're scared or have messed things up so badly already.

Pastor Peter Richard Hartford: But the depiction of God you are talking about sounds like it takes God's transcendence too lightly. I'm sure too that it satirizes decent theologians who are trying to make the Word of God clear. That's why I don't go to movies much anymore – they make fun of everything, even sacred things.

Pastor Harvey Boston: Well, my friend, you are right about one thing: *Oh, God!* is a mischievous movie. It dares to put forward the proposition that far too many people only want to think of God as the Great Bookkeeper in the Sky. At one point in this movie, the theologians submit a list of questions for Denver to ask Burns. As if God should have to take a quiz to prove that he is the Answer Man. The movie reminded me that Jesus never locked God up into one image or parable and that St. Paul proclaimed a God whose wisdom is foolishness! I got to thinking after watching this film about all the odd ways the Holy One has spoken to us throughout history and the very ordinary individuals chosen to be his messengers. Who are we to question Him?[16]

It is striking that this debate, however, although it does nervously examine the moral and religious message of the film, does not query the casting or portrayal of God by the Jewish actor George Burns. This depiction is close enough to the paternalistic, elderly and benign figure of tradition for this not even to be questioned by these religious leaders.

Bruce Almighty and its sequel, *Evan Almighty* (2007), demonstrate a similar approach to God to that of the Burns movies. In these films, Morgan Freeman, dressed in a white suit, plays God, as he hands over the reins of control to a mortal for a week to try his hand at running the world in a better way. Freeman imbues God with warmth towards mankind; this deity is loving, powerful and firmly in control, wanting to pass on to humans his messages of the importance of family, loving kindness and faith, in order to make the world a better place.

Bruce Almighty might at first seem radical in its portrayal of God by Morgan Freeman, for its depiction of the deity as black. This was not so groundbreaking, however, since the deity had been played by Rex Ingram in the 1936 film adaptation of the 1930 Pulitzer Prize-winning play *The Green Pastures*. Freeman's skin colour was not regarded as controversial, and some indeed felt that the casting reflected modern audiences' ease with African-American spirituality. This is perhaps an over-optimistic reading, as Scott Hughes explained:

> the reality behind this portrayal is probably rather more prosaic. While Bruce Almighty's God does embody some of the main tenets of black Christianity ... his appearance here as an African-American owes more to the simple wish to cast Freeman than one to explore racial or theological issues ... The creative team's principal aim was to present God as a more 'personal' and less 'generic and pious' figure, and that His being black was not a demand of the screenplay. Rather, it was on account of his track record in playing authority figures ... , together with his gift for conveying wisdom and sense of comic timing, that Freeman was considered, from very early in the movie's development, an ideal actor to take on the role.[17]

As a film directed by a professing Christian, Tom Shadyac, the movie was far from heretical. Michael Elliott, a Christian film critic, stated that '*Bruce Almighty* is very respectful of God and the relationship between God and man. ... The spiritual messages being delivered by the film are ones which Christians will especially recognize and support.'

More radical are those rare movies in which God is played by a female. Despite the traditional paternalistic ideas about the Judaeo-Christian God, two such examples can be found. In *Dogma* (1999), the role is played by Alanis Morissette, as a young woman with long, wavy, dark hair, dressed first in a long, tunic-style sleeveless dress and carrying a flower, and then in a metallic silver-laced bodice, fitted jacket, flip-flops and white, ruffled, chiffon, tutu-esque miniskirt. She does not speak, her voice being too powerful for human ears to bear,[18] her words being heard through the figure of Metatron (Alan Rickman). In an overt overturning of earlier cinematic depictions, Metatron says ironically, 'Tell a person that you're the Metatron and they stare at you blankly. Mention something out of a Charlton Heston movie and suddenly everybody is a theology scholar.' The female hippie-style God in this film is an explicit rejection of the traditional interpretation as represented in the public mind by Charlton Heston. Another female depiction from the twenty-first century was that of Whoopi Goldberg in *A Little Bit of Heaven* (2011), in which Goldberg sported a white flower in her hair and wore a gold-trimmed, white, flowing, robe-style dress, reminiscent of the traditional godly garb, which is perhaps more suited in style in the modern world to a woman than a man. This female God lends a maternal, nurturing element to the portrayal that only adds to the positive nature of the depiction. A similar approach was that of the faith-based fantasy film *The Shack* (2017), which cast the actress Octavia Spencer, well known for her roles in *The Help* (2011) and *Hidden Figures* (2016), as God.

Not all portrayals of God are as benevolent as these. A more comic and satirical take on God is that in the movie *Religion, Inc./A Fool and his Money* (1989), in which George Plimpton played God as a self-satisfied, middle-aged figure with an unexpected penchant for tax loopholes and a liking for playing tennis. A similarly sardonic depiction featured in the controversial animated series *God, the Devil and Bob*, a sitcom based on the idea of God (voiced by James Garner) and the Devil (voiced by Alan Cumming) challenging each other over the fate of the world. This God wants to destroy mankind and start again, but feels unable to take such drastic action because he's 'not that kind of God'. He makes a bet with the Devil, whereby the Devil selects one person who must prove they have improved the world in some way, and if he cannot, God will indeed wipe out the world. Despite the Devil's choice of Bob, a beer-drinking, porno-watching car-plant worker from Detroit, he does save humanity in the pilot episode, after which the series involves God's engaging Bob in various plans to help out and improve the world. This God has a pot belly, white hair and thick white beard, wears sunglasses and a Hawaiian shirt, and is visually styled on Jerry Garcia of The Grateful Dead, who died the previous year. He is, in the words of one review, 'an ageing, genial hippie',[19] who has a benign attitude towards the world and mankind as a whole.

Rather more negative are Irvine Welsh's God in *The Granton Star Cause* (1994), and Maurice Roeves' in *Acid House* (1998), both of whom are portrayed as foul-mouthed, Scottish drunks, worn out by humanity's insistence on blaming them for everything that goes wrong in their lives. More recently, a Belgian film entitled *The Brand New Testament* has God as an abusive father who lives in a shabby flat in Brussels and takes sadistic pleasure in making people miserable through the rules he invents and puts in place via an outdated DOS computer. A violent slob in T-shirt, long shorts and checked dressing gown, he has greying hair and stubble in place of the flowing white beard of traditional representations.

Such antagonistic depictions have reached a peak over the past two decades, in which God, and in particular the God of the Old

Testament, has become an anathema to film makers. Both physically and ideologically, there has been a radical alteration in how the deity is portrayed. The review of *The Brand New Testament* describes the God of this movie as 'more the Archie Bunker variety, played by "Man Bites Dog's" Benoit Poelvoorde as a domineering white-trash shlub in a wife-beater T-shirt and ratty bathrobe'.[20]

This negative perception of God is echoed repeatedly in the post-modern world, perhaps most strikingly in the two great Biblical epics of 2014, *Noah* and *Exodus: Gods and Kings*. Although in *Noah* God himself, called throughout 'The Creator', is never seen or heard, his message is conveyed through the character of Noah, who is, in the words of the director, Darren Aronofsky, 'a dark, complicated character' who experiences 'real survivor's guilt' after the flood.[21] He is also a religious fanatic who continually judges others harshly, leaving a young woman to die in a trap, and coming very close in his misguided beliefs to murdering his own newborn granddaughters.

Despite the fact that Aronofsky and Ari Handel, the producer, are both Jewish by birth and upbringing (though Aronofsky at least is a self-proclaimed atheist), and that they were very keen to locate the film in the tradition of Midrash, Biblical exegesis, the depiction of God in this movie is distinctive and sends a message that is clearly at odds with traditional Jewish and Christian ideas. In place of the opening words of Genesis, 'In the beginning God created', the film tells us on two occasions, 'In the beginning there was nothing', and while it states that 'the breath of The Creator fluttered against the face of the void, whispering, "Let there be light"', this is a rather abstract depiction and from that point on, there is no further mention of God in the creation story, until we are told that he made man and woman. Nor is this very minimal role in creation even necessarily the truth, for it is stated by Noah, while the running text at the beginning of the movie does not mention God at all, leaving open the possibility that this is merely human belief as opposed to truth.

This, in fact, is the case throughout the movie. No 'Voice of God' is ever heard; rather we see Noah's dreams, and hear the words of Methuselah and Noah, explaining their beliefs. It even seems that Noah may have hallucinated God's will after drinking a potion given to him by Methuselah. Certainly Noah is a religious fanatic. Some, at least, of his beliefs are mistaken, and lead him to commit evil, even to the point, as already mentioned, of determining to kill his own newborn granddaughters, a viewpoint and decision the audience is clearly not meant to endorse. If, then, Noah is wrong about this, is there not a good chance that he is wrong about everything else too?

He believes in 'the creator', and thinks he understands what that deity wants – but that does not necessarily imply that the creator actually exists. In fact, Noah is a tortured soul, who sees his misguided ideas disintegrate, leaving him with nothing, surely an interpretation inspired by Aronofsky's atheism. The movie goes further than this, however, for if God is real, he is harsh and unreasonable, repeatedly demanding terrible sacrifices from Noah, and implacably decreeing the deaths of millions, including presumably innocent children, without even answering Noah's pleas. So we are left with the idea that if God does not exist, Noah's beliefs are empty and false, while if God does exist, he is cruel and implacable.[22]

The film *Exodus: Gods and Kings* takes this view even further. This version of the tale of Moses leading the Children of Israel out of Egyptian servitude is a far cry from DeMille's classic epic movie of 1956, *The Ten Commandments*. In place of the authoritative Voice of God, in *Exodus: Gods and Kings* (the plurals in the title are surely no coincidence), we have an 11-year-old boy who appears to Moses as a theophany, and who is capricious and cruel, uttering lines such as 'sometimes children have to die' (see Figure 3.6). Although Ridley Scott declared of the child-God character, Malak, 'Malak exudes innocence and purity, and those two qualities are extremely powerful', it is malevolence and harshness that shine out far more than the qualities mentioned by Scott, and in fact Malak is a less merciful and compassionate character than Pharaoh. Moses himself, a warrior with a sword rather than a leader with a staff, is a tortured and anguished soul, as played by Christian Bale, who said of the character, 'I think the man was likely schizophrenic and was one of the most barbaric individuals that I ever read about in my life.' It is, in fact, entirely possible that this 'God' is merely the hallucination of a crazed man, which is in keeping with the general move to provide rational explanations for the Biblical events. As one review put it, the movie 'barely concedes the miraculous', and is perhaps, 'Ridley Scott's personal vision of God and his wrangling through his art with the consequences of what saying "I believe" means',[23] an interpretation that naturally led to some consternation on the part of believing viewers. For the majority, however, in a secular world, this vision of God is perhaps uncontroversial and a truly twenty-first-century take on the Judaeo-Christian deity.

This negative attitude towards God is a relatively new trend on screen; traditionally God was unquestionably good, and evil was represented by the Devil. Such ideas are reflected also in portrayals of the Olympians gods, since, apart from Zeus, the Olympian god who features most centrally on screen is Hades, to whom we now turn.

HADES

In 1934 Disney produced a 10-minute animated feature entitled *The Goddess of Spring*, which told the story of Persephone and Pluto, also known as Hades.[24] With long pointed ears and fingers, horns, black hair and a hooked nose, this figure erupts from the Underworld in a fiery volcanic explosion, accompanied by thunder and lightning, laughing menacingly. He is dressed in red, with a black cloak topped by a white collar, reminiscent of standard depictions of vampires. Approaching Persephone, he first bows low, enticing her to become his queen, but on her refusal, seizes her hand and sweeps her up into his arms, carrying her off, and descends once more into the flames, accompanied by his army of black, pitchfork-armed imps.

Much in this depiction is associated not with the classical god Hades, but with Christian conceptions of Satan/the Devil. There are of course many fundamental differences between Lucifer and the god of the Underworld, but as both are negative, powerful, supernatural figures, film makers have been less troubled by these distinctions than scholars, and have frequently conflated the two figures, attributing Satanic and other demonic elements to Hades. These elements include the cloak mentioned above, and in particular the colours red and black, both of which are associated with sin. Black is the colour of evil, contrasted with the purity of white, while red is linked to fire, lust and blood.[25] Fire in particular, inspired by the concept of

Figure 3.6 Malak (Isaac Andrews) in *Exodus: Gods and Kings* (2014). Chernin Entertainment/Scott Free Productions/Babieka/Volcano Films.

the flames of Hell, is associated with the Devil. As a result of the repression of polytheism by the Church, and the subsequent identification of Satan and his angels with the gods of paganism,[26] other divine pagan elements were adduced to the depiction of the Devil. From the god Pan, as well as the Celtic god Cernunnos, in particular, came the cloven hoofs, tail, horns, goatee beard, large phallus, big nose and wrinkled skin of popular depictions. He sometimes has female breasts, particularly common in seventeenth-century portrayals; these are very likely to have come from the goddess Diana.[27] Not every aspect of the traditional appearance of the Devil comes from pagan gods, however. He is also sometimes winged, a tradition that arose due to the conception of him as a fallen angel.[28]

The whole range of depictions of Satan have been utilised by film makers. Often he has been avoided altogether, with his spirit possessing humans, or seen as an unseen force (*Rosemary's Baby* (1968) and (2014), *The Omen* (1976) and its sequels, the later *Omen* remake (2006), *The Passion of the Christ* (2004)). This could be because, rather as Voldemort must not be named in the Harry Potter series, actually picturing the Devil is one step too far even for a horror movie. More likely, however, is that it is just not easy to portray the Devil convincingly. Some have portrayed the Devil as a red-horned creature with hooves, a forked tail and a pitchfork (*Legend* (1985), *The Simpsons* (1989–, episode from 1993), *South Park* 1997–, episode from 1999), *Tenacious D in The Pick of Destiny* (2006), to give a few random examples). Others have him in human form, but with some of these Satanic elements, such as horns (e.g. *Little Nicky* (2000), *Horns* (2013)), or with other supernatural aspects such as staring eyes or bloodlessly white skin (*The Passion of the Christ*, *The Collector* (2004–6)). On other occasions, as with the cinematic depictions of God, he is portrayed as human in form (*Bedazzled* (1967), *Mister Frost* (1990), *The Witches of Eastwick* (1987)). In such cases he is frequently well dressed, suave, elegant and attractive.

Some of these elements also frequently feature in depictions of Hades, so often conflated with Satan in popular culture. Hades' fiery hair and dark greyish colouring owe much to Satan in Disney's *Hercules*, for example, in which the influence of Dante and Christian tradition is notable. The Christian attitude towards Satan perceives him as being in competitive struggle with God for the immortal souls of men. Whereas all ancient Greeks would end up in the Underworld, regardless of their behaviour or lives, good Christians will go to Heaven, realm of the angels and saints, rather than Hell, where the Devil rules supreme. Disney's Hades is in part a Lucifer figure, who has been cast out of heaven and schemes to return, here portrayed as a fast-talking, manipulative salesman figure, who hates his job as lord of the Underworld and plots to overthrow Zeus. In this version, Hades has become the villain of the plot, in place of Hera, who hated and persecuted Hercules in the Greek myth because he was the result of one of Zeus' extramarital affairs. Like Sleeping Beauty's Maleficent, Hades is the agent of darkness, who plots to bring about the destruction of good. All that is evil comes from him in this portrayal. Thus it is Hades who sends creatures such as the Hydra and the Erymanthian boar to attack Hercules, not as part of an atonement process in the course of twelve labours performed as penance for Hercules' murder of his own children, but purely from enmity.

Hades is also a comic villain, and his swift patter voiced by James Woods was, according to Nik Ranieri, the supervising animator for the character, 'based on a Hollywood agent, a car salesman type'.[29] This epitome of 1980s capitalist consumerism is, in the end, one of Disney's least frightening and funniest villains, an interpretation that therefore undercuts this portrayal of the Devil. Despite his megalo-maniac tendencies and shallowness, this Hades is not actually mor-ally evil – more distasteful than repugnant.

Disney's influence also extends to the portrayal of Hades as a character in the fifth season of the television series *Once Upon a Time* (Season 5, 2016). Played by the 58-year-old Greg Germann, who based his portrayal on Disney's, this god of the Underworld is smartly dressed in jacket and tie, but has short, light-brown hair that turns to blue flames when he is angry, in a nod to the earlier produc-tion, as well as, once more, to the figure of Satan, to whom he owes more than to the Greek god himself.

As with the rest of the characters and stories in this production, this programme gave a new twist to the ancient stories, and to Hades' mythology itself. In this version, Hades is still a god, but is the younger brother of Zeus, and, jealous of his brother, it was he who killed their father, Kronos, and attempted to steal the all-powerful 'Olympian crystal'. As a result, in the struggle between the brothers over the crystal, Zeus hurls a curse at Hades, stopping his heart. In order to break this curse, Hades has continually been searching for his true love, whose kiss will start his heart beating again. Since he is despised by all, this proves a difficult task, and it is only when he meets someone equally evil, namely Zelena, the Wicked Witch of the West, that he is able to fall in love; but she proves to be his undoing, ultimately sending him into oblivion.

Hades in this incarnation is evil and manipulative, in a constant struggle with the heroes of the programme, Emma Snow and Captain Hook, and their allies and friends. He is a jealous god, with regard both to Zeus and to those who arrive in his realm, whom he is very loath to release. His behaviour is often vindictive and cruel, and he seems to have few, if any, redeeming features. Nevertheless, against the fantasy background of this series, he is actually a sympathetic character, who seems to suffer from the loneliness that stems from being King of the Dead. Once again like Disney's Hades, he is also a smooth talker, with comic overtones. Although he ultimately manipulates and lies to Zelena, there is actual chemistry between them at some points, and he somehow manages to evoke viewer understanding.

In the two Percy Jackson movies, based on Rick Riordan's enormously successful books, Hades is also more of a pitiable character than a diabolical one, and once again is portrayed as a figure of dry, sardonic humour. The Underworld in this case is situated beneath the DOA Recording Studios in Hollywood – Percy, Grover and Annabeth enter the realm of Hades through the Hollywood Sign – in an ironic commentary on Tinseltown, with both its surface allure and its darker underbelly. Steve Coogan, who plays Hades, talks of 'marrying the sinister with the comic' so that the character would be 'genuinely threatening' but also 'laced with a little humour'.[30] In his portrayal, Hades is 'neurotic as well as Evil'.

This evil is represented by the fact that the god does possess a violent and terrifying temper, bears grudges for an extremely long time, and, like his father, Kronos, can be cruel, ruthless and devious. Unlike Kronos, however, Hades is not evil, but rather distant and bitter. In Riordan's version, this bitterness is caused by the fact that he was left to rule the Underworld himself, and possessed no home on Olympus, unlike the rest of his family, who fear and despise him. Additionally, Hades' children are outcasts, rejected by other demi-gods, and are not even, at first, allocated a cabin at Camp Half-Blood.

Because of this bitterness and rejection, Hades is a solitary and independent god, who rarely works with others. He is a stern father, although his attitude towards his son, Nico, softens as the series progresses. As judge of the Underworld, Hades is a strictly implacable, even harsh, enforcer of oaths and the laws of morality, but he is also honourable and just, as well as highly intelligent, a brilliant strategist who is skilled in debate. He is also industrious, fulfilling his time-consuming duties diligently.

Physically, Riordan's Hades bears little resemblance to Satan either. The Riordan wikia site describes him as:

a very tall, imposing and very muscular god with albino white skin (due to the little time he spent in the sunlight), intense black eyes that 'glitter like frozen tar', and were either the eyes of a genius or a madman, and having a mesmerizing, evil charisma, and shoulder-length black hair, with bangs usually covering most of his forehead. According to Persephone in *Percy Jackson's Greek Gods*, when Hades is passionate, his black eyes 'flare with purple fire'.

His voice is also described as oily. In *The Demigod Files*, he is described as having a beard. Hades often wears black flowing robes with evil souls threaded into the cloth ... Hades' black robes are tied at the waist with a white cord. His cowl is pushed back, revealing dark hair shorn close to the scalp.[31]

This Hades can also transform into Pluto, his Roman identity, who in this case has a slightly different emphasis in characterisation. As Pluto, he wears modern clothing – a dark suit, black tie and grey undershirt.

In the films, despite the trappings of Cerberus and Charon, the connection between Hades and Satan is rather more pronounced than in the books. On screen the Underworld is actually identified as 'Hell', and Hades' palace is a dark Gothic mansion lit by candles and with roaring flames in the fireplaces. In this interpretation, the god is portrayed as an ageing and impotent rocker, clad in black leather and a trendily ripped black shirt, partnered with a Goth Persephone (Rosario Dawson) who is dressed in a low-cut, black and purple lace dress with a bodice, bustle and high-heeled boots. Coogan talks of the decision to play Hades as a rock star rather than having 'pointy horns and a tail, you know, with an arrow on the end of it, like you expect the Devil to be portrayed',[32] indicating his identification of the two, while Dawson also identifies the Underworld absolutely with Hell:

> It's quite poignant to see these two people – gods – struggling, hating and fighting and have it look like a disastrous Hollywood marriage. ... That's how Hell is depicted. Honestly, if I had to spend eternity listening to those people arguing all the time, I'd kill myself over and over again. ... It would just be awful. I think that's where you feel the descent into Hell, listening to these two people.[33]

The connection between Hades and the Devil is also highlighted by Hades' transformation, in a roar of flame, into a fire-breathing, drag-on-like monster, in response to Grover's surprise at his appearance.

Ralph Fiennes' Hades in the remake of *Clash of the Titans* from 2010 is a much more sinister, Voldemort-like figure. He is the main antagonist in this movie, and the influence of Disney's *Hercules* can be seen in that this Hades is bitter and turns on the other gods as a result of the sense of betrayal he feels because Zeus shut him down in the Underworld. In *Wrath of the Titans* (2012), after again attacking Zeus, he then has a change of heart and sides with his brother, demonstrating that he has a conscience and is capable of remorse and pity. In appearance, he is a humanised but still fearsome figure. In an interview, Fiennes described the god as follows:

> Well a voice that . . . you know . . . it's been choked with the fumes and the dust and the grit and the smoke and the kind of Hellish place where there's no fresh air. It's damp. . . . He's been sort of compressed by the weight of the world on him and the spiritual weight of so many dead people who have lost their lives. There is the pain and the suffering and the guilt and the agony of the dead souls, the lost souls he's surrounded by. . . . It's a bit literal but we had to go somewhere, so yeah, the hair is a bit matted and long, and the beard is long. All the male gods have armour but his armour is corrupted and corroded by water and residue . . . It's rotting armour, rotting metal.[34]

Despite the reference to a 'Hellish place' and 'smoke', the tones of Hades' realm are muted. Like Disney's, its dominant colour is grey, and water and damp the main features, as opposed to the fiery red of Satan and his abode. Unlike in the animated movie, however, this god is not a fast-talking comic act, but rather a figure weighed down by the cheerlessness of death. Although this pessimistic portrayal is closer to Greek views of death than many other depictions of the Underworld, it is, nevertheless, a long way from how the Greeks themselves viewed the god of the Underworld, a point that one fan-fiction writer makes amusingly in a story called 'Mount Olympus Movie Night':

> 'I mean they always portray me as their devil. Always! I'm just a simple God of Death. And I'm probably the least evil and the least cruel of you! . . . I mean what did I ever do to them? Nothing! Nothing at all!' Hades ranted: 'I gave in to Demeter; I gave in to Orpheus, to Hercules. I don't sleep around on my wife; I don't have any illegitimate children. I don't kill mortals for fun or send them mental illnesses or drive them into waging wars. I'm just as nice as Hestia or Hephaestus and yet they always make me evil and guys like you Zeus or you Poseidon are suddenly paragons of virtue and good.'[35]

This is a fair point. The Greek Hades or Pluto, king of the Underworld, was a feared deity in the ancient world, a cruel master of the shades who never relinquished any of his subjects, but this reflects the inevitability and immutability of death, rather than any inherent evil in Hades' character. To the Greeks, his realm included Tartarus, a place of eternal torture for evil-doers who committed outrageous sins against the gods,[36] and the fields of Elysium, where the heroes relaxed in never-ending enjoyment, but these were areas associated with the age of mythology and heroes, rather than the natural destination of the normal man. By Virgil's time, the Underworld (and its ruler) had altered somewhat to include a philosophy whereby it was a place where virtue is rewarded and vice punished. In Virgil's *Aeneid*, for example, ordinary sinners suffer torment and the virtuous get to a paradise that is an idealisation of the life led by Greek and Roman gentlemen. This paradise is reached through a cycle of rebirth and reincarnation which is broken only through virtuous behaviour, enabling eternal peace to be reached. Yet Hades himself is no more than guardian of this realm, rather than being the ultimate evil or representative of an ancient form of Hell. Although he has the Furies as his assistants, these female spirits of justice and vengeance, who persecute evil-doers with devilish and fiendish torments, feature in the Underworld only in the case of extreme criminals who are damned to eternal torment. Their central duties really lay in the world of the living where they could punish evil-doers – in particular those who committed murder, unfilial conduct, offences against the gods or perjury – with madness or disease.

This god has little in common with the Satan of either Jewish or Christian traditions. Unlike in Christianity, in Judaism, the Satan is an angel working at God's bidding , and the word always appears with the definite article, 'the Satan', rather than as the name of a figure. His role is that of a legal prosecutor, rather than a tormentor of sinners,[37] and he neither rules over a kingdom of demons nor torments the evil after death. In contrast, in mainstream Christianity, Satan is in overall control of Hell, which is contrasted with Heaven, where God reigns supreme. Satan is sometimes known as Mephistopheles or Beelzebub, although each of these is often also identified with a demon rather than the Devil himself. Origen, in the second century, made connections between Lucifer, the Prince of Tyre and Dragon, identifying all as Satan.[38] Other Christian theologians conceived of the Devil as the serpent in the Garden of Eden, the accuser of Job and the tempter of Jesus. At the heart of this depiction is the idea that the Devil is the ultimate enemy, at constant war with God, competing with him for men's souls. As Jeffery Burton Russell writes: 'Satan is the prime adversary of Christ. Satan tempts people; he causes illness and death. He obsesses and possesses individuals and tempts human beings to sin.' By the fourth century he had evolved as a fallen angel who rebelled against God, and in some versions, inspired other angels to follow his lead.[39]

Many of these elements are aspects dating back to the medieval period, or even earlier, but other depictions have also come to the fore over the past five centuries, and these show a wide variety of approaches. In the words of one review of a recent exhibition held at Stanford's Cantor Art Center, entitled *Sympathy for the Devil: Satan, Sin and the Underworld*, 'Over the past five centuries, artists have variously depicted the devil as a fanged, horned demon; as an armored, Apollo-like army leader; and as a tailor of Nazi uniforms.'[40] In general, as time passed, the horned, bestial monster took on a more human aspect as the more superstitious elements of religion lessened in the period of the Enlightenment. The same review continues, quoting Bernard Barryte, curator of the exhibition:

> 'By the 18th century, he's ennobled, almost looking like an Apollo', Barryte says – as seen in Thomas Stothard's *Satan Summoning His Legions*, from 1790. . . . People interpreted the figure less as demonic creature and more as heroic rebel against the oppression of the paternal god.'

The influence of John Milton's *Paradise Lost*, which portrayed Satan as an almost tragic hero, struggling to overcome his own doubts and weaknesses, also played a role in the humanising of the Devil at this time. This developed further into a depiction of Satan as a crafty and deceitful figure. In place of the fearsome, bestial figure, this suavely smooth, sly character, influenced strongly by works such as Goethe's *Faust* and Mark Twain's *The Mysterious Stranger*, enticed men to sin through temptation and persuasion, trapping them through attraction rather than terror.

Such portrayals may, in fact, be behind the occasional depictions of Hades in which he does not appear to possess Satanic elements. In the mid-1990s, Hades featured in *Hercules: The Legendary Journeys* and its spin-offs, *Young Hercules* (1998–9) and *Xena: Warrior Princess* (1995–2001). Three different actors played Hades in these series, and the appearance of the god differed with each. Mark Ferguson in 1994 appears more like Zeus than Hades, with no Satanic elements at all. Dressed in a white tunic and cloak, with a laurel wreath in his brown wavy hair, this Hades is not at all threatening, is relatively young, and is in fact rather weak, his kingdom being terrorised by Cerberus, who has got loose and has proved impossible to catch. Erik Thomson's Hades, in contrast, was a far more menacing figure, clad in trousers, cloak and breastplate all in black. He was still entirely human, however, with close-cropped hair and a military appearance. Although the third depiction by Stephen Lovatt appeared slightly more devilish, in that he was clothed in red and his realm had fiery elements, he was actually more like a Plantagenet prince than Satanic, his clothing consisting of a long, cloak-like robe, which he wore along with a crown that sat atop his neatly cropped hair.

PATRIARCHAL MALE GODS: SOME CONCLUSIONS

Clearly there is a strong overlap between both the depiction of Hades and Satan, and that of Zeus and God, on screen, with the appearance of these Greek gods owing much to traditional representations of the Old Testament deity and to the Christian Devil. Equally clearly, these representations, marked by paternal white hair and beard and flowing robes on one hand, and fire, horns and pitchforks on the other, have been influenced strongly by Renaissance painting and the reception of this art.

It is also notable that there are two different versions of Hades, one inspired by Satanic elements, in which he is the ultimate evil and the villain of every plot, and another in which he is far less threatening, and indeed a comic figure. In general, this less negative attitude towards him is seen in more recent productions, particularly under the influence of the Disney version. Although Satanic elements remain, especially in the association with fire that often figures as a feature of the screen Hades, he is, generally speaking, far from terrifying. Such an aspect is likely to be a result of the weakening of the role of Christianity, with its attitude of fear towards the Devil and his works, in the contemporary Western world, where Satan holds little sway.

Similarly, there have been radical, but parallel, changes in the portrayals of both Zeus and God on screen over the past half century or so, as film makers moved from reverence and awe, even in the case of the Olympian king of the gods, to a far more pejorative representation. The ultimate deity is now regarded as capricious and cruel, at odds with modern liberal ideology. As one review of *God, the Devil, and Bob* pointed out, when discussing the difficulty of depicting God in the modern world:

> Today, our culture has a new openness to the supernatural, to 'spirituality.' God may well come back into vogue, as long as He is egalitarian and tolerant, not 'judgmental' against sin but rather nice, making no exclusive truth-claims and not demanding too much of us. All that infinite stuff, all that unimaginable talk of a Trinity, the notion that God became incarnate in Jesus Christ – that will have to go. But a generic deity will be OK. That is exactly the kind of god that the Bible does not allow us to believe in.[41]

Obviously such alterations reflect changes in a society in which religion – at least in the form of mainstream Christianity – plays a far smaller role than in the past, and is even ridiculed and regarded as at best futile and at worst dangerously harmful by many, in a world in which religion is often cited more as the justification for extremist ideas than as a revered system of belief. How attitudes towards religion impact upon the depiction of other gods will be the subject to which we now turn, in an examination of both Jesus and the remainder of the Greek male gods as portrayed on the modern screen.

NOTES

1 Llewellyn-Jones (2013).
2 See Harryhausen and Dalton (2003: 155).
3 Trzaskoma (2013: 25).
4 <http://variety.com/2015/film/festivals/the-brand-new-testament-review-cannes-film-festival-1201498770> (accessed 10 May 2018).
5 These statues do not necessarily reflect the divine post-mortem apotheosis, and often predate the emperor's death. See Hallet (2005: 224–70).
6 Gwynne (1995: 249). See also Bober and Rubinstein (2010: 51).
7 Pausanias, *Tour of Greece* 5.11. 1f. Translation Dowden (2006: 26).
8 Dowden (2006: 27).
9 See Annibale Carracci, *Zeus and Hera* (1597); Peter Paul Rubens, *Cupid Supplicating Jupiter* (about 1614); Anton Losenko, *Zeus and Thetis* (1769); Jean-Simon Berthélemy, *Prometheus Creating Man in the Presence of Athena* (1802); Christian Griepenkerl, *The Theft of Fire* (1878).
10 <http://latimesblogs.latimes.com/entertainmentnewsbuzz/2012/03/wrath-titans-costume-armor.html> (accessed 10 August 2017).
11 <https://www.youtube.com/watch?v=ZwU7LTsvLU4> (accessed 10 May 2018) (at 2.25 mins).
12 <http://www.moviefone.com/2011/11/09/immortals-luke-evans-interview/> (accessed 10 May 2018).
13 <http://www.victrolux.com/L2/ggg_one/ggg_fs_main.html> (accessed 10 May 2018).
14 <http://www.radiotimes.com/news/tv/2018-05-25/troy-fall-of-a-city-blackwashing-casting-black-actors-greek-myth/>; <http://www.radiotimes.com/news/tv/2018-03-10/troy-fall-of-a-citys-hakeem-kae-kazim-calls-out-deep-insecurity-of-blackwashing-critics/>; <https://www.express.co.uk/showbiz/tv-radio/926754/Troy-Fall-of-a-City-blackwashing-Zeus-actor-Hakeem-Kae-Kazim-Achilles-Netflix-BBC>; <http://variety.com/2018/tv/news/troy-fall-of-a-city-casting-diversity-bbc-netflix-1202707708/> (all accessed 28 May 2018).
15 Scott Hughes, <https://www.theguardian.com/culture/2003/jun/20/artsfeatures> (accessed 10 May 2018).

16 <http://www.spiritualityandpractice.com/films/reviews/view/5922> (accessed 10 May 2018).

17 Scott Hughes, <https://www.theguardian.com/culture/2003/jun/20/arts features> (accessed 10 May 2018).

18 'Human beings have neither the aural nor the psychological capacity to withstand the awesome power of God's true voice. Were you to hear it, your mind would cave in and your heart would explode within your chest. We went through five Adams before we figured that one out' (Metatron in *Dogma*).

19 <https://www.theguardian.com/theobserver/2001/apr/29/features. review57> (accessed 10 May 2018).

20 <http://variety.com/2015/film/festivals/the-brand-new-testament-rev iew-cannes-film-festival-1201498770/> (accessed 10 May 2018)

21 <https://www.theguardian.com/film/filmblog/2012/aug/13/russell-crowe-noah-darren-aronofsky> (accessed 28 November 2018).

22 A final option is presented by Emma Watson's Ila at the end of the film, namely that God gave man, in the form of Noah, the choice to elect for mercy or destruction; but this case leaves man in a more powerful position than God, and therefore does not sit any more comfortably with believers.

23 <http://ncronline.org/blogs/ncr-today/exodus-gods-and-kings-stunn ing-barely-concedes-miraculous> (accessed 10 May 2018)

24 Available at <https://www.youtube.com/watch?v=JuVRi9XzNpk> (accessed 2 August 2018).

25 Ogechukwu (2012: 54).

26 Russell (1981: 70); Kelly (2006: 177, 208).

27 Russell (1984: 68); Levack (2006: 33).

28 Kelly (2006: 277).

29 <https://www.mouseinfo.com/new/2017/07/zero-to-hero-the-making-of-hercules-panel-at-d23expo/> (accessed 2 February 2018).

30 <https://www.youtube.com/watch?v=UffFJErEsJY> (accessed 13 February 2018).

31 <http://riordan.wikia.com/wiki/Hades> (accessed 2 May 2018).

32 <https://www.youtube.com/watch?v=dp7brpoQDGo> (accessed 13 February 2018).

33 <http://www.dailyrecord.co.uk/entertainment/celebrity/rosario-daw son-it-was-wild-to-play-a-goddess-1049587> (accessed 13 February 2018).

34 <https://www.youtube.com/watch?v=B1itxZqlVdg> (accessed 14 February 2018).

35 <https://www.fanfiction.net/s/6108369/1/Mount-Olympus-Movie-Night> (accessed 1 March 2018).

36 As Morford and Lenardon state, 'Tradition developed a canon of myth-ological sinners who suffer there forever: Tityus, with vultures tearing at his liver; Ixion, bound to a revolving wheel; the Danaids, vainly trying

to carry water in sieve-like containers; Sisyphus, continually rolling a rock up a hill; and Tantalus, tantalized by food and drink' (2003: 349).

37 See e.g. Federow (2012: 11–12).

38 See Russell (1981: 31).

39 Ibid., 31. See also Kelly (2006: 199).

40 <https://www.fastcodesign.com/3034309/the-changing-face-of-satan-artistic-depictions-of-the-devil-1500-to-today> (accessed 18 January 2018).

41 Veith (2000).

4 *Physiology and the Physical Appearance of the Divine (2): Screening the Olympian Males and Jesus*

SCREEN GODS, GODS ON SCREEN

Discussing *Percy Jackson and the Lightning Thief* (2010), in which he played Zeus, Sean Bean muses, 'It's every kid's dream in some way . . . to realise that you're part of the gods and you can become part of their world.'[1] Bean was talking about the premise of the Percy Jackson fantasies, but could just as easily have been talking about the status of the actor himself in the modern world, in which celebrities are analogous in many ways to ancient deities. Another website declares, 'To many women in the world Sean Bean is a Greek God'; this identification was attributed to his charisma and authoritative presence, his 'godlike' deep voice, his seductive power as evidenced by his role in 1993 as Lady Chatterley's gamekeeper, and the fact that he is 'one of the few men in this world that can look extremely masculine and dangerous wearing a "skirt"' (as seen when playing Odysseus in Petersen's *Troy* (2004)).[2]

Such an identification is not unusual; as Evans and Wilson explain, there is a close connection between the ancient gods and stars of the cinema:

> If we take a journey back to the earliest civilisations of man, we find then a primitive, but highly functional 'star system' in the shapes of the early gods and goddesses. They may have been far removed from the Hollywood award ceremonies, but weren't these the 'Oscars' of their times? They had specific gifts, were the 'best in their categories', and had a timeless quality that qualified them for the Hall of Fame. Like a Marilyn Monroe or a John Wayne they

personified what they did in a unique way. They all lived together in a world that was half real and half fantasy ... when Hollywood became a latter-day Olympus, the 'Home of the gods' became the home of the stars of the 'A' list.[3]

This is all part of a huge and powerful system that was developed in the early days of the film industry. As McDonald emphasises, 'the American film business has employed, and continues to employ, regular strategies for exploiting star performers in the production and consumption of films'.[4] Such a process explicitly and implicitly utilised the figures of the Greek gods, making direct parallels between screen gods and the Olympians. The American fan-magazine *Photoplay* from 1928 ran a full article extolling the connections between the two. 'Hollywood is the world's new Olympus. Hollywood is bringing back the glory that was Greece', it declared, and goes on to compare in table form the beauty, intelligence and even vital statistics of 'Early Greek' and 'a composite of 69 "Modern Hollywood" Apollos and 72 Venuses'.[5] Thus, as Michael Williams suggests, 'classicism first shaped the discourse of stardom, ... stardom appropriated models of fame from other visual arts, and ... antiquity might have provided paradigms for fandom through the idol/worshipper metaphor'.[6]

There are many ways in which there is an overlap in the perception of classical gods and modern celebrities, particularly screen celebrities. Firstly, like the divinities, a star is literally larger than life when projected onto the big screen. Stars embody the wish-fulfilment of the fans who worship them. Such a connection feeds a desire for more information, in particular about the private life of the famous personality, whose scandalous exploits, reported in tabloid newspapers and magazines, exert fascination. Again in parallel with tales of the Greek gods, such stories titillate the reader with the interplay between the elevated power of the star and the salacious titbits that hint at a darker or tainted side. Yet, paradoxically, despite this urge to discover imperfections, the enthrallment with stars centres on the idealisation of their beauty or attractiveness, and in particular, sexual allure and magnetism. They are regarded as physically superior to ordinary mortals, possibly even perfect. Despite common gender stereotypes, such attraction is as common for females as for males; in a recent article on a 'problem page' of a British newspaper, a reader asked plaintively, complaining about his girlfriend's attitude towards such figures, 'How can I stop my girlfriend perving over actors on television?'[7]

The idolisation of celebrities is more than just a physical attraction, however; fans also identify with them, forming a powerful parasocial relationship with both characters and actors, as the initial attraction starts with a fictional character, but is then extended to the actor playing that character. Later roles played by the same actor may also then become influenced by earlier ones, in a conflation of fiction and quasi-fact revolving around the identities of both celebrity and fictional character. This is what Monica Cyrino describes as the use of a celebrity 'star text' that is interpreted by viewers. Almost forty years ago, Richard Dyer emphasised how the image of such stars can affect both the meaning and the effect of a film;[8] as Cyrino succinctly summarises,

> when a famous actor takes on a role, they bring one or more previous roles to the new performance; thus their star text powerfully influences how an audience engages with their previous roles within the new performance.[9]

When these previous roles are actually divine, the impact is even greater, and goes a long way towards creating an identification between the star, with his semi-divine star status, and the godly role he is playing. Thus Laurence Olivier both imparts divinity to Zeus, and becomes himself more godly by playing the role; Kellan Lutz' role as Poseidon in *Immortals* (2011) lent an element of immortality to his Hercules; while Robert Powell's identity is merged with that of Jesus to such an extent that photographs of the actor are hung up in churches.[10] By their roles being recorded for posterity in celluloid, the images of these actors become eternal; it is not for nothing that we talk of being immortalised on film. Like the statues of the ancient deities, the filmic representation of gods keeps them from ageing, preserving their perfection, and provides a symbolic representation of their divinity and its significance for the contemporary audience.

THE GREEK PANTHEON ON SCREEN

How, then, do the Greek male gods appear on screen? Most commonly they function as part of the wider group of Olympians, in which the individual gods are often hardly distinguished between in anything more than the most superficial manner. There are a number of ways in which film makers choose to present these deities. One approach, perhaps the most common traditional way of depicting the gods on screen, is as dressed in long, white tunic or toga-like robes, often trimmed with gold, and with the individual gods differentiated by means of their various iconic symbols. In this way, the depictions echo the Homeric epics, with their attribute-bearing names of gods, and ancient Greek art, such as found on vases and reliefs, where the figures are stylised and their symbols representative of individual deities.[11] The black-and-white depictions, such as the early *Le Tonnerre de Jupiter* (1903), *Vamping Venus* (1928) and *Night Life of the Gods* (1935), follow this route, but it continues into colour depictions as well.

In the Ray Harryhausen movies *Jason and the Argonauts* (1963) and *Clash of the Titans* (1981), all of the gods wear white robes, in imitation of sculpture, but the individual gods are not marked out with their usual symbols, and there are only slight variations to suggest character; Zeus for instance wears a long-sleeved tunic beneath his himation, whereas Hephaestus is bare-chested.[12] This lack of distinctive features is compensated for by the use of kinds of actors whose own personas give hints as to the character of the god being played, as Lloyd Llewellyn-Jones states:

> But cinema audiences cannot be trusted to recognize the signs spelled out through costumes and sets. Other methods need to be adopted to ensure that film viewers recognize different gods and, moreover, appreciate the essential qualities that individual gods incorporate. Therefore the on-screen image of the god and the movie star who plays the deity are often merged in the audience's subconscious in order to clarify the type of god being portrayed.[13]

In general, though, Harryhausen's aim was to highlight the distinction, not between the different gods (with the exception of the gulf between Zeus and the other gods), but between mortal and god. To this end he explains that he dressed the actors 'in white togas, which were distinctly different to the humans' more earthy colours',[14] rather than to emphasise the different natures of the individual gods.

The only male gods apart from Zeus to feature in either of the two films are Hermes, Poseidon and Hephaestus (the former in *Jason* and the latter two in *Clash*). In *Jason*, the messenger god Hermes (who appears first disguised as an elderly man) is marked out by his traditional symbols of caduceus and winged helmet, in this case of bronze, and considerably younger than the character he had assumed, although still not in the first flush of youth. Played by the 45-year-old Michael Gwynn (most famous for his later appearance as 'Lord' Melbury in the first episode of *Fawlty Towers*), this Hermes is actually far from godly in appearance. His divinity is represented by his huge stature when compared to mortals, demonstrated as he morphs into godly shape, growing to dwarf Jason who is doll-like in comparison.[15]

In *Clash of the Titans*, neither Jack Gwillim's Poseidon nor Pat Roach's Hephaestus carries the traditional symbols of the god from ancient iconography (for Poseidon the trident, for Hephaestus hammer and tongs, and/or a symbolic emphasis on the god's lameness). There are slight variations in clothing, with Hephaestus being younger, darker and more muscled than the other gods, and shown working in his forge on Olympus, his occupation emphasised by his bare chest under his himation. Poseidon meanwhile looks to be almost of an age with Zeus. Neither figure is particularly attractive or godly, and both, like the goddesses, are clearly differentiated from the king of the gods, seated on his throne and surrounded by halo-like laser rays.

More recent portrayals utilise the same approach to depicting the gods. *Saturday Night Live* (1975–), for example, screened a number of sketches featuring the Olympians between 2011 and 2016, and in each, they are clad in white cloaks and tunics, and paired with their iconic symbols. A similar approach is taken by *Titans of Newark* (2012), where the gods wear the usual white, flowing, 'classical-style' robes, occasionally teamed with iconic symbols, most notably in the case of Hermes who wears his standard golden winged helmet. *Hercules: The Brave and the Bold* (2013), described as 'An Independent Adventure Film' by 3 Kings Productions, also dresses the gods in what appears to be sheets tied over the shoulder, in white or, in the case of Ares and Hades, black. In a reversal of tradition, the god of war is middle-aged in this production, while Hades is a younger man. So too in *For the Love of Zeus* (2015–18), Dionysus and Poseidon, like Zeus, are costumed in white tunics or togas, with wreaths on their heads, although both Hades and Apollo wear black jerkins. The reason for dressing Hades in such a manner is not only an association with death, but seems to be linked to the fact that, like Apollo in this portrayal, he is again played here as a younger god. Dionysus, on the other hand, despite being a second-generation Olympian in classical myth, is older in this case.[16]

Not all productions depict the Greek gods mainly in statue-inspired white, however; occasionally they appear in modern dress. In *A God Named Pablo* (2010–15), for example, Neptune is clothed in a cream suit with blue shirt and Apollo an open-necked black shirt. Because, in contrast to the traditional white-robed approach, such costuming gives no hint of something more than mortal, it is more common for film makers to search for some means with which to create the impression of godliness, however. In Disney's *Hercules* (1997), for example, the gods were surrounded by glowing light, and although they retained the Greek-style clothing, both they and their garments were brightly coloured. The predominant hues of Olympus were pink, orange and gold, creating an atmosphere of fantasy and magic, whilst also echoing traditional depictions of heaven through the inclusion of clouds and golden gates at the entrance.

Similar forms of fantastical depiction in order to create a sense of otherness are found in a number of productions, a fact that is unsurprising in light of the fact that these works fall into the fantasy genre. The gods in *Hercules: The Legendary Journeys* (1994 and 1995–9) and its spin-offs, *Xena: Warrior Princess* (1995–2001) and *Young Hercules* (1998–9), fall into this category. Hephaestus, Apollo and Ares all appear prominently in *Hercules: The Legendary Journeys*, while Poseidon features in *Xena*. Fully anthropomorphised, the Olympians in these productions are colourful beings, who wear a range of vaguely medieval-styled or fantasy-inspired clothes and – apart from Zeus, Poseidon and Hades – are young and mostly handsome. The only exception among the younger gods is Hephaestus, who has a scarred face and a limp as a result of his being cast off from Olympus, an episode that has left him self-conscious. He is highly skilled, making amazing objects including a shield that makes its bearer invisible, but he is tormented, especially in his love for Aphrodite, for whom he has pined for centuries on end, but who does actually love him in this version.[17] As played by Jason Hoyte, Hephaestus appeared in one episode of *Hercules: The Legendary Journeys*, one of *Xena* and five of *Young Hercules*, while Julian Garner took the role in one episode each of *Hercules: The Legendary Journeys* and *Xena*.

The other Olympian who appears most centrally is Ares. Played by Kevin Smith as a handsome schemer with Van Dyke beard, he is dressed in black leather trousers and black studded jerkin over a bare chest, with elaborate wrist guards, and armed with a sword. The Hercules and Xena Wiki describes him as follows:

> Ares is the god of war and violence. He is primarily the patron god of Sparta, but armies from all city-states offer prayers to him before going into battle. Though he represents the physical aspect of war, Ares is far from some mindless thug. He is, in fact, a brilliant strategist, preferring to plan his battles carefully rather than going into a fight with his proverbial guns blazing. Whenever possible, he seems to like the methods of getting other people to do his work for him or finding ways to get his enemies to destroy themselves. . . . Despite the often chaotic results of his worshipers' actions, Ares sees himself as a subtle strategist, as befits the god of war, rather than the god of brawling. He also exhibits [a] curious mix of sportsmanship and cheating when convenient for him.[18]

Depicting the gods as fantasy characters is the most popular method in the recent movies based on Greek mythology: the two

Percy Jackson movies (2010, 2013), *Clash of the Titans* (2010) and its sequel *Wrath of the Titans* (2012), and *Immortals*. In some cases, the Percy Jackson approach to portraying the gods is very traditional. Thus Zeus, Poseidon,[19] Apollo and Hephaestus are depicted as ancient Greek heroes, in armour consisting of cuirass, skirt and shoulder plates. Poseidon is sometimes shown with his trident and Hephaestus is the only black god, but there are few distinguishing features between the Olympians. Their palace is a mixture of classical pillared marble and 1920s Art Deco, is in keeping with the idea that they live atop the Empire State Building in New York.

This mingling of the two worlds is a feature of both books and movies and presented effectively on screen through the depictions of the gods, who, despite their anthropomorphic appearance even on Olympus, take on a noticeably more human and less supernatural look when in the world of humans, an element explained by the fact that it is forbidden for gods to have contact with humans.[20] Thus in the opening scene of *Percy Jackson and the Lightning Thief*, Poseidon emerges from the water in New York harbour in ancient Greek dress and of gigantic stature, towering over the scene, but as he strides landwards he alters, shrinking to normal human height, and wearing normal clothing as he meets Zeus, also wearing ordinary clothing, on the Empire State Building. Similarly both Hermes and Dionysus, who interact in the real world (Hermes as a courier and Dionysus as the manager of Camp Half-Blood), wear individual styles of modern dress.

Clash of the Titans (2010) and its sequel also dressed their gods in armour, but this was based not only on Greek mythology but on manga. The director of *Clash*, Louis Leterrier, a big fan of Masami Kurumada's *Saint Seiya* manga, explained that the armour worn by the gods in the film was a sign of homage and respect to *Saint Seiya*.[21] The costume designer for *Immortals*, Eiko Ishioka, explains that 'Based on Greek mythology we can create our own mythology of the story.' Rejecting the 'traditional, historical research', she aimed to create her own 'unique mythological vision'. In tandem with director Tarsem Singh's idea, she states that her creations are not pure Greek mythology, and that the audience are not historians; taking what she described as 'one very far out idea' and combining it with another aspect, that of 'very traditional, historical research' she aimed to create something new by fusing the two. Thus her gods have some traditional elements: the naked torsos, greaves, arm bracelets and peplum-style armour, popular in movies about the ancient world, as well as some of the iconic symbols such as Hermes' winged helmet and Poseidon's trident. These are, however, combined with elements of the fantastic, in particular with a preponderance of gold, the creation of over-large stylised helmets and armour. This Olympus is suspended in space, looking out over the globe, and made of traditional white marble, carved with reliefs, and decorated with porphyry, but also looks radically modern, with clean lines, a definite sparseness of design and no columns in sight.

THE DEPICTION OF INDIVIDUAL MALE GODS

Hermes

'Whoa! Excuse me! Hot stuff coming through! Excuse me, one side, Ares', gabbles the thin blue god in a short white tunic, helmet cap on his head, caduceus in one hand and a bunch of flowers in the other, as he rushes into the gods celebrating Hercules' birth, his winged sandals whirring noisily as background accompaniment. With his fast speech reflecting his speed in other ways, and with the flower delivery echoing the Mercury logo of FTD florists, the audience is in no doubt as to his identity.[22] This is Hermes, the god who, after Zeus and Hades, appears most frequently on screen. Partly because he has recognisable iconic symbols, and partly because he is a god who interacts frequently with mortals, as an intermediary between man and the gods, Hermes is seen far more often than the other Olympian deities as a stand-alone god. The emblems of helmet-shaped hat, winged sandals and caduceus staff are almost invariably present when he appears. This is so even in children's programming, as in the case of *Wishbone*, a children's television series that aired between 1995 and 1998, about the eponymous dog, of high intelligence, who imagines himself in the role of characters from classic books and gets involved in similar real-life adventures. In one episode from the second season, 'Roamin' Nose', Wishbone plays Aeneas, forced to flee the neighbourhood as the result of a gas leak. Peppered with comedy, and starring a very cute dog, this series is also heavily slanted towards education, as Wishbone's introduction to the *Aeneid* demonstrates:

> You know, the hero in a book called the *Aeneid* was forced to leave his home too. The *Aeneid* is an epic poem, written around the year 19 BC by the Roman poet Publius Vergilius Maro, Vergil to his friends.

The episode goes on to give an abbreviated version of the *Aeneid*, with Mercury featuring as the messenger sent by the gods to Carthage to remind Aeneas of his destiny. Played by Billy E. Jones, this Mercury moves in a flash of light. He is dressed in a short white tunic with a red-striped border at the neckline, a short white cloak pinned at the left shoulder, and, as usual, a helmet, this time trimmed with gold laurel leaves and wings. Similarly, the animated French children's television series *Jason and the Heroes of Mount Olympus*, from 2001–2, depicts the gods as anthropomorphised animals, with Mercury as a rabbit, but still with a pteruges-style skirt and winged sandals and helmet. The depiction in an episode of *Sabrina, Teenage Witch* (1996–2000; 'Thin Ice', 2001), aimed at teen viewers, also maintains the traditional depiction, with Patrick Bristow's Mercury dressed in white tunic and golden winged helmet.

Several adult productions also follow the same route. In 1966, Donald O'Connor's elfin depiction in *Olympus 7-0000*, one of the ABC Stage 67 series, featured a silver-clad god with shiny bowler hat with wings on the brim and a small, silvery stick intended to represent the caduceus. Typically, the connection with mortals is stressed, with *Olympus 7-0000* being Hermes' phone number. Mercury in *Hercules in New York* (1970), played by Dan Hamilton, is clad in traditional Greek-looking garb when on Olympus, where he wears a short tunic and has a gold laurel crown on his dark curls. When in the mortal world, however, he is dressed in a dark suit, white shirt and dark tie, although he does still fly, apparently not needing winged sandals or helmet to do so. Also from the same era, but rather different in tone, *Up Pompeii!* (1969–70) features the god played by Bunny May as 'Hermes the Messenger'. Again he is portrayed stereotypically, his skin painted metallic silver, and wearing a short, pale blue tunic, silver cloak, and winged silver helmet and shoes. He carries a large caduceus, also made of silver, as well as a roll of papyrus on which the message he is delivering is written.

Another version in which Hermes is depicted as metallic looking, but this time with a twist, is in the modernised *Odyssey* adaptation, *Toast with the Gods* (1995). The synopsis of this strange film on youtube reads:

> A surreal adaptation of Homer's epic classic 'The Odyssey'. Small-time drug dealer Toast must journey through the underworld of Seattle to save his sexy wife Penelope, a Brigitte Bardot-ish stripper, who has been abducted by a depraved bunch of madmen. Just like in the epic tale, Toast encounters a bizarre series of characters and situations, even real-life gods and goddesses who help him on his way back home.[23]

In fact, very few gods, goddesses or monsters feature in the movie, Hermes being one of the major exceptions, and he is shown as a bronze figure, clad only in a loin cloth rather than in tunic or classical-style clothes, giving the appearance of a bronze statue come to life, and with none of his usual iconic symbols. Also modernised is Michael Feast's Hermes in *Prometheus* (1998), where he is costumed in metallic silver, though in this case not in ancient Greek-style dress but in a boiler suit, and his helmet is more like a miner's and has no wings.

Unusually, the portrayal of Hermes in two versions of the *Odyssey* depicts the god without his usual symbols. In Franco Rossi's *L'Odissea* from 1968 the god is played by Peter Hinwood. Clad in a white, homespun-looking tunic, he is young and attractive, with his fair hair styled into large curls, and light plays on his face, indicating his godliness. His enigmatic smile as he gives Odysseus instructions, and his confident and somewhat aloof expression and tone, reflect his divine remoteness and that mortal affairs affect him little. A similar approach is taken in the 1997 version of *The Odyssey*, starring Armand Assante, in which Hermes is played by Freddy Douglas and sports a bare torso, with gleaming six-pack. His hair is elaborately curled and highlighted with gold, lending a divine sheen to the loincloth-clad deity as he hovers, arms crossed, in mid-air, while Odysseus struggles to climb the sheer cliff to Circe's lair (see Figure 4.1). Even less elaborate is the Hermes from *Troy: Fall of a City* (2018), who, like the other gods in the production, is dressed in simple, woollen cloak and tunic. Played by the Irish actor Diarmaid Murtagh, Hermes' identity is known only because he is named as such by Zeus, and through his responsibility as messenger god, in summoning Paris to judge the beauty competition.

Apollo

Apollo most commonly features as an offscreen presence through his delivery of prophecies via a seer,[24] but occasionally appears in person as well. The most extended appearance of the god as a stand-alone figure is in the *Star Trek* (1966–9) episode 'Who Mourns for Adonais?'[25] In this episode, broadcast on 22 September 1967, the crew of the *Enterprise* are captured by the god Apollo, played by the tall, rugged, handsome Michael Forest, dressed in a mid-thigh-length gold chiton and with a gold laurel crown on his head (see Figure 4.2). His words, delivered in a Shakespearean manner, echo and boom with divine presence, and before the eyes of the landing party he grows to enormous size. With its golden clothing, white pillared temple and huge size, the depiction is reminiscent of Harryhausen's *Jason and the Argonauts* from four years before, as is the ancient

Figure 4.1 Hermes (Freddy Douglas) in *The Odyssey* (1997).
American Zoetrope/Beta Film/Hallmark.

garden setting, possibly meant to represent Mount Olympus. The god is anthropomorphic, and has power, enabling him to render the *Enterprise*'s communicators and transporter room powerless. Capturing the landing party from the starship, Apollo addresses the ship's crew as his 'beloved children', and declares that they are to serve and worship him as their god, a command that Kirk defiantly refuses. The conceit here is that Apollo was one of a group of aliens that visited Earth fifty centuries ago, and were godlike, though not in the sense that the ancient Greeks believed them to be. He is indeed the real Apollo, and he and his companions thrived on the love, worship, loyalty and attention of the ancient Greeks, but left Earth when mankind outgrew them, and returned to their home planet. Apollo explains that the gods are immortal, but even they eventually reach a point of no return; they 'spread themselves upon the wind . . . thinner, and thinner, until only the wind remained'. Without worshippers, the aliens grew weaker but lacked the strength to leave their home planet, and, over the course of time, all but Apollo discorporated.

Despite the threat posed by Apollo, Greek civilisation, as represented by the god, is lauded in this version, with Kirk remarking

Figure 4.2 Apollo (Michael Forest) in *Star Trek* (1966–9) episode 'Who Mourns
for Adonais?' (1967). Desilu Productions/Norway Corporation/
Paramount Television.

that the Greek gods had once been a major inspiration for mankind,
driving civilisation to new heights in art and philosophy. Pondering
regretfully, he says: 'Would it have hurt us, I wonder, just to have
gathered a few laurel leaves?', although polytheism itself is roundly
rejected as he declares wryly, 'Mankind has no need for gods. We find
the One quite adequate.'

Apollo appears briefly in other television productions. He features
in one episode of the Canadian children's drama *MythQuest* (2001),
in which two teenagers travel into myths in search of their lost father,
The episode, entitled 'The Oracle', centres on Delphi, and depicts
Apollo with none of his traditional symbols. He is young, with short
dark hair, and wears a cream-coloured chiton and cloak, his divinity
indicated only by his echoing, digitally enhanced voice, but he is also
depicted as a true god, and the visions he sends to the Pythia are
genuine.

A far more prosaic depiction is that in the heavily (and rightly)
slated television series *Olympus*. A joint Canadian–British fantasy
production that premiered in Canada, the USA, the UK and Ireland
in April 2015, the series ran for only one season of thirteen episodes,
before thankfully being cancelled. In this production, the Olympian
gods hardly appear on screen at all, despite the premise of the plot:

The story of how several brave men and women banished the gods from
Olympus to the unconscious realm, a place dubbed as the Kingdom of Hades,

or the underworld. A young man, Hero, attempts to find the truths of his past and shed light on the future, which will inevitably link back to the gods themselves.[26]

One of the few exceptions is Apollo, who, for reasons that are both unclear and unexplained, appears to one of the characters in the form of a young man gathering rats in a sack. It is striking that as opposed to most other depictions of the deities, this god is dwarf-like in stature in comparison to mortals, upon whom the series is indisputably focused.

Poseidon

Striding majestically from the sea onto land, his enormous stature shrinking as he takes on mortal form in the world, Kevin McKidd's Poseidon is a thoroughly modern god of the sea, and indeed his role is unusually prominent on the contemporary screen. Although in ancient Greece, where the sea played a major part in daily life,[27] Poseidon featured prominently, Poseidon/Neptune is seen alone on film only rarely. Where he does appear, the depictions, as is to be expected, focus on his connection to the sea, as for example in the children's cartoon *Sponge Bob Square Pants* (1999–). Since Sponge Bob lives in a giant pineapple under the sea, there are a number of occasions on which he comes into contact with 'King Neptune'. This character himself appears in a few different versions, sometimes clearly as a god, with his name being used in phrases such as 'Dear Neptune', 'Neptune preserve her!' and 'Oh my Neptune!', although he does not seem definitely to be worshipped by the animals and beings that live in the sea. Similarly, in the first season of the programme he features in an episode entitled 'Neptune's Spatula', in which he has godly powers and offers as a prize in a competition that the victor will become a god in his kingdom, which is said to be Atlantis. Physically Neptune is a merman, with a fish tail in place of legs, and green in colour, and he wears a gold belt and wrist bands as well as a crown. His torso is heavily muscled, and he sports auburn, flowing, shoulder-length hair, full beard and moustache. In the *Sponge Bob Square Pants Movie* (2004), however, he appears rather differently, in a more cartoon-like depiction, making him rounder, without muscles, dressed in an ermine-trimmed short red jacket and carrying a trident, with his facial hair rather more orange in colour, and his head balding under a crown. He is also here explicitly portrayed as a king rather than a god, the ruler of the underwater kingdom. It seems that

the productions waiver between different ideas regarding Poseidon/
Neptune, sometimes portraying him as a version of the Roman god
of the sea, and sometimes as mortal, a king of the sea and a member
of a dynasty (a portrait on the wall in 'Neptune's Spatula' is said to
be of Neptune XIV). In none of the portrayals, however, is he a positive character, always exhibiting tyrannical and bullying behaviour
to his daughter and subjects.

Poseidon also appears twice in the television series *Once Upon a
Time*, an American fantasy series that ran from 2011 to 2018. The
premise of the show is that the members of the town Storybrooke, in
which the series is set, are actually characters from fairy tales transported to the modern world, but robbed of their original memories,
as a result of a curse. Over the course of its seven series, it expanded
to borrow elements and characters from wider sources, including
Greek mythology, among them Poseidon, also described as 'the sea
king'. One of his symbols of power is his trident, which his mermaid
daughter uses to transform her tail into legs, in a motif reminiscent
of Disney's *The Little Mermaid* (1989), to whose King Triton this
Poseidon also owes a debt. Appearing first in the fifteenth episode of
the fourth season, Poseidon is played by the 70-year-old black actor
Ernie Hudson, and sports full armour decorated with swirling sea
motifs and seaweed-like patterns, greaves, a cloak and the usual trident. He is a rather tragic and bitter character, having lost his beloved
wife to a pirate attack, although he does undergo a certain amount
of rehabilitation as he makes his peace with his daughter in his final
appearance.

In none of the modern depictions is the god of the sea portrayed
particularly favourably, reflecting the negative attitude towards the
sea deity in the ancient world that has carried over to the modern,
even in the guise of children's cartoons and fantasy drama. Even in
movies where the god does not actually appear, such as *Poseidon*
(2006) and *The Poseidon Adventure* (1972, 2005), the deity's very
name represents the malevolent force of the sea. The most positive
portrayal of the god is undoubtedly in the Percy Jackson books and
movies. Played by the blue-eyed, brown-haired McKidd,[28] he is of
slighter build than Zeus (Sean Bean), and when in godly appearance is
dressed in scale-like body armour worn over a tunic and paired with
his trident, but when he moves through the mortal world he does so
in everyday casual clothes, dark trousers paired with a hoodie. As the
father of the hero, Poseidon is generally benevolent to Percy, a proud
and loving parent, with a rather sardonic sense of humour, but he is
also an absentee father, and the strained relationship between father

and son is the defining theme in the first movie.[29] Nor is Poseidon as a character perfect in any way; he is proud and obstinate, possesses a fearsome temper and displays a leaning towards implacable vengeance, albeit to a lesser extent than his brother, Zeus.[30] Even in this relatively benign depiction, the power and threatening nature of the sea god linger on.

Dionysus

Dressed in leopard-print shirt, and with brown, shoulder-length hair, 'Mr. D', played by Stanley Tucci in *Percy Jackson and the Sea of Monsters* (2013) is the sardonic head of Camp Half-Blood, forbidden by Zeus from drinking his beloved wine, which turns to water when poured.[31] 'You know the Christians have a guy who can do this trick in reverse. Now there's a god!' he quips in frustration, a somewhat impotent figure, far removed from the powerful character of the original Greek god. Dionysus, or Bacchus, god of wine and the theatre, was a deity who has provided an inspiration for artists of all kinds for millennia; yet he appears relatively rarely on the modern screen.

The most common sightings of Dionysus are in filmed versions of stage productions, be they *The Bacchae* or opera (*Ariadne auf Naxos* (1965), *Vom König Midas* (1963)), which fall outside the scope of this study. Beyond this, he has a part in one episode of *MythQuest*, entitled 'Orpheus', in which the god is played by the 26-year-old Terry Chen, who is of ethnic Chinese origin, perhaps a nod to Dionysus' exotic nature and travels to the East (although admittedly not as far east as China!). Dressed in a brown, gold-trimmed tunic, and with a laurel wreath on his head, this Dionysus has a goblet in his hand and is found celebrating at Orpheus and Eurydice's wedding feast. He is described as someone whose philosophy of life is to 'live without barriers to pleasure', and who thinks that it is 'wonderful to be selfish'.

Dionysus is a rather more sinister creature in the *Young Hercules/Xena: Warrior Princess* programmes. Featuring in one episode of *Xena*[32] and three of *Young Hercules*,[33] this Bacchus is a horned monster, more reminiscent of Hades than of the god of the vine. In the earlier show, he is played by Anthony Ray Parker, and in the later by Kevin Smith, but in both cases the actor wears a prosthetic head and complicated make-up that took between six and eight hours to apply.[34] His skin in *Xena* is greenish in colour and reptilian in appearance, with scale-like armour, while in *Hercules* he is redskinned but equally monstrous. Described as the 'god of good times', he commands a cult of young women whom he has turned into

vampire-style monsters named Bacchae, and is in every way an evil
villain who must be destroyed.

Both the scarcity of appearances by Dionysus on screen, and the
negative depiction of him on the rare occasions when he does feature
independently of a larger group of Olympians, are striking, especially
when one considers the frequency of productions of *The Bacchae*,
and the possible attractions of a god of wine and liberated sensu-
ality. Perhaps cinema and television producers are too conscious of
the mainstream nature of many of their audiences to willingly take
this route? The fact that many mythological presentations are fantasy works, aimed at younger audiences, may also be a contributory
factor in avoiding this deity, and in portraying him as at least partially bestial, more of a monstrous Pan figure than the Olympian god
of the vine and the theatre.

JESUS ON SCREEN

For many people, ever since he played the role of Jesus in Zeffirelli's
Jesus of Nazareth (1977) Robert Powell's face is that of Jesus.[35] So
great is the identification that iconography which is undoubtedly that
of Robert Powell is found in churches, homes, cars, schools, offices
and holy grottoes all over the world. The actor himself talks about
an instance when he was filming in Venezuela over Easter, and on the
Sunday morning he had a lie-in while the Italian crew went to church.
'They all came back giggling at lunchtime', he relates, recounting that
they told him, 'You have no idea. It's a good job you didn't come with
us to church, because behind the altar, the icon is you', and explains
that 'They had found a magazine photograph, blown it up, and that
was it.'[36]

Powell, a Caucasian, with his piercing blue eyes, beard and
shoulder-length brown hair, was part of a long tradition that set
down the details of appearance for a celluloid saviour.[37] In the words
of Reinhartz, 'the cinematic Jesus is almost always of medium height,
with medium brown hair, a short brown beard, and piercing blue
eyes',[38] and he is clad in white, often wearing a cowl, hood or veil
over his head, framing his face, from which his cerulean eyes gaze
out penetratingly, as he looks benignly and calmly at the world (see
Figures 4.3 and 4.4) . Jeffrey Hunter in *King of Kings* (1961), jok-
ingly described as 'I was a teenage Jesus', was firmly in this mould,
a fair, good-looking, traditional Western Jesus, with 'dreamy blue
eyes'.[39] This can of course lead to a very generic cinematic saviour;
this, to Powell, was actually a positive thing:

The reason for Jesus' success over 2,000 years plus is the fact that he is who-
ever you wish him to be. He is not a person. He is not a person with characteristics or idiosyncrasies or mannerisms, you can impose on him whatever
you like. However you wish your Jesus, to be, that is your Jesus, and that is
why people can take him with them wherever they go and everybody has
a different one, a different image in their head. I think that that's what we
allowed in our film. The tens of thousands of letters that we got all said the
same thing, 'it's exactly how I imagined him to be', on that level we succeeded
in spades, we really did. We managed to make it so non-specific.[40]

The reason that Powell's Jesus matches up so closely to common
perception is that he epitomises iconic characteristics that are
common to Western Christian ideas, as Joan E. Taylor explains:

His image is found repeatedly in countless churches and Christian buildings.
He is usually somewhat European: a man with nut-brown hair (sometimes
blond) and light brown or blue eyes. He has a long face and nose, and long
hair and a beard. His clothes are also long: a tunic down to the ground, with
wide baggy sleeves, and a large mantle. He is fairly well-tended (combed hair,
good teeth, clean) and his clothes look newly washed.[41]

Yet it is fairly certain that none of these characteristics were present in the historical Jesus at all, since he would have had a Semitic
appearance. Although various attempts have been made on screen to
reflect his Jewish heritage and background, this does not extend to
his physical appearance. Jesus, according to a computer-generated
reconstruction of a Judaean Jewish man from the first century, published in 2001 by BBC Worldwide/Reuters, would have had 'a full,
square face, dark curly hair, dark eyes and abundant facial hair',[42] yet
he is almost invariably portrayed as Western European, not only in
cinema but in all other media as well. These are elements that are the
result of years of influence from Renaissance art, nineteenth-century
paintings by artists such as Gustave Doré and James Tissot, and most
of all, the religious imagery of Warner Sallman in the first decades
of the twentieth century.

Nevertheless, to portray the Christ is not merely to embody physically what audiences think of as the correct and authentic look of
Jesus. Ivan Butler's comment on the casting of Max von Sydow in
The Greatest Story Ever Told (1965) encapsulates the complexity of
the issue:

Max von Sydow is a strong, virile, compassionate and even at times a humorous Christ. Edward Connor describes him as the best since H. B. Warner
[DeMille's Christ] – it is arguable that he even surpasses the earlier performance. Warner, for all the beauty, tenderness, and dignity of his portrayal,
or perhaps because of these very virtues, never quite convinced as the Son
of God. Warner was the 'gentle Jesus' of the child's bedside as well as the

Teacher, the Healer, the Reformer, the Man of unquenchable will and inner determination. Von Sydow satisfies one on all these points, but in addition is also the trudger from place to place through the hot dusty countryside, the craftsman's son. The physical strength to undergo the strains imposed on Christ is evident in von Sydow – with Warner one occasionally has doubts in this respect.[43]

To show Christ on screen is clearly no easy task. If there are difficulties in depicting both Zeus and God cinematically, in a way that conveys their power and other essential qualities (which vary according to the message being promoted by the film maker), the problem of portraying Jesus is even greater. How does one express divinity in the form of a man who was not yet divine?[44] Can such a sense of divinity be communicated to those who believe in Jesus as Christ and practise Christianity, and indeed to those who do not? How can potential financially damaging offence be avoided? Who is fit and worthy to play a role held in such awe by many viewers? Should an already well-known actor be utilised, or someone with no previous roles to colour audience expectation? How should a screen Jesus convey the multifaceted elements present in the various interpretations? Powell, forty years on, recalled the difficulties of playing Jesus and his own solution to the dilemma:

> Franco Zeffirelli and I originally thought that we could combine the divine Christ with the human one and that we would be able to show the human side of him, but we discovered that it was just not possible.
>
> You go as an actor and work subjectively but the moment you start to try and play him as a real person you lose the divinity completely. With this story, the most important element that this character has to be is extraordinary. So from that moment on, I played it objectively without any recourse to giving him any particular idiosyncrasies, quite deliberately avoiding the normal human things. To try and play a god and get the idea of it is a shortcut to a nervous breakdown. So, I backed off completely. I found a way of doing it that was counter to the actor's normal approach.[45]

These issues are not, of course, new; Passion plays have been staged since medieval times and face the same question of how to cast Jesus (and other figures), but in an explicitly religious act, for an audience of believers, the issue is somewhat less complicated.[46] For film makers, whose aim is not only, or not even in most cases, to educate but to entertain, and just as importantly, make money, the portrayal of Jesus is a complex matter. As Jocelyn Noveck puts it:

> depicting Jesus on the screen has always been a tricky business, one that balances weighty theological concerns – how divine to make the son of God, and how human? – with more earthly ones, like how best to sell movie tickets?[47]

Figures 4.3 and 4.4 Jesus (Max Von Sydow) in *The Greatest Story Ever Told* (1965), George Stevens Productions, and Jesus (Robert Powell) in *Jesus of Nazareth* (1977). ITC (Incorporated Television Company)/ RAI Radiotelevisione Italiana.

Yet these issues have not deterred film makers. For many years, the solution, a nod to the holiness of the character, was not to show his face at all. This is the approach taken by *Ben-Hur*, and indeed by various other peplum movies in which Jesus is shown through the eyes of other characters, a decision taken in part at least in order to comply with the censorship laws in different countries.[48]

Avoidance was not the only answer, and other film makers were attracted enough by the idea of portraying Jesus' life in celluloid to develop the genre, whilst still making every effort to maintain and demonstrate a high level of veneration. As early as 1912, *From the Manger to the Cross* showed the life of Christ in a full-length production running at over an hour in total, a trend that developed into the fully fledged biopic with Cecil B. DeMille's *The King of Kings* (1927).[49] During the golden age of the epic movie in the 1950s and the two decades following, the Jesus movies continued to flourish, with movies such as *The Robe* (1953) and *Ben-Hur* (1959) retelling the story of early Christianity, and biopics such as *King of Kings*, *The Greatest Story Ever Told*, *Jesus of Nazareth* and *The Jesus Film* (1979) appearing. Most films took a conservative and traditional approach to the tale, particularly in the various television adaptations such as *Jesus* (1999) and *The Bible* (2013). Even Zeffirelli's *Jesus of Nazareth*, groundbreaking as it was for its setting of the story in its historical and Jewish context, was also very reverential and traditional in other ways. *The Miracle Maker* (1999) was innovative in its use of stop motion animation but told the story utterly conventionally, presenting 'the bare events of the gospel narratives, without adornment or invention, without idiosyncratic "explanations" or editorial spin, without elaborations for the sake of amusement or excitement'.[50]

Some movies demonstrated a less conventional attitude, however. Pasolini's *The Gospel According to St. Matthew* (*Il vangelo secondo Matteo*) (1964) was a stark black-and-white movie with a rugged Italian peasant setting and commensurate Jesus; *Jesus Christ Superstar* (1973) recast the story as a rock musical. Franco Rossi's *A Child Called Jesus* (1987) focused on the childhood of Christ, about which there is little evidence even from the Gospels, and therefore was able to be more creative and speculative. Two movies from 2006, *Color of the Cross* and *Son of Man*, interpreted the story as one of racial oppression and cast black actors as Jesus (Jean-Claude La Marre in *Color of the Cross* and Andile Kosi in *Son of Man*). *The Messiah*, a 2007 Iranian movie, brought a different non-Christian interpretation to bear on the tale. Perhaps most famously, Martin Scorsese's *The Last Temptation of Christ* (1988), based on Nikos Kazantzakis' controversial 1955 novel, presented a flawed Jesus, who was subject to fear, doubt, depression, reluctance and even lust, while Mel Gibson's *The Passion of the Christ* (2004) mixed Jesus biopic with horror movie, in a version 'steeped in guts and gore'.[51] The trend of finding new and innovative ways to retell this ancient story continues, while the popularity of the tale for film makers is not in any way diminished. In 2016, there were no fewer than four Hollywood movies about Jesus: *Risen*, *The Young Messiah*, *Last Days in the Desert* and *Ben-Hur*, all of which, in the postmodern world, attempt to fill in gaps in the Biblical narrative.

CONCLUSIONS: CROSSOVERS AND RECONFIGURATIONS BETWEEN CHRISTIANITY AND THE PAGAN GODS

There is no doubt that Christianity and paganism have influenced one another in their depictions of the gods. Satanic elements in the depiction of Hades abound, reflecting a confusion between the roles of the Greek god of the Underworld and the Devil. Similarly, many of the elements in the classic portrayal of Jesus have their roots in the ancient pagan world. Jesus' long hair and beard, for example, mark him out as a philosopher-teacher, but also as a younger incarnation of Zeus himself.[52] The halo which surrounds his head

is an adaptation of Apollo's nimbus of sun rays. Jesus' long robe
and baggy sleeves, as well as his sometimes luxuriant hair, evoke
Dionysus, a god with whom he shares a great deal through the motifs
of death and rebirth. White clothing, reflecting purity, may also be
influenced by the marble statuary with which the pagan gods were so
often associated. The aim of these borrowed elements of iconography
was to associate Jesus with divine aspects of these other gods, and
emphasise his role as a supreme deity.

Given the common roots and symbolism, it is therefore striking
how different the figure of Jesus on screen is from that of the pagan
deities. There are a number of reasons for this. Firstly, Jesus' age at
the time of his ministry and crucifixion ('around thirty' according
to Luke)[53] puts him at a definite stage of life, limiting the possibilities of actors taking on the role. In contrast, a Greek god may be a
young man in the prime of life (particularly in the case of Apollo, but
also applicable on occasion to Ares or Dionysus) or an older figure
(Zeus, Poseidon, Hades); or he can be eternally youthful as in Tarsem
Singh's interpretation.

Such fluidity allows for a far wider range of representations than is
possible (or at least has so far been seen) with regard to Jesus. While
the Greek gods have, equally inaccurately, in general been portrayed
as Western European, there is far more licence to adopt innovative
portrayals and casting when dealing with gods who are no longer
worshipped than there is with Jesus himself. Although the casting
of a black actor in the role of a god or hero continues to provoke
outrage among some, as the recent reaction to *Troy: Fall of a City*
reflects, this is not always the case: Ernie Hudson's role as Poseidon
in *Once Upon a Time* and Jay Pharoah's as Apollo on *Saturday Night
Live* provoked very little reaction. Even in the case of *Troy: Fall of
a City*, the opposition was more to Achilles' and Patroclus' casting
than to that of Zeus, by people objecting to the ethnicity of the
heroes, which seemed to them to go counter to 'the truth', whereas
since Greek gods could change shape and appearance at will, the idea
of a deity choosing to appear as black was less problematic for them.

What does emerge from a comparison between Jesus and the
Greek gods on screen is, in fact, the high level of uniformity in almost
all depictions of Christ, and its lack in those of Apollo, Hermes and
Dionysus. When these gods are portrayed, despite the fact that Greek
art does show a certain level of common elements in its iconography
with regard to these deities, there is no rule when it comes to hair and
eye colour, height, build and dress, all of which change from production to production, with multiple interpretations and presentations,

and with the symbolism recurring more than any physical features. This is in startling contrast to the portrayals of Jesus, most of which strongly resemble one another. It seems that the lack of necessity to conform to beliefs gives film makers a freedom that they are denied with the Jesus biopics, which feature a character with an established (if inaccurate) appearance. If this is so with regard to the male gods, how much more so might it be expected to be when depicting female goddesses, of which there is no Judaeo-Christian equivalent, and to which we will now turn our attention.

NOTES

1 <https://www.youtube.com/watch?v=2ixsyfZ4gv4>   (accessed   13 August 2018).
2 <http://cashthefilmfanblog.blogspot.com/2010/01/why-zeus-why-stark-why-sean.html> (accessed 13 August 2018).
3 Evans and Wilson (1999: 2).
4 McDonald (2000: 1).
5 Williams (2017: 1).
6 Ibid. 5.
7 <https://www.telegraph.co.uk/family/relationships/dear-graham-nor ton-can-stop-girlfriend-perving-actors-television/> (accessed 12 August 2018).
8 Dyer (1979).
9 Cyrino (2018: 94).
10 See p. 84.
11 Hansen (2004: 7).
12 Llewellyn-Jones (2007: 429).
13 Llewellyn-Jones (2007: 429).
14 Harryhausen and Dalton (2003: 155), also quoted by Llewellyn-Jones (2007: 429).
15 Llewellyn-Jones (2007: 430).
16 Played by Ken la Kier, in his mid-forties.
17 She even declares profoundly 'Beauty's not just what you look like. It's also what you are inside.' Quoted by Robert Weisbrot (1998: 147).
18 <http://hercules-xena.wikia.com/wiki/Ares> (accessed 3 August 2017).
19 See also below for more on Poseidon in particular.
20 According to Nathan Fillion, the actor who played Hermes, in an interview in TV Guide <http://www.tvguide.com/news/nathan-fillion-per cy-jackson-sequel-1063341/> (accessed 10 August 2017).
21 <http://www.cbr.com/clash-of-the-titans-reimagined-by-masami-kuru mada/> (accessed 10 August 2017).
22 Florists' Telegraph Delivery or FTD was founded on 18 August 1910. In 1914, the company adopted Mercury (Hermes in Greek) as its logo, the

company emulating the speedy messenger. To reflect its global presence, FTD became Florists' Transworld Delivery in the 1960s. See <http://findingmickey.squarespace.com/disney-animated-features/hercules/8271214> (accessed 9 August 2018).

23 <https://www.youtube.com/watch?v=i97tU8BZ7S8> (accessed 6 September 2017).

24 See Chapter 7, on human–divine interactions.

25 On this episode, see also Wenskus (2002: 130–2); Winkler (2009: 86–90).

26 <https://en.wikipedia.org/wiki/Olympus_(TV_series)> (accessed 6 September 2017).

27 See Larson (2007: 57).

28 In the books, the god is described as having black hair and green eyes.

29 <http://www.kevinmckiddonline.com/percy-jackson--the-olympians-the-lightning-thief.html#.Wbebq7IjHIU> (accessed 12 September 2017).

30 See <http://riordan.wikia.com/wiki/Poseidon> (accessed 12 September 2017).

31 Dionysus is played by Luke Camilleri in *Percy Jackson and the Lightning Thief* but appears only briefly amongst the other gods in their hall on Olympus, situated above the Empire State Building in New York.

32 'Girls Just Wanna Have Fun' (1996).

33 'Lyre, Liar' (1998); 'Fame' (1998); 'The Lure of the Lyre' (1998).

34 Weisbrot (1996: 198).

35 On the traditions surrounding how Jesus is depicted, see Chapter 2, pp. 29–34.

36 <https://www.youtube.com/watch?v=OacW3VFxbdw> (accessed 29 November 2018).

37 See Malone (1989); Jones and Tajima (2015).

38 Reinhartz (2007: 48).

39 Medved and Medved (1980: 96).

40 <https://www.history.co.uk/shows/robert-powell-the-real-jesus-of-nazareth/articles/speaking-for-jesus-an-interview-with-robert> (accessed 9 August 2018).

41 <https://www.irishtimes.com/culture/books/what-did-jesus-really-look-like-as-a-jew-in-1st-century-judaea-1.3385334> (accessed 23 May 2018). Taylor's ideas are elaborated at length in her book (2018).

42 The image can be viewed online (website also cited by Reinhartz (2007: 265)) at <http://www.lightplanet.com/mormons/basic/christ/physical_appearance.htm> (accessed 23 May 2018).

43 Butler (1969: 48–9), also quoted by Hawkins in *The Christian Century*, 801, available online at <https://www.religion-online.org/article/jesus-on-film/> (accessed 24 May 2018).

44 Despite the interesting examples that may be found, for reasons of space I exclude from this study those 'Christ-figure' films in which characters

are presented as resembling Jesus in a significant way, but are not actually Jesus himself.

45 <https://www.history.co.uk/shows/robert-powell-the-real-jesus-of-nazareth/articles/speaking-for-jesus-an-interview-with-robert> (accessed 9 August 2018).

46 For a discussion of the Oberammergau passion play, see Shapiro (2000).

47 <http://www.stuff.co.nz/entertainment/9802432/Casting-Jesus-Was-he-really-hot> (accessed 23 May 2018).

48 Reinhartz (2013: 91).

49 For a brief yet full outline of Jesus films in the twentieth century up to 1988, see Singer (1988: 44–5).

50 <http://decentfilms.com/reviews/miraclemaker> (accessed 23 May 2018).

51 <https://www.theguardian.com/film/2004/feb/29/melgibson.markkermode> (accessed 23 May 2018).

52 Poseidon also shares the iconography, but it seems more likely that the king of the gods is the model here rather than the god of the sea. There may also be influences from the Graeco-Egyptian god Serapis.

53 Luke 3:23–38.

5 *Gendering the Divine (1): Greek Goddesses on Screen*

THE MOVIE DIVA

I'll never forget the first time I saw her, it was in *My Gal Sal* in 1942, and her name was Rita Hayworth. I couldn't take my eyes off her, she was the most perfect woman I had ever seen. The old cliché 'screen goddess' was used about many stars, but those are truly the only words that define that divine creature. . . . I was stunned and amazed that any human being could be that lovely.[1]

These are the words of one (female) fan about one 'screen goddess' or 'diva', but the reaction is a common one. If screen celebrities and deities have much in common, as already argued, how much more so is this true in the case of the adored and idealised film actress, idolised especially by men, although also held up as an ideal by women, who is often actually described as a goddess? Yet what commonalities are there between the divine and the screen actress? And what does an understanding of this issue contribute to our understanding of how divinities are, and have been, viewed?

Turning first to the ancient world, it is a given that the lives of ancient women in general, and Athenian women in the classical period in particular, were very circumscribed. The only area in which women participated fully was that of religious practice, where they worshipped and served goddesses who were believed to wield great power, in a period when women were actually socially and politically subordinate to men.[2] Although worship of the goddesses enabled women to take on roles that far exceeded the possibilities offered to them in other walks of life, nevertheless the nature of the goddesses was intrinsically connected with gender issues, and in particular, sexuality. Each of the female deities is to a certain extent defined with regard to her sexual behaviour: Athena is virginal and sexless, masculine in her attributes; Artemis virginal and chaste; Hera is the protector of the home and legitimate birth, and persecutor of extra-marital relationships; and Aphrodite is the goddess of sexual love. Thus the gender and femininity of the deity are an intrinsic aspect of her function and how she is regarded.

How do these aspects overlap with screen divas? First of all, a screen goddess is epitomised by her beauty. The classical conception of the body dominates glamour photography, and stresses the screen goddess' unattainable beauty. Secondly, she is remote and untouchable; such stars are regularly described as being out of reach and belonging to a different world or plane of existence. Another fan quote expresses this, saying 'Film stars ... seemed very special people, glamorous, handsome and way above us ordinary mortals.'[3] So remote are these stars that they take on a separate life from their actual personas; few people really expect to meet the actresses who are so described. With the arrival of the internet and new media such as fanfiction, things have moved into a new realm, as fans can imagine and write themselves into scenarios whereby they interact with the perfect character and/or actress, but they still have no expectation that such meetings could ever really take place. The goddess remains far off, on her exalted plane.

Thirdly, the screen star inspires devotion and reverence; her perfection must be acknowledged and honoured. The use of the word 'goddess' suggests the intensity of the devotion felt by the spectator. As Jackie Stacey points out, worship of stars as goddesses also:

> involves a denial of self, found in some forms of religious devotion. The spectator is only present in these quotes as a worshipper, or through their adoration of the star. There is no reference to the identity of the spectator or suggestion of closing the gap between star and fan by becoming more like a star; these are simply declarations of appreciation from afar. The boundaries between self and ideal are quite fixed and stable in these examples, and the emphasis is very strongly on the ideal rather than the spectator.[4]

Finally, the screen goddess, like any deity, has the power to influence her followers' thoughts, dreams, fantasies and even actions. The use of the religious term reflects the special status of the star, who exerts influence over her devotees simply through her nature. In extreme and more sinister cases, she may even drive people to obsession, resulting in excessive fan following and even stalking. Such events can be compared to the madness inspired by divinities in their worshippers, examples of which occur throughout classical mythology.

There are of course, as already discussed, both male and female stars of the screen that inspire such reactions from their fans and spectators. Yet while female film stars are called goddesses, male stars are not given the epithet of god. It seems that the influence of Judaeo-Christian tradition is strong here; even in the modern secular world, to call an actor a god has at best an irrelevant, and at worst an uncomfortable, almost blasphemous ring to it. The term "goddess' was first coined and popularised in the 1920s, when the Western world was far more conservatively Christian in outlook; since a female deity does not exist in Christianity, the label did not have the threatening subversive overtones that the masculine form would have. It seems that the separation between God and man in the Western tradition was absolute; for a concept such as a female deity, which had no place in such a mindset, the boundaries could merge much more easily. Thus when watching a Greek goddess on screen, viewers are aware of three interacting aspects: the goddess, the character and the actress, all of which possess overlapping elements of divinity that contribute to the overall aura of perfection and mystique surrounding the figure of the female deity.

Such an aura in the modern world surrounds celebrities, particularly stars of the screen, whose status evolved in tandem with the cinema itself. As one group of researchers argued:

> By the late 20th century, members of the high-status group had come to expect obsequious deference, exact significant financial tribute, and lay claim to legal privilege, as aristocratic and caste elites did in earlier centuries. But the new status system was different. It was born out of capitalism and mass media, and its dynamics reflected the conditions of the modern era. This system is called celebrity.[5]

Such words have only become more relevant as the power of celebrity status has increased incrementally in the global society of the second millennium. Yet the celebrity status of the actress is also bound up with her physical appearance, and to some extent objectifies her. At the same time, the twentieth and twenty-first centuries have seen more radical alteration in the status and role of the female than any other period in history. Women have moved from disenfranchisement to legislation granting equality to the 'me too' phenomenon of 2017–18. An examination of the depiction of female divinities on screen, therefore, provides an opportunity to consider how far these portrayals reflect these wider societal evolutions affecting both gender and celebrity, in a rapidly changing world.

THE GREEK GODDESSES ON SCREEN

Hera/Juno

A disembodied voice is accompanied by a pair of floating eyes with irises of peacock feathers. In the final episode of the fourth season she at last appears in person, a majestic figure in black, with a collar of peacock feathers, bodice decorated with crystals in shades of turquoise, blue and purple, and an iridescent cape with matching crystal trim on the shoulders. Such is the portrayal of Hera in *Hercules: The Legendary Journeys* (1994 and 1995–9), with the use of the peacock, the bird sacred to the goddess in the ancient world, a constant theme, featuring as a symbol of Hera in both her own appearances and that of her minions.

Hera, played by Meg Foster, here fulfils the role of primary villain. This is made clear by the opening credits, and by the delightfully cruel and wicked portrayal of the goddess herself, as she sneers at Hercules in smug loathing in their interactions. The goddess is blamed for, and is usually behind, every ill that befalls the young hero in this production, sending a stream of monsters and enemies to attack him (the hydra, minotaurs, executioners, Echidna, the Water Enforcer, the Fire Enforcer, the bounty hunters and so on). She also steals Prometheus' torch in order to remove fire from the earth, in an antithesis of the beneficiary role he often symbolises, and chains Prometheus himself to the rock, thereby depriving the Earth of his knowledge of the gift of medicine as well. Eventually, Hercules kicks the queen of the gods down to Tartarus in a satisfying reversal of the fate she had planned for him, a fitting retribution for this cruellest of deities.

A similar conception of Hera is also behind her appearance, at least tangentially, in the low-budget Korean horror/porn movie *Hera Purple: Devil Goddess* (2001). This film tells the story of a woman named Haerim, who suffers from vivid and disturbing nightmares in which she is possessed by the goddess Hera, and in which she attacks men in various violent and sexual ways. It emerges that the woman was raped as a child, and her victims in the dreams, which parallel real-life murders plaguing the city, are her rapists. The justification for her possession by the queen of the gods, and the title of the movie, is that Hera also 'avenged herself against the men who destroyed her'.[6]

Such depictions are a nod to ancient myth, in which Hera constantly persecutes the illegitimate products of her husband's liaisons with other females, both mortal and divine. Hera's forced marriage to Zeus is not a happy one, an aspect which, in a patriarchal society, makes her a veangeful figure, the stereotypical nagging, scheming, shrewish wife in constant bitter struggle against her husband and his infidelities.[7] In *Hercules: The Legendary Journeys*, the marital tension is also exploited after she is restored from Limbo by Zeus, and at first suffers from amnesia, ironically resulting in a happy relationship with her husband for a brief time, before having her memories restored by Ares and thus reverting to her usual role of harassment.

Another production that features Hera's state of conflict with Zeus centrally is the remake of *Jason and the Argonauts* (2000). In this version, Hera and Zeus appear in the sky as lordly and powerful beings, shown from the waist up, lounging in the midst of clouds with the tiny mortals below them. As Llewellyn-Jones explains,

> Their bodies blend into the hazy cloud formations, suggesting that the gods are not fully anthropomorphic nor is Olympus anything physical; the gods *are* Olympus and Olympus becomes corporeal in the figures of the gods.[8]

Played by Olivia Williams, aged 32, this is a more youthful Hera than is often seen, her dark hair falling in waves to her shoulders, and her clear grey-blue eyes, flawless skin and calm expression give a Madonna-like impression. She also has very natural looking make-up, which contrasts with the heavily made-up, exotically Oriental appearance of Medea, a technique that highlights the difference between the divine, who has no need of beauty aids, and the mortal.

This beautiful, divine couple, in keeping with mythological tradition, are, however, in a state of constant warfare due to Zeus' philandering and Hera's jealousy. They tamper with the lives of mortals in order to carry on their own private battles, the subject of interference in this case being Jason, and then also Medea, whom Hera causes to fall in love with the hero by sending Cupid to shoot her with his dart. Despite this intervention, Jason and Medea's passion for each other is portrayed as true love, and a contrast to that of the divine couple, providing a lesson for Zeus and Hera themselves, to the extent that Hera declares to Zeus that Jason and Medea put them to shame. Leaving aside the irony of the love of this particular couple being touted as the ideal, this declaration points up a message of the production: that the mortals are in some ways superior to the gods, a fact that Hera realises, even if Zeus does not.

This greater understanding in Hera, in contrast to the powerful but sometimes rather dim Zeus, is also seen in Harryhausen's *Clash of the Titans* (1981), where she is portrayed more positively than Zeus, who is described as harsh and uncaring as he plays his games with the mortals in whose lives he meddles.[9] A similar depiction is that of the strongly sanitised Disney's *Hercules* (1997). Since the king and queen of the gods are here portrayed as happily married, with Hercules their beloved and adored son, all negative elements are removed from Hera.[10] Physically, there is a strong resemblance between Hera and Aphrodite, in that both have pink skin, darker pink dresses and blonde hair, but Hera is more stately, with a less figure-hugging, more modest dress, and elaborate hairstyle and crown. In this adaptation, Hera is in many ways superior to Zeus, acting as both his conscience and the voice of reason, and persuading him to the right course of action in matters that he treats casually. In particular, in the animated series she has elements of great power. She is able to wield Zeus' lightning bolts as skilfully as her husband, who in one episode is forced to admit that Hera helped him to defeat the monster Typhon, as well as other enemies, but it seems that she, as a loving – and subservient – wife, allowed Zeus to take the credit for these achievements in order to maintain his image as invincible. In general, in contrast to her husband, Hera is sensitive, reasonable and balanced, even separating from her husband at one point due to his callousness, although ultimately Hercules is able to reunite his parents.[11]

Hera's main role in the Disney productions is that of mother figure, protective of Hercules, objecting to Zeus letting the newborn play with his thunderbolts. In the animated series *Hercules* (1998–9), she gives sensible advice to her son, balancing the very macho Zeus with more level-headed parenting, and reflecting her ultimate characterisation here. She is a kind and loving mother to Hercules, and breaks down in tears over her son's disappearance when she finds his cradle empty after his capture by Hades' minions. Such ideas hark back to Hera's ancient roots; probably an earth-mother figure in origin, her cult was pre-Hellenic and widespread, with temples dedicated to her predating those to Zeus in several places. She was the queen of heaven, whose emblem was the pomegranate, symbol of conjugal love and fruitfulness, and whose associated animals are the colourful peacock and the valuable cow.

Despite her original villainous role in the series, this aspect also comes through in *Hercules: The Legendary Journeys*, where Hera eventually ends her feud with Hercules, and in *Xena: Warrior Princess* (1995–2001), where she supports Hercules as he tries to stop Zeus from killing the pregnant Xena, whose child will bring about the demise of the reign of the gods. In a veritable rehabilitation of her character, the queen of the gods has now grown to love mankind, which she regards as her offspring, and works to assist Hercules in defeating Zeus.

Such ideas may also be behind the title of the 2007 American coming-of-age movie *Juno*, which also obliquely features Hera in her guise as the Roman queen of the gods. The eponymous heroine, a sparky and independent-minded high-school girl, becomes pregnant and, instead of going through with an abortion, decides to give her baby up for adoption. She finds a family in the classified ads, and then she carries on as if nothing unusual had happened, continuing to go to school and live a normal life. Although loving, and in wonder at, her unborn child, she is still prepared to give it away because she understands that this will be best for both mother and baby. The connection here, tenuous as it is, is with the name of the lead character, as Sonja Livingston points out:

> Juno is named for the Roman goddess. Wife to Jupiter, the goddess had no shortage of causes for jealousy and spite, but in her manifestation as Lucina, Juno was said to help ease the pain of childbirth. In the ancient world, women and girls ripped the braids from their hair as they labored, loosening their clothes and calling out to the [sic] Juno Lucina for help. The name Lucina is thought to come from the Latin word for light because a newborn was said to have been 'brought to light' with Juno's intercession – but isn't it equally possible that Juno was called *Lucina* for the way she helped provide the world with new light, for what baby does not shine brighter than the sun itself?[12]

Hera in the ancient world was more than just a mother figure, however. Queen of the gods, revered and worshipped, she was a complex deity with multifaceted areas of influence. The classical Hera is therefore often described as having been an appropriation of a pre-existing Great Goddess archetype in the territories conquered by Indo-European invaders.[13] Nevertheless caution must be exercised. As Vinciane Pirenne-Delforge and Gabriella Pironti point out:

> In the case of Hera, the main clues for understanding the various aspects of her persona are the notions of marriage, legitimacy, power, and sovereignty. This definitional structure of the goddess is largely rooted in the relationship with her husband and brother, the king of the gods. Therefore, any attempts to reconstruct a 'prehistory' of Hera as a 'great goddess' independent from Zeus has more to do with modern expectations and fantasy than with ancient evidence.[14]

Whatever her origins, the ancient power and dignity of the goddess do linger on in film. Harryhausen's *Jason and the Argonauts* (1963) demonstrates the reverence in which Hera was held. At her first appearance in the film, Briseis is shown kneeling in devout supplication before the enormous cult statue, while, as Llewellyn-Jones explains:

> Hera appears on screen in shadow, swathed in black veils and standing behind the statue, from whence she promises the girl help. While she does not inhabit the statue, she is identified as the power the statue represents.[15]

When shown on Olympus, Hera is clad in white and gold, her blonde hair plaited and curled into elaborate ringlets, and topped by a gold crown. She is a mature woman, regal in bearing, befitting the role of queen of the gods. Her power is also evident, an impression intensified by the casting, since the goddess was played by Honor Blackman, aged 38, already familiar to British viewers as Cathy Gale in the television series *The Avengers* (1962–4).[16]

She is also a somewhat severe character, in both Harryhausen movies. Hera has a smaller role in the second film, *Clash of the Titans* (1981), where she is played by Claire Bloom, partnered with Laurence Olivier's Zeus, opposite whom Bloom had played in Olivier's Richard III in 1955. At 50, she was considerably older even than Blackman had been, and her Shakespearean-trained diction lent dignity to the role. Clad in white, with none of the gold touches of the earlier movie, apart from her crown, she also wears a white veil atop her dark hair, adding to the matronly appearance. She is of stern disposition, showing little sympathy for Perseus and Danae ('Does it matter? The death of a girl or her child?'), and valuing human respect for the gods above mercy or morality. In contrast to the Godlike Zeus, who declares, 'Hundreds of good deeds cannot atone for one murder', she pleads for forgiveness for Acrisius, who 'has always shown devotion to the gods of Olympus in the past' and has 'built magnificent temples and dedicated them to you, great Zeus, father of the gods'. Thus the ancient severity of the queen of the gods is transposed into a lack of humanity in this Hollywood interpretation.

In the earlier Harryhausen movie, such harshness had also been demonstrated, as the goddess turns on Pelias, who killed Jason's sister, his mother and his father, the previous king, Aristo; her anger is not because of these murders, however, but due to Pelias' having carried out one of them, that of Jason's sister, Briseis, in her temple, thereby desecrating it. As a result of this outrage, Zeus reluctantly agrees to allow Hera to help Jason on five occasions, corresponding to the five times that Briseis called upon Hera herself. Thus she becomes a patron and protectress of Jason, symbolised by the figurehead of the *Argo* in her likeness, which is animated on occasion as she opens her eyes and speaks to Jason. It is notable that it is only the hero who can hear and see her communication, however. This was a decision taken by Harryhausen, as he explains:

> The Hera figurehead, located at the stern of the vessel, was designed so that the eyelids opened and the eyes moved, but I drew back from making the mouth move, as I felt most audiences would liken it to a ventriloquist's dummy, and it would then become borderline comedy. In the end we decided that Hera would communicate with Jason in his mind.[17]

It also had the effect of strengthening the protection and patronage Hera exhibits towards Jason, intervening at one point when the *Argo* gets to the Clashing Rocks by sending a sea god to guide the ship through the narrow straits.

Hera's power also dominates in the recent retelling of the Trojan War, *Troy: Fall of a City* (2018), where she is played by a relatively unknown actress, 41-year-old Inge Beckmann. This goddess, like the other deities in the production, is determinedly lacking in glamour, with naturalistic make-up, dressed in muted colours, materials that look more homespun than elegant, and topped with a black cloak that seems to be made of feathers. She is a jealous goddess; when Paris chooses Aphrodite and hands her the golden apple, Hera lets out an echoing shriek of rage and disappears in a flurry of her cloak, to leave Paris with his hands clapped to his ears in terror.

Despite the dangerous potency and authority reflected in scenes such as these, and her role as queen, Hera is no equal partner with her husband, remaining firmly under Zeus' jurisdiction. This was the case, of course, in the ancient patriarchal society of Greece; according to one study, Hera becomes largely identified through the male, hanging on to what little power she has through the position of her husband.[18] Yet it is also a common element in the screen depictions of the goddess, where she is almost always depicted together with Zeus/Jupiter as his consort; this is the case in the Harryhausen films, for example, and also in the 1988 television movie *Goddess of Love*, where she is portrayed as Zeus' wife and Aphrodite's mother. Here she is an attractive, cheerleader type of blonde-haired woman, dressed in ancient Greek costume, who trusts that her daughter will be able to make a man fall in love with her and so return to Olympus, from whence she has been banished, but admits ruefully that to do so without killing him might be a problem. In *Jason and the Argonauts*, although the fierce antagonism between Zeus and Hera, so often depicted in both the ancient world and the modern, does not feature, her relationship with her husband is one of subservience. Perhaps the most extreme case is that of *Xena: Warrior Princess*, where Zeus, furious with Hera's betrayal and her championing of mankind, kills his wife with 'the kiss of death', again exerting his dominance and subjugating the female, who now represents a mother figure, and humanity itself. Finally, in spite of Hera's power in *Troy: Fall of a City*, the goddess' role here is still clearly as the subservient wife of Zeus, who is firmly in authority over her as over the other gods who are shown (Athena, Aphrodite and Hermes). Despite the changes in society over the past decades, Hera does not seem to have evolved at all. She may be the queen of the gods, but she remains subservient to, and powerless against, her often oppressive husband, and her jealousy and spite are hallmarks that remain in the relatively rare portrayals of the goddess, who, because of this lack of evolution, is an uncomfortable figure in the contemporary world, unless portrayed in the least subtle of ways as a caricatured villain.

Athena/Minerva

A rather modern goddess wearing sunglasses and a pale blue minidress, with laced bodice ending in a bra style top, is played by Amanda Lister for a mixture of laughs and sexual titillation. Dressed in a bronze-coloured, long-sleeved dress and knee-high boots, her long brown hair held back somewhat severely under a crown, and made up with pale and luminescent eye shadow and heavy lipstick, Jane Fullerton-Smith's goddess seems stylised and dignified. Paris Jefferson strides around in gold armour, with bra-style top complete with Medusa's head to give an aegis finish, greaves, arm protectors and helmet-style headdress, teamed with high boots and miniskirt.

All three of these are not only depictions of the same goddess, Athena, but depictions that feature in interconnected shows. Lister played the role in *Hercules: The Legendary Journeys* and *Young Hercules* (1998–9), where she featured in only one episode, entitled 'The Apple', whose plot is inspired by the tale of the judgement of Paris. Fullerton-Smith was the goddess in *Young Hercules*, in which she took a role on the opposing side of arbitration, acting as judge in the episode 'Ares on Trial'. By far the most important of these depictions of Athena, however, is that of *Xena: Warrior Princess*. Played by Paris Jefferson, this Athena is a powerful, dignified and highly intelligent deity, a forceful figure, who is nevertheless benevolent towards mankind, using her powers to teach them to improve their lot. The goddess plays a pivotal role in the plot of the show, appearing in three episodes within the 'Twilight of the Gods' story arc that is the central topic in the fifth season.[19] In this series, after Hercules kills Zeus, it is Athena who rules on Olympus. Believing a prophecy that if Xena's daughter, Eve, is not killed, she will bring about the gods' destruction, she is determined to kill the child, and sets out to attack Xena's village, at the head of a huge army. After these events, believing Xena, her partner Gabrielle and Eve to be dead, Athena continues her rule on Olympus for the next twenty-five years, and is a commanding presence, although eventually, after discovering that Eve is still alive and attempting to attack her once more, she is killed by Xena.

The varied depictions, even within one syndicate, reflect the complex nature of Athena in the ancient world. Patron god of the city of Athens, worshipped by the Romans as the goddess Minerva, she was associated with wisdom, war and the useful arts (carpentry, weaving, manufacture etc.) in the ancient world. Although in origin a goddess of fertility, she developed into a warrior virgin figure, supremely worshipped and honoured in classical Athens, the cultural centre of ancient Greece, but still maintaining earlier aspects and connections with animals such as the owl and the snake.

In particular, the owl features as her symbol up to and including the present day, decorating the current Greek one Euro coin.[20] On screen, in the depiction of Athena in Harryhausen's *Clash of the Titans* (1981), where she is played by the classical and Shakespearean British actress Susan Fleetwood, the Athena symbolism is again conveyed by her owl, Bubo, which she carries on her hand like a falcon. The importance of the bird is stressed; when commanded by her divine father to send Bubo to aid Perseus, she declares 'Never!' and instead demands of Hephaestus that he make a mechanical substitute, saying defiantly, 'Let great Zeus rage till even Olympus shakes. But I will never part with you, my beloved Bubo.' Dressed in angelic white, and with dark curly hair, Fleetwood was 37 at the time, and with her background in the classics and unusually tall stature, she brought dignity and presence to the role. This was a statuesque, majestic goddess, a likely daughter for Laurence Olivier's Zeus with his Shakespearean inflections.

Fleetwood's Athena displays courage and an independent spirit, elements that also have their roots in the ancient depictions of the goddess. More than almost any other deity, she represented much of what the Athenians thought of as worthy and unique to their society (which is generally what is meant when the culture of ancient Greece is imagined), resulting in their pre-eminence in their known world. A proud figure who punished insult fiercely, as myths such as that of Arachne reflect, she was the product of Metis (intelligence) and Zeus, born from the head of her father rather than through birth from a female. Thus she combines wisdom and intelligence with a feminine aspect, albeit presented in a rather masculine manner.

This combination of factors has led to Athena having a strong identity in the post-classical world. As Susan Deacy writes:

> Athena is one of the Greek gods who has held a special appeal since Antiquity. Her connections with civilised values, the arts, learning, justice and intelligence have given her an emblematic value second only to Aphrodite . . . Her intriguing gendered identity has helped ensure her longevity, giving her a particular prominence within feminist and psychoanalytical thinking.[21]

With the move from paganism to Christianity, certain elements, in particular her capricious cruelty, were suppressed, and her association with wisdom and justice, and her patronage of civilised institutions and worthy characters, stressed. Her survival was aided by an association with the Virgin Mary, to the extent that temples to Athena were converted to shrines to Mary. With the explosion of art in the Renaissance, Athena's role as patron of the arts gave the goddess new popularity, while as a strong female figure, she was adopted by various female rulers in the sixteenth and seventeenth centuries as a means of bolstering their own positions. Thus her post-classical function became that of the strong female who embodied morality and upheld civilised, male values. As an allegorical figure, she became the figure of Liberty in France and Britannia in Great Britain, and influenced the depiction of the Statue of Liberty in the United States. [22] Her iconography features on the United States' highest personal military decoration, the Medal of Honor, where she is depicted holding a shield and the Union flag. She has also featured on European coins; the 100 Lira coin used in Italy until the introduction of the Euro portrayed Minerva with an olive tree. Due to her connections with intelligence, a number of academic institutions in the modern world have adopted her as a symbol. Perhaps the most striking contemporary usage of the goddess is the modern-day sculpture of Athena in Nashville Tennessee's Centennial Park, where she stands in the full-scale reconstruction of the Parthenon on the Athenian Acropolis (see Figure 5.1).

While she appears only infrequently on screen, it is as the goddess of wisdom that she is most clearly presented, even in the occasional oblique references, such as the name of Minerva McGonagall in the Harry Potter films, which represents the teacher's wisdom and virtue. In *Xena: Warrior Princess*, she is also an intellectual, as well as level-headed and honourable, valuing intelligence above all. Athena

Figure 5.1 Statue of Athena by Alan LeQuire at the Nashville Parthenon. Photograph by Bubba73 (Jud McCranie) [CC BY-SA 4.0 (https://creativecommons. org/licenses/by-sa/4.0)], from Wikimedia Commons, https://commons.wikimedia. org/wiki/File:Athena_at_Parthenon_in_Nashville,_TN,_US.jpg.

is also, however, bitterly opposed to Xena, due to the role she and Eve play in the fated downfall of the gods.[23] This is in sharp contrast to her role in Greek mythology, where she is the patron of heroes; an aspect highlighted by the TV miniseries *The Odyssey* (1997), starring Armand Assante, where Athena demonstrates a protectiveness towards Odysseus that is much in keeping with the Homeric treatment. One of only two gods who appears on screen,[24] and played by the legendary Italian actress Isabella Rossellini, this Athena has a luminous, supernatural glow to her pale skin. Aged 45 at the time, Rossellini is Hollywood royalty, the daughter of three-time Oscar-winning Swedish-born actress Ingrid Bergman and neo-realist master Italian director Roberto Rossellini. She was also the third wife of Oscar-winning director Martin Scorsese from 1979 to 1982 and the partner of legendary director David Lynch. Dressed in an olive-green chiton with a gold cord belt, aegis-style heavy necklace, gold sandals and a Bronze Age-styled helmet which she holds but does not wear, this Athena is a dignified figure who projects a majestic divinity in the role she plays in this production.

Athena's role as protectress of heroes and benefactress of mankind in general is also visible in the much panned, and unintentionally hilarious, *Hercules* of 1983.[25] Described by one website as 'a delirious mishmash of retro peplum and Eurocomics sci-fi', the movie opens with three of the gods, Zeus, Hera and Athena, situated, not on Mount Olympus, but on the moon, debating the fate of mankind since Pandora's jar has been opened, scattering evil in the world. On Athena's advice, Zeus crafts a soul of incomparable strength and righteousness out of the purest white light, and dispatches it to Earth to incarnate itself into an invincible champion, namely Hercules. Played by the Italian actress Delia Boccardo, then aged 35, in this incarnation Athena has long, wavy, white-blonde hair and again is dressed in white, but in this case with no classical overtones. Her floor-length, strapless gown is backed by a strange white gauzy piece of material marked with vertical white stripes, fashioned rather like a peacock's tail. On her head she wears a gold crown, adorned with pale blue stones. None of the traditional iconography accompanies this Athena, but, despite the wooden acting and the limited role any of the gods play in this movie, her role as goddess of wisdom does persist, for it is to her that Zeus turns for advice as how to prevent evil from gaining ultimate control of the world. Later in the film she is the champion of Hercules and his love interest in this film, Circe, defending them and declaring that 'they've had to work hard for everything they've won', against Hera's complaints that the hero has used divine magic. In the even more bizarre sequel to the movie, *The Adventures of Hercules* (1985),[26] Athena is played by 34-year-old Carla Ferrigno, wearing a long, flowing, white robe and cloak, gold earrings and necklace, and with her abundant curly blonde hair topped by a gold crown. Her one brief appearance is, again, siding with Zeus and appealing to him, on behalf of mankind, to send

Hercules back to Earth to save the world. Thus, even in these rather absurd productions, which owe little to the traditional versions of Greek myth, Athena is portrayed as the patron and defender of mankind.

Athena is one of the three goddesses depicted in the recent *Troy: Fall of a City*, although her role is relatively minor, even in a series in which the viewer is really given little more than glimpses of these gods. Her physical portrayal is striking, however. Perhaps the only occasion on which Athena has been portrayed by a non-Caucasian actress, the South African Shamilla Miller brings an exotic air to the role, with her dark beauty and piercingly powerful gaze (see Figure 5.2 below). Like Hera, she has a full-length cloak, but her tunic is much shorter, more like that of a man. In another nod to her classical attributes, her costume looks vaguely armour-like, with a bodice that is shaped like a breastplate during the golden apple scene, and material crossed over her chest in the episode in which she walks among the battle lines prior to the battle. As she walks, she, like Hera and Aphrodite, blesses her individual favourite heroes. This personal protection and favour are the sole role of Athena in this production, and she is a strong figure even though she does not seem to demonstrate the other attributes commonly ascribed to the goddess.

The battle association is one that has been played up more in recent years. In the Percy Jackon movies, Athena, played by Melina Kanakaredes, has a bigger role than any of the other gods except Zeus and Poseidon. Strongly identified with intelligence and reason, she is also the god of war strategy, but nevertheless tries to convince Zeus in the first movie that 'war is not the answer'. She has a positive relationship with her daughter, Annabeth, declaring herself to be very proud of her, and communicating with her telepathically. As opposed to the books, where she is inimically opposed to Percy, son of her enemy, Poseidon, there is no sign of animosity in the film, and she is overall rather less fearsome than in the novels. With long, curly brown hair, Kanakaredes is in her mid-forties, and while attractive, she is no page-three girl. Clad in the traditional long white dress, but with the bodice made of dull, metallic armour, this is a warrior goddess but with a much more unusual, gentler, maternal side as well.

A rather more violent portrayal is that found in *Athena, the Goddess of War* (2015). This is an action movie produced by the Maiden Network, a streaming service similar to Netflix, Hulu and Amazon Prime, but which 'focuses on female led action adventure and drama movies, tv series, comic books and audio books'. Their programming

Figure 5.2 Athena (Shamilla Miller) in *Troy: Fall of a City* (2018). BBC.

is available On Demand on television, computer, tablet and phone as well as on a Free Live TV service. Their website explains that:

> The network also serves as a platform for our Maidens to perform for their fans. Maidens are amazingly smart, amazingly beautiful and they aren't afraid to embrace both sides. It's about a woman's ability to be sexy and be strong. Here you will find women filling the lead roles of our films, television series and books in stark contrast to many mainstream studios that won't take the chance or risk. At the Maiden Network we wouldn't have it any other way.[27]

The movie, and other products put out by the network, are heavily influenced by comic books, from which the genre of heroine movies emerges, with heroines 'thrust into a series of challenges requiring physical feats, extended fights, extensive stunts and frenetic chases'.[28] Elizabeth Abele suggests that 'the key agency of female action protagonists is their ability to draw on the full range of masculine and feminine qualities in ever-evolving combinations'.

The potency of Athena, whether in the sense of physical warfare or of intellect, means that portraying the goddess is easier in some

ways for modern film makers, for she is far less oppressed by a patriarchal society than Hera, for example. She is generally portrayed as
a powerful figure, with independent agency. Unlike the other Greek
goddesses, her various characteristics – wisdom and intelligence, skill
in war, power, patronage – do seem to appear on screen in different
productions according to need, reflecting a level of comfort in treating this multifaceted deity in the modern world.

Artemis/Diana

Artemis, moon goddess and goddess of the hunt, appears in a single
shot in Disney's *Fantasia* from 1940, towards the end of the fifth seg-
ment ('The Pastoral Symphony'). Represented as goddess of archery
and animals, but most of all of the moon in this animation, the cres-
cent moon forms her bow, and she is accompanied by a small white
deer. Dressed in a short white chiton, with ribbons flowing behind
her, her right shoulder (although not breast) is bare as she pulls
back the bow, announcing the arrival of night through the release
of an arrow that twinkles in the sky. This depiction reflects much of
the iconography and elements of the ancient myths, which describe
her as *potnia therōn*, mistress of animals, with whom she is often
depicted, as well as being associated with the moon. Cold and aloof
as the moon itself, she is a chaste and virginal figure. In ancient statuary, she is usually dressed in a chiton, often with one breast bare, a
young and beautiful virgin.[29]

She is also swift to punish those who transgress, even unintentionally, an aspect that also lies behind some cinematic depictions of the
goddess, such as her fleeting appearance in Jean Cocteau's *La Belle
et la Bête* (1946), in which it is Diana who has turned the prince into
a beast. When the evil villain of the film, Avenant, breaks into the
'Pavilion of Diana', the statue comes to life and shoots him with an
arrow. Thereupon he is himself turned into a beast, while the prince
is restored to his true form. We have only the briefest glimpse of
Diana, dressed in a short chiton and cloak, decorated or covered with
leaves, as she lifts the bow to her shoulder and fires the arrow, but she
appears rather older than her traditional depictions. There is also no
explanation for why it is Diana who acts in this role, but it seems that
her tradition as avenger of wrongdoers, combined with her huntress
role and the wild and uncultivated element of her nature and setting,
are what motivated her inclusion in this movie.

Another French classic movie also gives a sighting of Diana, albeit
in the form of a model posing as the goddess for an artist. In François

Truffaut's 1968 film *La Mariée était en noir*, Jeanne Moreau plays Julie Kohler, a widow who hunts the five men who killed her husband on her wedding day. Her fourth victim is the artist Fergus, for whom Julie models as Diana/Artemis, dressed in a white chiton tied at one shoulder, and eventually killing the artist with her bow and arrow. The choice of Artemis again seems motivated by the archery element and by her inclination towards vengeance, which is supremely suited to Julie, a character obsessed with revenge.

Despite Artemis' virgin status and merciless tendencies, she is also the goddess of childbirth and children, having helped her mother give birth to her twin brother, Apollo. As Diana she is even a fertility goddess, especially venerated thus at Ephesus.[30] A multifaceted goddess, she is worshipped in wildly differing ways in the ancient world,[31] and some of this has spilled over onto the modern screen. In the first episode of the 1995 comedy *Four Rooms*, a very strange version of the goddess features. This surreal movie consists of four interconnected stories that all take place in a rather decrepit hotel on New Year's Eve. The first, entitled *Honeymoon Suite*, involves a coven of witches who resurrect the petrified Diana, and the description of the goddess, even in this bizarre comedy setting, is unusual to say the least. Invoked by the scantily clad women, the virgin goddess of the hunt is described here as 'Diana, O Great Beautiful One, O Goddess Bride' and 'Goddess of Light, Goddess of Lust', a depiction that is a far cry from her classical roots. Seen only from the neck up when she appears, Diana emerges as if from water, so that her short blonde hair looks slicked back, and with her lips heavy with full dark-red lipstick as she parts them in a sultry smile. The decision to incorporate Diana, rather than another goddess, in this scene seems based on her connection with the moon, and thereby the night, rather than any of her more traditional qualities.

Another depiction that deviates somewhat from the traditional portrayal is that in the *Hercules: The Legendary Journeys/Xena: Warrior Princess* syndicate. Although Artemis appears only occasionally in these series, she has none of the aloofness or vengeful elements of other characterisations. The earliest appearance of the goddess is in *Hercules: The Legendary Journeys*, where she is portrayed as a sporting type, 'able to do more than ten thousand push ups in one day'.[32] She is portrayed here as the middle child of three divine sisters, coming between Athena and Aphrodite, whose birth order is reversed here, in contrast to many variants of classical myth. Artemis also replaces Hera as the third goddess in the divine beauty contest in another deviation from ancient sources, in the episode entitled 'The Apple' (1996), based on the judgement of Paris. Played by Rhonda McHardy, she has long red hair, is dressed in a short yellow tunic with the stomach section cut out, giving it a bikini-like appearance, and wears a slim gold fillet round her forehead. This look is maintained throughout the different series. Thus in *Xena: Warrior Princess*, Artemis appears in the episode 'Motherhood', along with various other gods, and in this case she is depicted as a huntress, with a short yellow tunic, worn with a golden belt at the hips and bodice adorned with gold at the breasts and down the sternum, and a quiver full of arrows on her back. Played by Josephine Davison, who also voiced the character in the animated movie *Hercules and Xena – The Animated Movie: The Battle for Mount Olympus* (1997), she has long, red, curly hair, topped with a fillet-style gold crown, and takes an active part in the battle. The only variation is the single episode of *Young Hercules* in which she appears, 'Inn Trouble' (1998), where she is seen only as a blue hologrammic light shape, although it is clear that she is still wearing a short tunic or skirt.

This more powerful and athletic depiction is the forerunner of the most recent screen incarnations of Artemis, who has been glimpsed only rarely in cinema or television. She appears briefly in *Clash of the Titans* (2010), clad in a short grey tunic, with one breast covered in silver metal, in keeping with her traditional depictions. Here she features only as part of the pantheon, however, and has no speaking role. In *Immortals* (2011), she does not even appear.

Where elements of the goddess can be seen, however, is in various other screen depictions of strong, warrior-archer princesses. From as early as 1941, with the birth of the character of Wonder Woman, whose alias is Diana Prince, this archetype has grown in popularity. In film, it developed, ironically, from 1970s Blaxploitation movies, where actresses such as Pam Grier, described as 'the biggest, baddest and most beautiful of all female heroes in popular culture',[33] in the words of David Cox, 'gleefully punched, kicked and shot men, kicked them in the testicles, and stabbed them with hairpins, broken bottles and metal hangers'.[34]

With the growth of feminism and changing attitudes towards, and roles of, women, film heroines have become stronger, more independent and powerful figures, taking on roles usually assigned to men, although this in itself raises questions about female empowerment, for it may be argued that a woman taking on a man's traditional role in film makes her only male in nature, rather than a strong woman on her own terms. This is a point made by the actress Natalie Portman, who declared that, 'The fallacy in Hollywood is that if you're making

a "feminist" story, the woman kicks ass and wins. That's not feminist,
that's macho.'[35] Similarly, Martha McCaughey and Neal King raise
the question of whether female action heroes may be 'phallic women'
who 'reproduce male domination'.[36] Especially when it is remem-
bered that the prime audiences for many such films are men rather
than women, it is hard to avoid the conclusion that there is as much
female objectification here as there is emancipation.

Nevertheless, the female action figure, for whatever reason, is one
of the descendants of Artemis on the modern screen. The influence
of Atalanta, probably in herself originally a version of the goddess
Artemis, under whose protection she fell, can also be seen in these
depictions. Together the two figures present an example of a strong,
female, archer archetype that has found resonance in modern screen
adaptations. Katniss Everdeen in *The Hunger Games* (2012) owes
a great deal to Artemis.[37] Although Katniss is not a perfect copy
of the goddess, as Hansen emphasises, 'when the narrative begins
Katniss strongly evokes the figure of Artemis because of their shared
status as bow-wielding hunters'. Likewise, Katniss is more at home
in the natural wilds than in urban surroundings, and is a virginal
figure, whose 'romantic and sexual innocence' is 'a running theme
throughout', as well as a protector of children.[38] Similarly it has
been argued that the character Lisbeth Salander has traces of the
Atalanta/Artemis figure in *The Girl with the Dragon Tattoo* (2011),
as does Anastasia Steele, the main character in E. L. James' *Fifty
Shades of Grey*.[39] In recent years, figures such as Andromeda in
Wrath of the Titans (2012) and Gal Gadot's *Wonder Woman* (2017)
perpetuate the archetype.

All these characters, according to Bolen, 'ventured into the wilderness of emotion and sexuality', a point she expounds as follows:

> These are young women who call upon their intuition, depth of feeling and
> courage to go beyond previous limits; who feel fear and outrage and have to
> adapt and endure and not give in or give up. Each has an inner spirit that is
> not subdued, a will that is not broken. Each in her own way is a quirky, inde-
> pendent, courageous person who is in uncharted territory – the metaphoric
> wilderness, the realm of Artemis.[40]

Rarely, then, does Artemis appear on screen in the form recognised
in the ancient world, and when she does, as an archer or moon goddess, it is in a very two-dimensional and superficial manner. Where
the deity does have influence, however, is as the figure behind strong,
female warrior characters, such as Atalanta and the Amazons, of
whom she was patron, and who embodied the ideals that she represented. In their elements of empowerment, such ideals are ones with

which contemporary society can identify in some way, thus allowing for the Artemis/Diana figures to come to new prominence.

Aphrodite

Troy: Fall of a City gives a central role to Aphrodite, who bribes Paris with the promise of Helen in order to win the golden apple, and thus becomes the ultimate cause of the war and the city's destruction. Played by Lex King, this goddess of love has long, flowing, red-gold hair, is tall and slim, and is generally costumed in a short green two-piece costume that is reminiscent of a swimsuit, topped occasionally by a long green cloak. Since Paris and Helen are deeply in love, she is the patron of Paris, and is shown supporting him; but she is powerless, in that she is ultimately unable to assist him in any way, since Zeus does not allow the gods to take sides. Perpetuating the dumb blonde stereotype in a manner that might seem surprising in the twenty-first century, she is also of limited intelligence, since she does not even understand the true nature of the curse on Troy, which she believes that Paris' suicide attempt had cancelled.

Despite her obvious beauty, and the patronage of love, there is very little sexuality about this Aphrodite, who, like the other gods in the series, seems more remote and aloof than passionate, perhaps a result of the problems inherent in portraying a sexual goddess in the 'Me Too' climate of 2017–18. Herein lies the nub of the difficulty with depicting this goddess, whom the Etrsucans knew as Turan, the Romans as Venus, the Greeks as Aphrodite.

In order to understand the ancient goddess, however, it is important to take into account that the concept of love had quite different connotations for the ancient Greeks than it does for the modern Western world. There were several different kinds of love in classical Greece: there was *philia*, the love of human solidarity, an affectionate love between friends, close family members, usually between equals.[41] There was also *agapē*, the verbal form of which, according to Lidell and Scott's *Lexicon*, means 'greet with affection' and 'show affection for the dead', but which appears as a noun mostly in a Christian context, meaning 'the highest form of love, charity' or 'the love of God for man and of man for God'. Neither *agapē* nor *philia*, however, were the domain of Aphrodite, who presided over only erotic sexual love, or *eros*. As Froma Zeitlin points out, 'The Greeks themselves divinized carnal desire in the figure of Eros, attesting to the enduring power of this most essential of human instincts.'[42] Eros as a divine figure was usually held to be the son of Aphrodite, who was a feminised version of the erotic quality.[43]

Partly due to the inferior social status of women in ancient Greece, attitudes towards heterosexual sex and sexual love were complex. What might be today considered infatuation was, to the Greeks, a form of madness, a mental illness. Erotic love was more of a frightening danger, an attack by the arrows of Cupid/Eros, than an exciting and romantic rite of passage.[44] Women, as beings able to incite such feelings, were regarded with suspicion. Thus Socrates wrote, 'women are the weaker sex ... being born a woman is a divine punishment since a woman is half way between a man and an animal'.[45] Talking of Spartan women, Aristotle thought that the comparative freedom of the Spartan constitution had caused nothing but trouble, declaring that 'in the Theban invasion, ... they were utterly useless and caused more confusion than the enemy'.[46] He believed that 'the male is by nature superior and the female inferior as one rules and the other is ruled. This inequality is permanent because the woman's deliberate faculty is without authority like a child's.'[47] Thus *eros* flourished between man and woman, or between an older man and a younger, and was thought to be egocentric and object-oriented, and far inferior to *philia*, which was between equals.

The idea that sexual love was dangerous, and Aphrodite a goddess who posed a threat to man, has bled through into modern receptions. One of the earliest appearances of Venus in a central screen role is in the 1948 movie *One Touch of Venus*. This film is based on F. Anstey's story *The Tinted Venus* (1885), a tale loosely based on that of Pygmalion, but where in Ovid's original version, Pygmalion prays to Aphrodite to grant his statue life, in this movie (and the Anstey book), Venus herself replaces Galatea. The plot involves a wealthy department store mogul named Whitfield Savory who has bought a statue of Venus for $200,000, which he places in the store. Eddie Hatch, a window dresser, while under the influence of alcohol, kisses the statue, causing it come to life. Venus, played by Ava Gardner, then falls in love with Eddie and leaves the store, causing Eddie to be accused of stealing the statue. She then turns up at Eddie's apartment, where he hides her from his girlfriend, Gloria, who is a paranoid shrew of a woman, and his roommate, Joe. Enchanted by Venus' singing a love song, Joe falls in love with Gloria, while Venus, having returned to the store, is discovered sleeping on a sofa by Whitfield, who in turn becomes besotted with her. This is revealed to be no more than infatuation, however, for his true love is his secretary, Molly. At the end of the movie, Venus is recalled to Olympus by Jupiter and returns to her pedestal. Whitfield and Molly remain together, as do Joe and Gloria, with Eddie the only one left alone, until the arrival of a new salesgirl who is a doppelgänger of Venus herself.

One Touch of Venus is basically a light and frivolous comedy, yet its portrayal of the goddess of love has serious undertones. This is underscored by the choice of Ava Gardner, who had shot to stardom in the noir film *The Killers* (1946), where she played a femme fatale, the beautiful and deadly Kitty Collins. Such a role would have helped create an impression of Venus as a sexually alluring but dangerous figure when she appeared in the much lighter movie. Her sexual attraction is emphasised in the movie poster, in which the words 'The gal who invented love' are emblazoned over her head, applying equally to both Venus and Ava. She is also, unusually, dark-haired rather than blonde, adding to the sense of a somewhat threatening figure. This impression is only increased by Venus' narration of the harsh manner in which she had treated former lovers; she explains, for example, in a tale that has no basis in Greek mythology, that she turned Hippolytus into an owl because he irritated her.

The remake of the movie from 1988, in a version entitled *Goddess of Love*, starring Vanna White, presents a quite different style of Venus. On the Rotten Tomatoes website, the listing for the movie reads:

> The famed Wheel of Fortune gameshow letter-turner Vanna White makes her acting debut in this sub-par TV-movie. White stars as the goddess Venus, who goes after the love of a present-day man. The silly film was universally panned by critics.[48]

This movie was a variation on the theme of its predecessor forty years earlier, and was an attempt to capitalise on the success of the profitable 1987 movie *Mannequin*. Also a modern-day adaptation of the Pygmalion story, this film featured not Aphrodite but rather a young woman from ancient Egypt who was transformed into a statue in the twentieth century by the gods, in order to prevent her having to marry against her will. While bearing obvious similarities to *Mannequin*, *Goddess of Love* owes more to the plot of *One Touch of Venus* in its use of the Greek goddess.[49] There are differences in portrayal, however, particularly with regard to Aphrodite herself, who is in this version given a back story. The movie opens on Mount Olympus, 'Ages ago' according to the text on screen, and presents Aphrodite – who explains that she prefers to be called Venus – being found guilty of sexual misconduct and, as punishment, banished from the realm of the gods.[50] At this point, Hera wonders if Venus will ever be allowed to return to Mount Olympus, to which Zeus answers,

'Perhaps. Some day. She will return when she has won the heart of a man ... and prove that she can keep his love without killing him', thus setting up the lesson about the nature of love to be learned by the goddess, and by extension the audience, in this banal TV movie.

As a means of accomplishing this end, Venus, meanwhile, has been turned into a statue which in the late twentieth century ends up in the 'L.A. City Museum'. The plot continues in a similar vein to the earlier movie, with the hero, Ted, slipping the ring onto the finger of the statue and bringing Venus to life, with mayhem and an eventual moralising message ensuing.[51] In contrast to *One Touch of Venus*, the goddess here is not played by a movie star who exudes sexual allure, but by the vapid, although physically attractive, former Miss World, Vanna White. Blonde and slender, with a beautiful face, she nevertheless lacks charisma and screen presence. This produces a rather dissonant portrayal, for although she lacks the temptress appeal of Ava Gardner, with her fresh-faced, innocent beauty this Venus, in the decade of *Fatal Attraction* (1987), is a threatening and violent deity. She is prepared to 'crush' anything or anyone that stands in her way, a fact demonstrated by her destroying a lamp with a cartoon-like ray special effect from her finger. Despite this attitude, White is so insipid that it is very hard to believe in her as a divinity of any sort, let alone one with power and jealous vindictiveness. It is perhaps in the end unsurprising that where the young man in the 1948 movie abandoned his mortal love in favour of the (screen) goddess, in the later one he stayed true to her, and in a romanticised twist, the mortal couple teach the goddess about true love. As a result, she proves to Zeus that she has learned this and seems to be forgiven for her sins, although she is then, rather bewilderingly, transformed back into the statue at the end of the movie, albeit with the caveat that Zeus might relent towards her later.

In the ancient world, Aphrodite was a powerful deity, whose complexity reflects not only ideas about sexuality, but also her pre-classical origins and the varied attitudes and customs throughout the Greek-speaking world.[52] According to most Greek traditions, Aphrodite predates Zeus, being born from the castration of Uranus by Kronos.[53] She actually resembles Zeus more than she does other goddesses. Although married, she has sexual relations with other gods and mortals; she is highly sexualised; and she also has a jealous spouse, Hephaestus. Altogether an ambivalent goddess, she is 'simultaneously powerful and weak, adored and humiliated' in the ancient texts.[54] This characterisation is most closely caught in the television series *Hercules: The Legendary Journeys* and *Xena: Warrior Princess*, in which she has a recurring role. Like the other gods in these series,

Aphrodite has elements of selfishness and self-aggrandisement, demonstrating what seems to modern eyes arbitrary favouritism, but which echoes a fair amount of ancient tradition. Despite these qualities, Aphrodite is actually one of the most likeable of the gods in these shows, and often provides some comic relief, as well as giving the audience insight into the internal politics of the gods.

In her first appearance, she is scheming and manipulative, spiteful and mercurial, but soon develops into a more compassionate and high-spirited character, albeit still somewhat volatile. She is the mother of Cupid, with whom, partly due to her own wilful and shallow personality, her relationship is tense, especially when she tries to manipulate him and force him to fire his arrows for her own ends. She does actually care about her son, however, begging Hercules to save him from Hera's curse. Hercules' bond with her is depicted as that of an indulgent older brother who loves but is somewhat exasperated by his irritating and spoiled little sister. She also has a close relationship with Ares, here portrayed as her brother rather than her love interest, although the ancient tradition of the sexual connection between the two has echoes in the episode when Ares loses his divinity, as a result of which Aphrodite goes insane, since 'War and Love must exist in cosmic balance.' Since Aphrodite has by this stage formed a close relationship with Gabrielle, despite being in conflict with Xena, she does not side with the gods in the war between Xena and the Olympians,[55] with the result that she and Ares are the only two gods who are not killed and survive into the new order of the world.[56]

Physically, Aphrodite is blonde and full-breasted, and habitually dresses in revealing corselette-type tunics in pale pink, made mostly of lace and chiffon. Later, in *Xena*, her lingerie style of clothing remains, but becomes a more sophisticated black by the time the battle between Xena and the Olympians takes place. Since the same actress, Alexandra Tydings, played the goddess over the whole five-year period, the divinity does age a little in these productions, being almost thirty by the release of the final episode in which she figured,[57] a somewhat unexpected depiction of idealised female beauty in a production aimed at teens.

It is with regard to the idealisation of beauty, in this case through art, that Aphrodite frequently appears. The goddess is the subject of two of the most famous pieces in the history of European art, the *Venus de Milo* and Botticelli's *Birth of Venus*, and one of the most common contexts in which she is seen on screen, as in the rest of popular culture, is via reference to the latter. Terry Gilliam explored this piece of art twice, the first time in a short musical animation

from 1971 in *Monty Python's Flying Circus* (1969–74). This clip
parodies the great work of art, featuring an animated drawing of a
meat grinder, the 'meat' of which becomes the hair of Venus on her
shell. Romantic background music accompanies the goddess. After a
few seconds, a hand emerges from the water and tweaks the goddess'
nipple, as if turning a dial, whereupon the music changes to a bright
circus-like tune, in time to which Venus dances, her limbs twirling
acrobatically. Discussing this animation, Gilliam talks of the source
of his interpretation, which sees Aphrodite as:

> something violent and ugly and meat . . . The raw materials that make up our
> physicality. And there she is sublime. And then, of course, being naked and
> beautiful, she kind of turns me on in a sexy kind of way. Why wouldn't . . . ?
> So if she's going to turn me on, I'm going to turn her on, and she has some-
> thing that looks like a radio dial that you switch on. So that's what her nipple
> becomes. A hand comes in and turns it on and she dances for me.[58]

Seventeen years later, Gilliam revisited the Botticelli Venus motif in
The Adventures of Baron Munchausen (1988), a fantasy-adventure
film, in which Venus, played by Uma Thurman in her earliest film role,
ascends from a pool on a giant clam shell (see Figure 5.3). The shell
opens to reveal Thurman standing in a pose reminiscent of Botticelli's
painting, against a backdrop of colours that echo that of the picture. She is naked, partially covered only with an artfully draped
cloth, but then attendants rush to cover her quickly with white gauzy
pieces of cloth that somehow turn into a lovely dress that recalls
Botticelli's *Primavera*.[59] She has no embarrassment or shame regarding her nudity; Gilliam says of this that he was inspired by Botticelli's
painting where, 'Everyone's rushing in to get her clothes on. . . . she's
so beautiful and confident and statuesque, and there's all this activity
at the edge of the picture. . . . "Clothes on! Oh Jesus! Don't look! She's
naked!", and that kind of conflict in reaction to the painting intrigues
me.'[60] Talking of the allure of Venus in this movie, he continues:

> I remember when we had screenings of the film, with a lot of young men in
> there, there would be a moment when she would look at them straight into
> the audience – and they would go quiet. . . . On one hand, they're all getting
> very excited by her because she's this full-figured beautiful girl, then suddenly
> she looks at them. 'Oh, what are you looking at?' I always loved that reaction.
> I think he is doing the same thing. Venus is not ashamed, she's not hiding,
> she's, 'This is what I am.' It's bold and I love that about her . . . she is the
> ultimate male fantasy.[61]

Echoing the ancient tradition canonised as early as Homer, in this
version, Hephaestus/Vulcan is unappreciated by his wife, who scorns
the perfect diamonds he makes for her, and flirts and dances with the

Figure 5.3 Venus (Uma Thurman) in *The Adventures of Baron Munchausen* (1988). Prominent Features/Laura-Film.

Baron. In the end, however, Vulcan shows himself the superior force, as he pulls Venus down from the sky where she is floating with the Baron, by the same red rope that had pulled her up from the depths at the beginning of the scene, abusing her as a 'whore' and 'strumpet' as he does so. Her retort is that she is a goddess who can do as she likes, but she is quelled by her husband, who declares himself 'THE God'. At the end of the scene, Venus, however, calms her husband down by seducing him, reasserting her ultimate but less obvious power over his blunt force and violence.

This homage to Botticelli's Venus is typical in that it serves as a short cut for ultimate female beauty and sexual attractiveness in multiple pop culture references, often depicted only very briefly on screen. Thus in an episode of *The Simpsons* (1989–), entitled 'The Last Temptation of Homer', Homer meets a new co-worker to whom he is strongly attracted, and imagines her naked, on a conch shell, with two winged Cupid-style characters holding a piece of material across her naked body. Botticelli's painting has been spoofed by the Muppets on several occasions, most commonly with Miss Piggy taking the role of the goddess.[62] Similarly, the first appearance of Artemis in *Hercules: The Legendary Journeys* also evokes the iconic paining, with the goddess appearing from the sea inside a giant clam-shell, which opens and which she then uses to windsurf.[63] This motif is repeated in *Hercules and Xena – The Animated Movie: The Battle for Mount Olympus* as she surfs across the sea and down the slopes of Mount Olympus.

Given Hollywood's fixation on physical beauty and romance, it is perhaps surprising how infrequently Aphrodite/Venus, goddess of love, has actually been depicted on screen. She is seen only briefly in Harryhausen's *Clash of the Titans* (1981), featuring in the background for much of the time, but does have a handful of lines, and also provides Perseus with his new sword. The role was played by Ursula Andress, who had been a sex symbol ever since she had become the first Bond girl in *Dr No* in 1962, and had appeared in Playboy on seven occasions by the time *Clash of the Titans* was released. As Monica Cyrino points out, the early first appearance in *Dr No* as she emerged from the sea in her, what would become, iconic bikini, would have been in the minds of the audience watching *Clash*:

> Thus, the bikini scene would have had the effect of reinforcing Andress' identification with the sea-born goddess Aphrodite in *Clash of the Titans*, as the movie audience would certainly be aware of her nearly mythical emergence from the waves of Dr. No's Caribbean island in the earlier film.[64]

Cyrino goes on to point out another connection between the actress and her part that no doubt added to the romance surrounding her:

> An extra-cinematic association between the actress and the Greek goddess of love was also at work during the filming of *Clash of the Titans*, as Andress became romantically involved with her much younger heroic co-star Hamlin, and gave birth to a son, Dimitri, her only child, at the end of the shoot. So after being cast as the perfect Aphrodite, Andress seemed to live the part.[65]

This also points to another issue of note; Andress was (and is) undoubtedly beautiful but, still, was 44 at the time of filming, and therefore perhaps older than might have been expected for the epitome of beauty and sexual love. With her severe expression in the movie, and her distinctly covered-up appearance in her demure, floor-length, white dress, whose sleeves cover her arms completely when extended, she actually bears no more or less resemblance to a sex goddess than do any of the other female deities in the movie. It is her reputation that creates the image of Aphrodite, producing an interesting case of intertextual influence between movies that actually owes little to the image on screen in the latter case.

Aphrodite's role in Disney's 1997 *Hercules* movie is tiny, although she features on occasion in the television series (1998–9), where she appears whenever an issue of love or romance arises. Voiced by Lisa Kudrow, she is a benevolent figure most of the time, but also with a temper, and rather flippant in attitude, with a relaxed 'valley girl' personality. Whenever she appears a musical jingle plays, which becomes a running joke as it annoys everyone, including her. It is mentioned that she is romantically involved with Hephaestus, although this is never elaborated on in the programme. Despite her pink skin, she conforms to stereotypical ideas of loveliness, being beautiful, slim, blonde and young. Her hair is waist length and her eyes a deep blue, lined with purple eyeliner and fringed with long eyelashes. She wears a purple, single-strapped dress, with a heart-shaped brooch on the strap, and a skirt reaching down to her feet with a slit at the front to thigh level. This is accessorised with a pair of gold high-heeled shoes and two gold ankle bracelets. Her divine luminescence is pink and gold. Being an animated character, there are no awkward requirements for her beauty to be anything other than the idealisation of feminine beauty, as envisaged by her creator.

In more recent years, Aphrodite has made few screen appearances, one of which was in the micro-budget gay romance *ECupid* (2001) about a long-term relationship on the rocks, in which Venus appears as a mentor figure. Played by Morgan Fairchild, who communicates by means of a strangely supernatural phone app, the characterisation is somewhat oblique, for she is only referred to as Venus in the credits at the end of the film, although the 'Cupid Software' which provides the app is created by 'Divinity'. Her role is to give the hero what he thinks he wants, but with the aim of teaching him (and the audience) a valuable lesson about love. Unusually, this Venus is in favour of monogamy, and the vapid, Disneyesque moral she promotes is explained when she appears in the form of a helpful waitress at the end of the movie, declaring, 'it's not what you know in your head, it's what you feel in your heart'.

Aphrodite starred centrally in the sadly short-lived 2008–9 romantic comedy series *Valentine*, in which the Greek gods are transposed to modern Los Angeles. In this production, Grace Valentine, played by Jamie Murray, is the modern incarnation of Aphrodite, who is here the matriarch of a family that runs a business called Valentine Incorporated, which brings soulmates together. She is unhappily and abusively married to Ari, a war contractor, who is really the god Ares. Her one true love, however, is Ray, the god Hephaestus, to whom she was previously married, and whom she regrets leaving for Ares thousands of years before. Her son Eros appears here as Danny Valentine, a young and irresponsible party animal, whose bow and arrows have been updated into a gun that shoots love at his innocent targets. His best friend is Leo, the reincarnated Hercules, who, somewhat ironically in light of traditional Greek myth, provides the moral compass of the group. Other characters include Phoebe Valentine, the Titan 'Goddess of the Oracle at Delphi', who helps the family find the soulmates who must be brought together, and a mortal, Kate Providence, a romantic novelist recruited by Grace when the gods' initial attempts at matchmaking prove unsuccessful.

Unusually, this Aphrodite is not blonde but brunette, and is far more elegant and refined than in most other productions. She exudes godly power, with her knowing and ironic quips and smile, but here it is exerted for good, as she channels it towards a enterprise that is, in keeping with twenty-first-century American ideals, 'both profitable and benevolent'.[66] The series also has comments to make about the altered nature of love and relationships in the contemporary world. As Danny complains to his mother, everything has changed, since 'Entire relationships are conducted through text messaging. Mortals are constantly creating substitutions for human interaction.' The result of this is that the gods' ancient methods no longer work, and they themselves, as irrelevant beings, are in danger of losing their immortality. This is presented as a negative point, sending a message about modern love through the medium of the perspective of the ancient goddess of love.

It is striking that in both the recent remake of *Clash of the Titans* (2010) and the Percy Jackson movies (2010, 2013) Aphrodite is barely seen and plays no speaking role. As one website says of Agyness Deyn's Aphrodite in *Clash*: 'her role is a little bit blink-and-you'll-miss-it – she's basically standing looking gob-smackingly beautiful in the home of the Gods, but you wouldn't necessarily realise it was her if you weren't looking out'.[67] Similarly, she is briefly seen but has no speaking role in the Percy Jackson movies; even a scene featuring her bikini-clad nubile daughters splashing in a rock pool was cut from the final version. She does not appear in *Immortals* at all.

The modern reception of this complex divinity, beloved in pop culture more as a symbol of female sexuality and love than for concrete mythological connections, is therefore interesting not because she is presented in ways that reflect her multifaceted nature in the ancient world, but rather because she is not; pop culture iterations of Aphrodite focus only on her symbolic epitomising of beauty and sexuality, and impose modern ideas of romantic love on a character that was an embodiment of an altogether different kind of love. Since the portrayal of a sexual goddess of love, beauty and desire therefore reflects contemporary ideas about women and sex, the lack of attention paid to her in recent years is striking; it seems that, in the age of powerful and empowered women, to say nothing of wide-ranging sexualities becoming the norm, the goddess of (heterosexual) sexual love is seen as having little to contribute.

GENDERING THE DIVINE:
SOME CONCLUDING THOUGHTS

How then, have the Greek goddesses been portrayed on screen, and how have these depictions been affected by the radically altering society in which they were produced? Contrary to what we might have supposed, there is little real evidence for change. Hera remains under her husband's authority, exhibiting more spite than positive attributes. In place of Artemis, it is the strong warrior figures inspired by her who predominate in movies. Aphrodite's role on screen is usually to titillate or symbolise female sexuality and/or romantic love. The way in which the growing status of women can best be reflected is not in their portrayal, but in the fact that film makers frequently seem to avoid using these goddesses on screen; none is seen very often, especially in recent years, and when they do appear, they are often two-dimensional and portrayed somewhat shallowly. Due to her more positive strong (and traditionally more masculine) qualities Athena is the goddess who fares best, in the sense that the screen portrayals display wider variation and depth of characterisation. Even she, however, cannot be depicted easily other than as a member of a patriarchal society, in that, while respected and even doted on by her father Zeus, she will always be subservient to him. On the one hand, the attraction of the Greek goddesses, especially for film makers who wish to sell their products, remains, in that they are beautiful, wonderful female beings, often clad in gauze or scantily; but on the other hand, blatant use of these elements is no longer acceptable in contemporary Western society. Unlike in Christianity and Judaism, female deities exist within pagan culture, allowing for a feminine slant and input to screen productions, something that in itself would be presumed to be of benefit for film makers aiming at a broad audience. Yet, paradoxically, it does not seem that these goddesses are, or at least have been to date, utilised easily within popular cinema. Turning now to the Judaeo-Christian tradition, we will consider if the same holds true for Biblical films.

NOTES

1 Quoted by Stacey (1991: 154).
2 Blundell and Williamson (1998: 1–2).
3 Stacey (1991: 154).
4 Ibid.
5 Kurzman, Anderson, Key, Lee, Moloney, Silver and Ryn (2007: 347).

6 <https://www.rottentomatoes.com/m/hera_purple_devil_goddess/> (accessed 7 March 2018).

7 Rippin (2003).

8 Llewellyn-Jones (2013: 10).

9 See Tomasso (2015: 150).

10 There is perhaps a hint of the negatively portrayed Hera in Disney's animated series *Hercules* (1998–9), in that she is more friendly with Hades, here the villain of the piece, than the other gods, and even persuades Zeus to attend the king of the Underworld's pool party. Nevertheless, this is a very minor element, and Hera remains one of the very few characters in the Disney repertoire who are rehabilitated by the productions, reinterpreting the villainous enemy as a benevolent character.See <http://disney.wikia.com/wiki/Hera> (accessed 7 March 2018).

11 See <http://hero.wikia.com/wiki/Hera_(Disney)> (accessed 7 March 2018).

12 Livingston (2015: 128).

13 Baring and Cashford (1993: Kindle Location 6248). See also Kerényi (1975: 114–47).

14 Pirenne-Delforge and Pironti (2015).

15 Llewellyn-Jones (2007: 431).

16 As a result of the role as Gale, Blackman also featured as a Bond girl in the 1964 movie *Pussy Galore*.

17 Harryhausen and Dalton (2003: 153), also quoted in Llewellyn-Jones(2007: 431).

18 Woolger and Woolger (1987: 175–225).

19 'Amphipolis under Siege', 'Motherhood' and 'Looking Death in the Eye'.

20 <http://151.12.58.141/virtualexhibition/today.html> (accessed 14 September 2017).

21 Deacy (2008: 141). For more on Athena as a feminist symbol, see ibid. 153–6.

22 Ibid. 144–9.

23 <http://hercules-xena.wikia.com/wiki/Athena> (accessed 7 May 2018).

24 The other is Hermes: see p. 78.

25 See Hughes (2011: 287–8).

26 Kinnard and Crnkovich (2017: 198).

27 <http://maidennetwork.com/menu_faq.html> (accessed 19 August 2018).

28 Abele (2013: 132).

29 Monaghan (2004: 127–9).

30 See Morford and Lenardon (2003: 209).

31 Fischer-Hansen and Poulsen (2009: 11).

32 According to the wiki website (<http://hercules-xena.wikia.com/wiki/Artemis> (accessed 13 November 2017)), she considers herself 'a jock'.

33 Schubart (2007: 41).

34 <https://www.theguardian.com/film/filmblog/2013/dec/12/female-

action-heroes-katniss-role-models-women> (accessed 19 November 2017).

35 Ibid.
36 McCaughey and King (2001: 2).
37 See Hansen (2015); Marlina (2015).
38 Hansen (2015: 162–4).
39 See Bolen (2014).
40 <http://womensenews.org/2014/08/artemis-archetype-arises-in-mod-ern-day-films-books/> (accessed 16 November 20170.
41 See e.g. Lindberg (2008: 1–2).
42 'Foreword' in Calame (1999: xiii).
43 For both Eros as a god, and *eros* as an emotion, see the introduction to Sanders, Thumiger, Carey and Lowe (2013: 1–8), with its excellent and thorough bibliography of recent studies on the subject.
44 See e.g. Thumiger (2013: 27–40).
45 Plato, *Timaeus* 42A–C, 90C, 91A (translation from Lee (1965)).
46 Aristotle, *Politics* 2. 1269b.
47 Aristotle, *Politics* 1. 1254b.
48 <https://www.rottentomatoes.com/m/goddess_of_love/> (accessed 5 February 2018).
49 The plot of the film is fully, and amusingly, summarised at <http://jabootu.net/?p=695> (accessed 5 February 2018).
50 See James (2011: 99).
51 Discussed in depth in ibid. 108–14.
52 See e.g. Smith and Pickup (2011), especially the introduction by Pirenne-Delforge (2011: 3–16).
53 Most famously, Hesiod (*Theogony* 173).
54 Finkelberg (2011: 63–4).
55 'Motherhood', Season 5, Episode 22 (2000).
56 Cyrino (2010: 142).
57 'Many Happy Returns', Season 6, Episode 19 (2001).
58 *Botticelli's Venus: The Making of an Icon* (2016).
59 I am indebted to Anise K. Strong for this observation, made during her talk 'Venus Born Again – From Phryne to Beyonce' at the Celtic Conference in Classics, Montreal, July 2017.
60 'Botticelli's Influence on Contemporary Art and Design', *Botticelli Reimagined* exhibition at the V&A Museum, 5 March to 3 July 2016, <https://www.vam.ac.uk/articles/botticellis-influence-on-contemporary-art-and-design>, available on youtube at <https://www.youtube.com/watch?v=DFGp71YRgvM> (accessed 4 February 2018).
61 Ibid.
62 'Hiroshi paints Oscar', *Sesame Street*, Season 22, Episode 2789, 10 January 1991; *The Muppets' Wizard of Oz* (2005); 'Museum Guards', *Bert and Ernie's Great Adventures*, Episode 4552 (2016); *The Furchester Hotel* (2014–17, 2016 episode).

63 'The Apple', *Hercules: The Legendary Journeys* (1996 episode).
64 Cyrino (2010: 138).
65 Ibid.
66 Ibid. 142.
67 <https://www.thecut.com/2010/03/agyness_deyn_is_in_clash_of_th. html> (accessed 12 February 2018).

6 Gendering the Divine (2): Holy Female Figures in the Judaeo-Christian Film

Who is Mary, mother of Jesus? Is she the young and innocent, blue-eyed girl epitomised by Olivia Hussey? A middle-aged Jewish European, such as Maia Morganstern? A Middle Eastern-looking young woman, as depicted by Keisha Castle-Hughes? Is she Caucasian, African, Asian? Does her race matter? How does her appearance affect the portrayal of the mother of God? What function does Mary fulfil in movies, particularly in the Jesus biopic? Most importantly, who do we – meaning the director or producer as well as the audience – want her to be? Similarly, who is Mary Magdalene? Is she a holy woman or a whore, or both? What part does she play in the cinematic Jesus tradition? In general, what are the roles of such figures in screen productions?

Female characters widen the appeal of a movie, making it more attractive to both women, who are able to identify with them, and men, who can objectify them, usually sexually. In Biblical films, however, no such figures can exist easily. It is true that the Old Testament deity has occasionally been depicted as a woman;[1] but this is a very rare occurrence indeed, and in general, movies featuring the Judaeo-Christian deities cannot include an element of the female divine. In Old Testament movies, little can be done to solve this problem; while female roles exist, their holiness stems from qualities of prophecy or being chosen by God, and therefore their role is discussed in the next chapter, in which human–divine interactions are explored. Within the Christian tradition there are two possibilities for females to take on enlarged roles; the Virgin Mary, who actually has elements of divinity herself, and Mary Magdalene, who interacts closely with the divine in human form.

THE VIRGIN MARY

Inevitably, the answers to the questions outlined above depend at least in part on the individual film makers' readings of the Gospels, their interpretations of how Mary has developed within Christianity, and the messages they wish to impart in their screen productions. In actual fact, Mary's role in the Gospels is relatively minor, a fact that allows film makers to develop her character in many different directions, while still, however, retaining that 'cloak of purity and sanctity in which she has been clothed by Christian tradition, theology, art, and popular piety'.[2] This tradition, developed from early roots in the Christian church, continued throughout literary and artistic history. In the tenth century, for example, the life of Mary was retold in poetry in *Vitae*, which elaborated on, and added to, the Biblical tradition. This process has continued throughout history, with the Madonna appearing in poetry, plays, novels and art.[3] With the advent of cinema, this provided a new outlet for the artistic expression of the mother of Jesus, where she takes on a much more prominent role. As O'Brien points out,

> Since the late nineteenth century, the film industry has added to Mary's vast pictorial legacy by capturing her image on celluloid. Writers have transformed the Scriptures into a script. Casting directors have sought an appropriate actress to incarnate the Virgin Mother. And filmmakers have encountered the tensions between religion, originality and profit for the film studios.[4]

Mary is therefore presented in a number of different ways, according to the needs of individual productions and the messages they promote.

The Divine Mary

The first question that arises when dealing with such tensions is that of the very nature of Mary: to what extent is she more than mortal? As with the portrayal of Jesus, depicting Mary on film is a challenge for film makers, but the problem is perhaps even more acute with regard to the mother of God than with Christ himself, for he at least is accepted as, and generally portrayed as, divine. This is not entirely the case with Mary, although she is sometimes regarded as having at least an element of divinity, depending on the tradition utilised. Such an aspect was perhaps inevitable; early Christianity itself needed a female figure as much as paganism had, and the influence of goddesses such as Isis and Diana on Mary has long been highlighted.[5] There are of course examples of virgin births in Greek mythology as well, a point noted at least as early as the third century, when Origen suggested that these cases were the result of God using paganism in order to prepare his people for the birth of Jesus. However, as O'Brien points out:

> it is the *differences* between the goddess myths and the New Testament Infancy Narratives that shed light on the unique nature of Mary for Christians. Mary is the opposite of a goddess because she is the woman who has given Christ his humanity, humility and the capacity to suffer and die. ... Mary could not be a goddess in the pagan sense because her motherhood supports the humanity of Jesus.[6]

Whatever the reason, the cult of the Virgin Mary has been widely accepted by various groups of Christians throughout history, and involves a range of practices and beliefs. Marina Warner summarises the doctrines concerning Mary as follows:

> Four dogmas have been defined and must be believed as articles of faith: her divine motherhood and her virginity, both declared by councils of the early Church and therefore accepted by most of the reformed Christian groups; the immaculate conception, sparing her all stain of original sin, which was proclaimed in 1854; and her assumption, body and soul, into heaven, which Pope Pius XII defined in 1950.[7]

According to Pope John Paul:

> The Church sees in Mary the highest expression of the 'feminine genius', and she finds in her a source of constant inspiration. Mary called herself the 'handmaid of the Lord' (Luke 1:38). Through obedience to the Word of God she accepted her lofty yet not easy vocation as wife and mother in the family of Nazareth. Putting herself at God's service, she also put herself at the service of others: a service of love. Precisely through this service Mary was able to experience in her life a mysterious, but authentic 'reign'. It is not by chance that she is invoked as 'Queen of heaven and earth'. The entire community of believers thus invokes her; many nations and peoples call upon her as their 'Queen'. For her, 'to reign' is to serve! Her service is 'to reign'![8]

All of these ideas turn Mary from fully human to a semi-divine or even totally godly figure, who has been, and continues to be, venerated in a myriad of ways, in different times and places, but particularly in the Catholic Church, where the cult of Mariology is central.

How then may Mary be conveyed as something in keeping with such beliefs? O'Brien argues that 'the concrete reality of the film set and the evident humanity of the actress who incarnates Mary ensure that the traditional trappings of goddess imagery are circumvented',[9] and this is true, but there are also a range of techniques favoured by film makers to indicate Mary's supernatural holiness. Firstly, in depictions of the nativity, lighting is used to create a glow on the face of the Madonna, often spreading out into a halo or nimbus effect. Other film makers use the artistic tradition, staging the actress in poses that recall, for example, especially the Madonna and Child motif so common in art, or specifically Michelangelo's *Pieta*, as the Madonna cradles her dead son in her lap; drawing on these existing motifs and connotations lends holiness to the character.[10] Music also provides a potent manner in which Mary's special nature can be manifest. Epic movies regularly use leitmotifs associated with different characters, and Mary is no exception. In *King of Kings* (1961), for example, the leitmotif used liberally when she appears is a sweeping one of redemption.[11]

The Realistic Mary

Despite such techniques, the emphasis in film is more often on portraying a 'real', historical, authentic Mary. Zeffirelli's production, with its attempt to ground the narration in a concrete historical and geographical setting, is perhaps the most obvious example of this, but Zeffirelli himself was well aware of the difficulty that ensues on so doing:

> When you have that face in front of you in the silence of the chapel in St Peter's, a ray of light falling upon it from above, you remove it entirely from any human context, from all reality. But when you see it in the world of Nazareth, with the chickens, the little donkey, at the loom, during the engagement ceremony, or on the journey to Bethlehem, you need human qualities approaching the sublime as convincing as possible, and beauty, too, not artificial or disturbing, but a true inner beauty.[12]

In other words, Mary must be human, but also transmit the sensation that she is also more than human in some way; even more than the anthropomorphic Greek goddesses, she must be both human and divine.

Notwithstanding the historical Mary's Middle Eastern background, and various very conscious efforts to place Jesus and his family within the context of Judaean Israel, few casting choices reflect this ethnic background. While Mel Gibson's *The Passion of the Christ* (2004) chose the Romanian Jewish actress Maia Morgenstern for Mary, and *Saint Mary* (2000), with its Iranian actresses, is another more Semitically accurate casting, such cases are rare. More recently,

Catherine Hardwicke was determined to cast a young teenage actress with Middle Eastern features, and selected New Zealand actress Keisha Castle-Hughes for the role, coaching her to use 'a light Israeli accent' for the part.[13] The Italian actress Margherita Caruso in Pasolini's *The Gospel According to St. Matthew* (*Il vangelo secondo Matteo*) (1964) presents a Mediterranean image, but most commonly in film, Mary conforms to Western European ideals of loveliness. Although a blonde Mary is not found, with various shades of brown being most popular, in many movies she does have blue eyes; *King of Kings*, *The Greatest Story Ever Told* (1965), *Jesus of Nazareth* (1977), *Jesus* (1999), *Mary of Nazareth* (2012) and *Mary Mother of Christ* (2014) all feature blue-eyed Virgins.

The Young and Innocent Mary

Some films cast a youthful actress as Mary, emphasising thereby her beauty and innocence.[14] Such movies tend to be ones that place more focus on Mary herself, emphasising her humanity and portraying her as a young girl, chosen for a unique role. Most notably, Zeffirelli's *Jesus of Nazareth* cast the 26-year-old Olivia Hussey as Mary, who, although she is aged a little through the use of make-up, at the Passion still looks younger than Mary Magdalene (see Figure 6.1). The length of this production, a miniseries running for six hours, enabled Zeffirelli to include many scenes and details hitherto not seen on screen, as he traced the story of Jesus from before the marriage of Mary and Joseph until the Resurrection. With Zeffirelli's stress on setting the tale blatantly in a Jewish world, including scenes such as the marriage of Mary and Joseph, Jesus' circumcision and his bar mitzvah, his youthful home life was greatly expanded, thereby inevitably increasing the role of Mary as well, and revealing her emotions and reactions to the scenes in a way rarely seen previous to this production.

As the title reflects, the 2012 television movie *Mary of Nazareth* places the emphasis on Mary rather than Jesus himself. An Italian–German–Spanish collaboration, directed by Giacomo Campiotti, it focuses on life events of the mother of Jesus, and depicts her in the context of her own family, introducing her in the company of her parents, Ann and Joachim. From the outset she is presented as special and under divine protection, as well as devoted to God, to whose service she is depicted as being dedicated in a service at the temple. She is shown as constantly exhibiting a childlike belief, as she faithfully succumbs to his will in place of her own desires. In keeping with

Figure 6.1 Mary (Olivia Hussey) in *Jesus of Nazareth* (1977). ITC (Incorporated Television Company)/RAI Radiotelevisione Italiana.

this portrayal, Mary is played by Alissa Jung, whose very youthful appearance belies her 31 years.

In a different vein, the 1985 French movie, *Hail Mary* (*Je vous salue, Marie*), written and directed by Jean-Luc Godard, is a contemporary retelling of the story of a virgin birth, in which Myriem Roussel, aged 24, plays the modern Mary. The youth of the actress in this case, however, is probably due to the updating of the story and consequent presentation of 'Marie' as a young, fertile but virginal twentieth-century woman. It is also the case that in this movie the central focus is on the eponymous character, and such elements of realism, replacing the religious messages, become more necessary. In the same fashion, the centrality of Mary to the plot of *Mary Mother of Christ*, listed as 2014 but still (by late 2018) not released, has influenced the casting. According to the movie publicity, this production follows Mary from her own youth 'to her struggles as a young mother caring for her child, Jesus, up to the age of 12 years old', allowing the audience to 'peer into Mary's life at ages 8, 15, 19 and 27'.[15] Since the emphasis is very much on Mary as a young woman, it is only logical that the actress playing the role was of similar age, and, indeed, this production features the youngest Mary on screen, the 15-year-old Israeli actress Odeya Rush. Similarly, Catherine Hardwicke's *The Nativity Story* (2006) cast 16-year-old Keisha Castle-Hughes as the mother of God, and emphasises her youth, a point encapsulated by Hardwicke's description of her as 'the most famous teenager in the world'.[16]

In all of these portrayals where emphasis is placed on the youth of Mary, the connection with beauty is also of paramount importance. It was a long-held tenet of the Church that the Virgin Mary was a symbol not only of purity and holiness, but also of beauty. In the twentieth century, both Pope Paul VI in 1975 and Pope John Paul in 1999 made reference to this.[17] On screen, therefore, Mary must be beautiful. Yet the nature of beauty is of course subjective, and varies from culture to culture and period to period. Pauline Malefane's Mary in Mark Dornford-May's adaptation of the narrative recast as an African fable, *Son of Man* (2006), is a rare non-Caucasian Mary. Debbi Morgan, in *Color of the Cross* (2006), is another.

The Wise and Mature Mary

Other productions focus only on Jesus as an adult, and hence show only an older Mary. One of the earliest full-length silent Biblical epics, Cecil B. DeMille's *The King of Kings* (1927), for example, focused just on the last weeks of Jesus' life, and shows the Virgin only as a mature woman, here played by a well-known silent movie actress, 33-year-old Dorothy Cumming. Similarly, Martin Scorsese's *The Last Temptation of Christ* (1988) and the 1999 miniseries *Jesus* portray only the mature Jesus, and the role of Mary was taken by Verna Bloom, then aged 49, and Jacqueline Bisset, 55, respectively. Maia Morgenstern, aged 42, played the role of Mary in Mel Gibson's *The Passion of the Christ*, which is even more focused, depicting only the last twelve hours of Jesus' life. Similarly, Debbi Morgan in *Color of the Cross*, which also concentrates on the end of his life, reinterpreting his persecution and death as racially motivated, was 50 at the time of the film's release.

Further productions depict the whole span of Jesus' life, thereby covering a much greater period. Of these, a few still use a mature actress for the role of mother of God. In *King of Kings*, Siobhán

Figure 6.2 Mary (Siobhán McKenna) in *King of Kings* (1961).
METRO-GOLDWYN-MAYER.

McKenna, then 38, appeared as Mary (see Figure 6.2), while in George Stevens' *The Greatest Story Ever Told*, 49-year-old Dorothy McGuire plays the Virgin Mary. In these epic movies, since Mary is only shown as a fully mature adult woman, this creates an, albeit perhaps unintentional, sense of agelessness and timelessness, which adds to the atmosphere of holiness surrounding her.

A few movies employ two different actresses to reflect Mary's ageing; in Pasolini's *The Gospel According to St. Matthew*, the 14-year-old Margherita Caruso played the young Mary, while Susanna Pasolini, almost six decades her senior, played her as an old woman. Less of a contrast can be seen in *Saint Mary* (2000), the Iranian film by director Shahriar Bahrani that portrays the life of Mary as depicted in the Quran and Islamic tradition. In this movie, the child Mary is played by the pre-teen Maryam Razavi, while Shabnam Gholikhani, aged 20, takes over as she becomes a young woman. The 2013 miniseries *The Bible* traces the events of the Gospels over its last five episodes, using two different actresses to portray Mary at different stages of her life, with 20-year-old Leila Mimmack taking on the role of the young woman, and the 54-year-old Roma Downey playing the mature Mary.[18] One movie, Fabrizio Costa's *Maria, Daughter of Her Son* (2000), even uses three actresses, one for the infant Mary, one for the child, and one for the young woman.

The Symbolic Mary

The figure of Mary is a trope that may be adapted to suit cultural and ideological needs, and becomes a symbol of various aspects of womanhood. Although she is the queen of Heaven, the perfect bride and an intercessor for mortals with God,[19] whose ultimate reward, according to Mariology, was to be assumed body and soul into heaven, these aspects are rarely seen on film. One exception is in *The Song of Bernadette* (1943), where the Virgin Mary, seen by both the audience and Bernadette, is shown as a saint, surrounded by a white halo and smiling broadly, placid and kind but remote.[20]

Mary's sanctity is also implied by the depiction of her as a wise figure to whom people turn for advice. Nicholas Ray's *King of Kings* presents her as such a character, as Walsh stresses:

> For Ray the important female character – and her role is greatly amplified – is Mary, mother of Jesus. Several characters (a camel driver, Lucius, John the Baptist, Mary Magdalene, and Jesus) come to Mary's home for counsel. In fact, in a homely scene, it's Mary who knows when Jesus must go to Jerusalem and that he will not return (to fix her chair).[21]

In this movie, it is also Mary who tells the parable of the lost sheep to Mary Magdalene, reflecting the former's role as wise moral guide. She is often depicted as being aware of and understanding Jesus' special role and destiny,[22] bringing an element of supernaturally granted prophecy to the character.

Some more subtle elements of symbolism are also used with regard to Mary. She is often costumed in either blue or red, both colours associated with her in Christian art, where they represent the rich dyes worn by the elite.[23] Blue in particular is associated with the Virgin in art, again perhaps an influence from the Egyptian goddess Isis; from the twelfth century onwards, the colour becomes brighter, recalling the colour of contemporary French stained glass windows. In film, this tradition is sometimes maintained, as for example in *The Greatest Story Ever Told* and in *Jesus of Nazareth* where she wears a blue robe. Red is more rarely seen, since it is more commonly associated with Mary Magdalene, but in Young's *Jesus*, Jacqueline Bisset does wears a red dress. Most commonly, though, directors use a 'realistic' approach, and recognising that simple peasant folk would not have access to such expensive dyes, Mary is clothed in beiges, browns, blacks and greys, in a more homespun look. Occasionally, especially in earlier productions, such as the 1903 *The Life and Passion of Jesus Christ*, the 1916 *Christus* and DeMille's *The King of Kings*, as well as in *Mary, Mother of Jesus* (1999), she is costumed in garb reminiscent of a nun, with white wimple and dark veil, and a full, long-sleeved robe, thereby conveying an impression of Christian holiness.[24]

Mary the Mother

Although Mary is held up generally in film as the model for women of all kinds, in particular she is the ideal of motherhood, with the Holy Family being depicted as a unit, in which Mary is protective of her son, teaching him about life in general and his faith in particular. Thus in Rossellini's *Il messia* (1975) she gives him his first tallith prior to the expanded scene of the young Jesus preaching in the temple, and explains its significance and her son's role in his religious tradition, fussing over him maternally as she helps him dress.[25] In *From the Manger to the Cross* (1912) she is shown in a tableau teaching him from a scroll, presumably the holy scriptures, and in several movies is also depicted teaching him to read.[26] Although in some Christian traditions, Mary also becomes a disciple of Jesus, with their parental–filial roles being reversed, this is rarely seen on screen, where her maternal aspect is emphasised and remains constant throughout the entire period.[27]

Mary the Feminist

Traditionally, the Church was able to use the example of Mary in order to make declarations about matters such as chastity and sexuality, in particular for women.[28] Nevertheless, the idea of what the perfect woman must be has altered over the history of movies more than at any period throughout history, and this is reflected in the films in which she features. Where differences over time can be seen in particular is with regard to Mary's agency and self-confidence. This is important theologically, since:

> The question of whether Mary received the Annunciation passively, or actively decided to partake of it, becomes a loaded question which potentially points to a co-optation of Mary as a religious icon into the causes of feminists and liberation theologians, who see her as cooperating with God freely and demonstrating exemplary qualities of faith, hope, and love which are to be emulated by those striving for social justice.[29]

Even in Hollywood, influenced by the developing theological approaches within Christianity, a change can be observed. From the 'silent icon in the days of early cinema', Mary develops and becomes a more complex character who doubts and questions whether she can be a mother.[30] In earlier films, she is, for example, more submissive and obedient, shown as accepting her role, either willingly or after a struggle.[31] With the changing ideas concerning gender roles, however, there is an alteration in her portrayal:

> From the late 1970s onwards, Mary on screen is not a reticent figure, despite the danger that her characterisation might be seen as anachronistic when viewed against the historical background within the diegesis. As the Catholic Church reflected changing attitudes to the status of women in two major publications (the US Bishops' letter *Behold your Mother* and Pope Paul VI's apostolic exhortation *Marialis Cultus*), so the filmic representations of Mary gradually took on a more self-determined angle.[32]

Thus Bernard Kowalski's *The Nativity* (1978), Fabrizio Costa's *Maria, Daughter of Her Son*, Kevin Connor's *Mary, Mother of Jesus* and Hardwicke's *The Nativity Story* all show an independent-minded and spirited Mary, with ideas of her own and the self-confidence to declare them, whether they involve speaking up during men's councils or expressing an opinion regarding the choice of her own husband.[33]

MARY MAGDALENE

> What would a biopic be without romance? But how to inject romance into the story of the celibate son of God? Very few movies about Jesus dare to involve him in affairs of the heart or the body; those that try are roundly chastised for their audacity. But this restriction does not prevent Jesus films from the silent era to the present from exploiting the aura of sexuality that has long surrounded one of Jesus' most famous followers, Mary Magdalene.[34]

The other female character who features in the Jesus hagiopics is another Mary, but one presented generally as a contrast to the Virgin, namely Mary Magdalene. In contrast to the Madonna, who is portrayed in a wide variety of ways, there is consistency in the depiction of Mary Magdalene; without exception, until the most recent 2018 production, she is seen on screen as a woman of loose morals, frequently conflated with the anonymous 'woman taken in adultery' mentioned in the Gospel of John. This is despite the fact that there are a range of presentations of Mary Magdalene within Christian tradition, not all of which refer to her as either a whore or sexually profligate; in the Gospels no mention is made of any kind of sexual activity, forbidden or otherwise.

Such a cinematic emphasis is unsurprising; in Reinhartz' words, 'Mary Magdalene provides the only opportunity for a female sexual and love interest within the otherwise chaste story of Jesus of Nazareth.'[35] What scantily clad beautiful goddesses do for films based on Greek mythology, Mary Magdalene must do for Jesus movies. Both in order to titillate and satisfy the audience, and to provide moral lessons, the fallen woman and her redemption is the motif that epitomises this Mary on screen. In fact, as early as the fourteenth century, associations can be seen between the Magdalena and the goddess Venus in art, with Giotto's *Mary Magdalene Taken to Heaven in a Shell*, with its definite Aphroditean overtones.[36]

It is only of help to film makers that the sources for Mary Magdalene in the Gospels are scant yet intriguing. The very paucity of references – her demons are expelled, she is at the foot of the cross, and she is the first one to whom Jesus appears after the Resurrection[37] – indicate closeness with Jesus but give few details. This allows for the development of character and background according to the whims and needs of scriptwriters and directors, and in particular for Mary Magdalene to be portrayed with blatant sexuality, filling the role traditionally filled by females on screen.

The fascination with, and scope provided by, the figure of Mary Magdalene are observable at the very beginning of the cinematic tradition, in DeMille's *The King of Kings*. This movie opens with a remarkable scene, described vividly by Pamela Grace as follows:

> Shortly after the title about the film's reverent part in Jesus' great command, the film opens with a scene in Mary Magdalene's pleasure palace. The skimpily-dressed Mary, whose costume combines elements of the lascivious pagan and the new woman of the 1920s, flirts with her elderly admirers and cuddles a tiger. The Magdalene is put out because her lover Judas has gone off to follow some carpenter from Nazareth. When Mary's admirers mention that the carpenter 'hath some power', Mary laughs at the preposterous idea, jumps into her zebra-drawn carriage, and rides off to retrieve her lover.[38]

From this licentious picture, DeMille proceeds to portray Mary (played by the sultry young beauty Jacqueline Logan; see Figure 6.3) as seeing the light, with Jesus casting out her demons, here depicted as the seven deadly sins, and turning her from tainted woman to redemption; through following a figure of holiness, she herself becomes holy.[39] The opening scene featuring Mary Magdalene then plays a similar role to those scantily gauze-clad females in movies set in the ancient world. Just as those films ostensibly denounce the slavery, nudity, paganism and values of earlier times, while actually providing an opportunity for titillating the audience with depictions of the things the films apparently condemn, so in *The King of Kings*, the sensual extravagances of the 1920s world are here rejected in favour of the purity and spirituality of Jesus – but only after the viewers have enjoyed the spectacle of those corrupt yet exciting dissipations.

Nicholas Ray's *King of Kings*, by contrast, presents a very different

Figure 6.3 Mary Magdalene (Jacqueline Logan) in *The King of Kings* (1927).
DeMille Pictures Corporation.

Mary Magdalene. In place of the self-assured vixen courtesan, this
film presents her as a troubled outcast. In this version she is the adulteress pursued by a bloodthirsty, stone-wielding mob that was surely
an inspiration for the scene in *Monty Python's Life of Brian* (1979),
who is saved by Jesus from stoning. Very aware of her own status,
when she seeks out Jesus in Nazareth, she tells his mother, expecting
to be rejected, 'I am a woman of sin. . . . I have done much evil.' By
following Jesus, however, she regains self-respect and social standing.
Played by Carmen Sevilla, she is outfitted with elaborate jewellery in
gold and turquoise; although unquestionably beautiful, she seems,
however, more of a tragic figure than a temptress, and by the time she
reappears, she is without jewellery. In *King of Kings*, in contrast to
the wicked Salome, Mary is not heavily made up, and appears more
pitiable than wicked. Most unusually, she is even dressed in a more
virginal white, rather than the more typical red. Similarly, Stevens'
The Greatest Story Ever Told also rehabilitates the character created
or popularised by DeMille. Stevens' Mary is dressed in scarlet and
guilty of adultery, when asked by Jesus if the accusations are true, she
looks down silently, demonstrating shame.[40] Both films show Mary

Magdalene reformed and as one of Jesus' disciples, within the group of his charmed circle.[41] Just as the Magdalena of the 1920s reflected contemporary attitudes to a changing world, so perhaps in the early 1960s an adulterous woman (for whose adultery no background is given) had more resonance than the sophisticated courtesan of DeMille's work.

One of the most interesting developments of the character is in *Jesus Christ Superstar* (1973), in which she has undergone another alteration. No longer a whore or even an adulteress, in this rock opera she is the loving, albeit feisty, companion to Jesus, although the relationship is fiercely resented by Judas, with whom a triangle of emotions is therefore created. In the words of Stephenson Humphries-Brooks:

> *Jesus Christ Superstar* updates DeMille's formula of sex, sadism, and mel-odrama. The updating results in a different interpretation of Magdalene as Ur-woman, or earth mother, Eve. She is no longer a courtesan who aspires to wealth and power but rather a sexually experienced woman (the film never calls her a prostitute) who loves Jesus and wants him as lover.[42]

Not only does she want him as her lover, but she seems to achieve this as well, in a blatant strengthening of the sexual aspect of the relationship between Jesus and Mary in this production. It is true that the sexual act is never definitively referred to or shown, but, as Reinhartz points out:

> Mary Magdalene is almost always in close physical proximity to Jesus as she cares for his physical needs – food, drink, rest, and, perhaps, more. They frequently embrace, with a fervor that steps beyond the bounds of platonic or spiritual friendship.[43]

In the changing world of the early 1970s, when not only whores but also adulteresses have gone out of fashion, Mary Magdalene has become a strong and passionate figure, whose humanity influences that of Jesus. Her love for Jesus makes her search in anguish to understand him, a struggle that expands and gives depth not only to her own character but also his, making him seem more human. The best-selling song from the production, 'I don't know how to love him', with its refrain of 'He's a man. He's just a man. And I've had so many men before, in very many ways, he's just one more', encapsu-lates this impression.

This depiction was taken to extremes by perhaps the most contro-versial of all Jesus movies, Martin Scorsese's *The Last Temptation of Christ*. Like the 1955 novel by Nikos Kazantzakis on which it was based, the film depicts Jesus' battle against various temptations, such as fear, self-doubt and, most controversially of all, lust, as he is shown imagining himself engaged in sexual activities. The figure with whom he is tempted to have sex, marry and settle down is, naturally, Mary Magdalene, and from the outset it is clear that Jesus has an intimate relationship with the woman, who, in this version, is a Jewish prostitute, whom he is also seen saving from a mob who want to stone her for prostitution and working on the Sabbath. In this film, Jesus is conflicted, torn between the path he believes God has ordained for him and his own desires. Depressed as a result of this struggle, he collaborates with the Romans, which leads an old friend, Judas Iscariot, who is one of the rebels, to be sent to assassinate him. Becoming convinced instead that his intended victim is the long-awaited Messiah, Judas persuades him to lead a rebellion against the Romans to free the Jews from their oppressive rule, although Jesus emphasises that his message is one of love for all mankind, rather than one of liberation as such. The conflict between Judas' plans for Jesus, Mary's desire for him and Jesus' own internal struggles are the pivot of the movie, the whole plot of which 'hangs on the interaction of Magdalene with Jesus and of Judas with Jesus', although Mary and Judas never actually communicate on screen.[44]

In this version, the role of the Magdalene was greatly expanded by Barbara Hershey, who played the role and was a prime mover behind the film's making; she had given Scorsese a copy of the original novel during the making of the film *Boxcar Bertha* (1972), which he directed and in which she starred, and had begged him for the role.[45] Having won it – after the series of auditions upon which Scorsese insisted so as to avoid charges of favouritism – she put heart and soul into the performance. As Babington and Evans emphasise:

> The Scorsese Magdalene is much the most developed version, her complexity lying not in an attempt to counter the stereotype of Eve's daughter but in exploring it in ways more wide-ranging and intense. Often foregrounded and played by an actress (Barbara Hershey) who brings not only intense sexuality but also a vivid, pained seriousness to the role, the character cannot be reduced to the sum of stereotypes.[46]

Although the film was attacked for its portrayal of Jesus' sexuality, this is actually depicted relatively subtly, especially in the earlier part of the movie.[47] It seems that Jesus and Mary were intending to marry, but that he abandoned her as a result of his vocation.[48] Since that point, Mary has come down in the world, and is now a prostitute working day and night. When Jesus arrives to talk to her, there is a shocking scene in which he has to wait awkwardly for hours on end to see her, as the long line of customers take their turns with her before he can enter, a situation which is clearly torturous for Jesus himself. Mary herself is an angry figure at this point, taunting him and exploiting his desire and his refusal to give in to it. Despite her resentment, however, it is clear that her fury stems from his rejection of her love, which still possesses her; in the end, she does give him her blessing as he leaves for the desert.

In appearance, this Mary Magdalene is unusual as well. She has light-brown hair and green eyes, and is clad not in scarlet or white, but in browns and blacks, thus removing all symbolism from the clothing. Most strikingly, she is heavily tattooed, an aspect that was apparently inspired by a *National Geographic* cover. Since the film had only a limited budget, Hershey applied the tattoo make-up herself, reapplying it every few days before the day's shooting.[49] The tattoos mark her out as exotic and different, perhaps even somewhat wild, but come with none of the pejorative elements so often associated with the character, who is here a flesh-and-blood individual, passionate and troubled, like Jesus himself.

Since *The Last Temptation of Christ*, Mary Magdalene has continued to develop and has undergone even more radical transformation as a figure in her own right, particularly under the influence of the societal changes in which women's roles have altered so thoroughly. One Italian–German television movie from 2000, *Gli amici di Gesù: Maria Maddalena*, told her story as part of a volume series, entitled in English *Close to Jesus*. This production portrayed her creatively as a woman bent on revenge after being divorced by her uncaring husband, and then gang raped, while pregnant by a Roman soldier, but who then finds Jesus and discovers that love is more fulfilling than revenge.[50] A few years later, in 2003, the publication of Dan Brown's *The Da Vinci Code*, and the subsequent film version of the book, popularised the idea that Mary had been the wife of Jesus, and possible mother of their child, but thanks to misogyny her story had been repressed and excluded from history.

Such ideas have led to a promotion of Mary Magdalene to a level almost equal with Jesus himself. This 'deification' of Mary has perhaps reached a culmination in the recently released movie entitled *Mary Magdalene* (2018), which tells the story of Christ's life from the perspective of Mary Magdalene herself.

This is very much a postmodern movie. The film's official synopsis reads:

> *Mary Magdalene* is an authentic and humanistic portrait of one of the most enigmatic and misunderstood spiritual figures in history. The Biblical biopic tells the story of Mary (Rooney Mara), a young woman in search of a new

way of living. Constricted by the hierarchies of the day, Mary defies her traditional family to join a new social movement led by the charismatic Jesus
of Nazareth (Joaquin Phoenix). She soon finds a place for herself within the
movement and at the heart of a journey that will lead to Jerusalem.[51]

Several points jump out from this summary. Firstly, the portrayal
of, and attitude towards, Mary are striking. In the second decade of
the twenty-first century, feminist thinking cannot allow for a passive
Magdalene. It was, in fact, the focus on Magdalene that persuaded
Mara to take on the role, as she explains:

> Most other films about Jesus are solely about him, and this time the film is
> about Mary Magdalene. We still see all of the things that we're used to seeing
> in biblical films, but we see it through her eyes. And seeing it through her eyes,
> we get to see it in a very different light. I thought this was a great opportunity
> to tell a version of the story that we hadn't seen before.[52]

This Mary, then, is not a prostitute; director Garth Davis and Mara
were keen to dispel what is now recognised as 'an historical distor-
tion introduced in 591 by Pope Gregory'. The refutation of the sexual
background here reflects both a desire to rehabilitate the character,
and a rejection of the exploitative passivity which such a profession
would imply. For the Mary of 2018 is a liberated woman, actively
searching for truth, but 'constricted by the hierarchies of the day'; the
subtext of this is surely that these hierarchies, while less blatant, still
exist in the present age. She is brave and rebellious – she 'defies' her
family, who are 'traditional', a term here used pejoratively; and in her
search, finds 'a place for herself', where presumably she is accepted
on equal terms.

Above and beyond the figurative meaning of this phrase, there is
a literal meaning, referring to a physical location, namely the city
of Jerusalem. Mary in this version leaves her small fishing village
to follow Jesus to Jerusalem. The urban setting of the movie was
another conscious innovation by Davis:

> 'I wanted to avoid doing something that had been done before', says director
> Davis, who is keen to present the story as one with deep contemporary reso-
> nances. 'Most biblical movies are shot in the desert and there's an "etiquette"
> about them. I wanted this to be more relatable, relevant and contemporary
> and I really wanted to avoid all the stereotypes.'[53]

Finally, returning to the synopsis, perhaps the most notable point
is that this is not a Jesus biopic, but a 'biblical biopic', centred on a
figure who has a very marginal role in the Bible, even if that role was
expanded by Christian tradition. Indeed, it is notable that the film
is not billed as Christian at all, or religious. This was a conscious

decision, and in fact, Mara was very determined to avoid religion; she was at first 'sceptical about playing the "apostle to the apostles"', since, having gone to a Catholic school, she had 'a lot of preconceived notions', and read the script for the first time 'with a very cynical outlook'. Rather remarkably, she told Garth 'very early on' that she 'didn't want to be in a "religious" movie'. Her views regarding the film, and both her approach and Davis', were actually to remove religion from Jesus' story. In Mara's words:

> I hope the audiences can take different things from the film. If people can put their preconceived notions about religion aside, they'll find something really beautiful in what Jesus was saying, not as a religious figure but just as a man. He was very much a Gandhi or Martin Luther King figure.

Accordingly, the review advises watchers to 'put religion to one side and discover something very beautiful in the new film *Mary Magdalene*'.

THE TWO MARYS

As the above survey indicates, there is a very broad spectrum of approaches to portraying both Mary, mother of Jesus, and Mary Magdalene. This is unsurprising; unlike the Greek pantheon, which possesses a number of goddesses who may be utilised, in Biblical films, all roles stereotypically filled by females – romantic love interest, sexual temptress, powerful role model, maternal carer, innocent virgin and so on – must be satisfied by these two figures.

Just as elements of the Greek goddesses (and others) were actually assimilated into the Christian figure of the Virgin Mary, so the same process takes place on screen, leading to her being depicted by actresses of different ages, ethnic backgrounds and appearances, and costumed in a variety of ways, although certain elements (blue eyes, blue dress) do frequently recur, as a result of Christian iconography. What brings all the depictions together is the element of purity and holiness, which characterises Mary, even as it is conveyed in different ways according to changing times and ideals. Thus Mary becomes progressively less passive and more determined and empowered over time, but the idea that she is a feminine ideal remains; it is the concept of what that ideal is that has altered, rather than attitudes towards the mother of Christ.

Similarly, with changing attitudes towards sexuality, the portrayals of Mary Magdalene have also been modified. In general, the sexual element remains, but an attempt is also made to rehabilitate her as she becomes the victim of rape, or has fallen into destitution. Thus, she also becomes a more powerful figure, who is restyled in keeping with contemporary ideas, and, in her latest incarnation, becomes a role model for the twenty-first-century woman, as a courageous and independent-minded female, whose heart is pure, and who battles against the constraints of patriarchal males who would seek to oppress her.

NOTES

1 See Chapter 3.
2 Reinhartz (2007: 68).
3 See Ebertshäuser, Haag, Kirchberger and Söll (1998); Boss (2007).
4 O'Brien (2011: 1).
5 See e.g. Benko (1993); Matthews and Muller (2005).
6 O'Brien (2011: 107–8).
7 Warner (2013: xxxiv).
8 'Letter to Women' (29 June 1995) <https://w2.vatican.va/content/john-paul-ii/en/letters/1995/documents/hf_jp-ii_let_29061995_women.html> (accessed 21 March 2018). Also quoted in Sanders (2002: 172).
9 O'Brien (2011: 108).
10 Reinhartz (2007: 84); (2010: 520).
11 Elley (1984: 47).
12 Zeffirelli (1984: 71–2).
13 Pringle (2006).
14 This idea of the never-ageing Mary is parodied in Luis Buñuel's *The Milky Way* (1969). See Reinhartz (2007: 84).
15 <http://www.imdb.com/title/tt0949757/> (accessed 19 March 2018).
16 Pringle (2006). Also quoted in O'Brien (2009: 294).
17 See O'Brien (2011: 4).
18 Downey, as President of Lightworkers Media, the family and faith division of METRO-GOLDWYN-MAYER, also produced the series together with her husband, Mark Burnett. The later episodes, in which Downey featured, were then adapted into an epic movie, entitled *Son of God*, which was released in 2014.
19 Warner (2013) *passim*.
20 Durley (2000: 67).
21 Walsh (2003: 144 n.39).
22 Reinhartz (2007: 79–83).
23 Staley and Walsh (2007: 204).
24 Reinhartz (2007: 85); Babington and Evans (1993: 108).
25 Reinhartz (2007: 72–3).
26 Ibid. 73.
27 Ibid. 83–5.

28 Smith (1980).
29 Kia-Choong (2013: 169–70).
30 O'Brien (2011: 40).
31 Babington and Evans (1993: 108).
32 O'Brien (2011: 73).
33 Ibid. 73–4.
34 Reinhartz (2007: 126).
35 Ibid. 129.
36 Erhardt and Morris (2012: 320); Griffith-Jones (2008: 180–1).
37 Luke 8:2, Mark 16:9 and John 20:1–18 are the main sources.
38 Grace (2009: 28–9).
39 See Kozlovic (2008). Lindsay (2015: 36–41), on the other hand, argues that Mary continues to be associated with these transgressive pleasures throughout the film, including at the Resurrection at the end of the movie, despite having been tamed by Jesus' miraculous healing power.
40 Malone (1989: 61); Reinhartz (2007: 132).
41 Babington and Evans (1993: 108).
42 Humphries-Brooks (2006: 60).
43 Reinhartz (2007: 144).
44 Humphries-Brooks (2006: 83).
45 <https://fictionmachine.com/2017/03/31/i-am-the-saint-of-blasphemy-the-last-temptation-of-christ-1988/> (accessed 27 March 2018).
46 Babington and Evans (1993: 109).
47 There is one brief shot of them making love, but it is from a distance and in any case is within the 'dream' or 'prophecy' section, in which the tempting alternative life choice is shown to Jesus while on the cross, as opposed to actually taking place.
48 One proposed scene of him jilting Mary at the altar was cut in the end from the movie.
49 <https://fictionmachine.com/2017/03/31/i-am-the-saint-of-blasphemy-the-last-temptation-of-christ-1988/> (accessed 27 March 2018).
50 <http://www.imdb.com/title/tt0244647/>; <https://cinemagazine.nl/maria-magdalena-gli-amici-di-gesu-maria-maddalena-2000-recensie/> (both accessed 28 March 2018).
51 <https://g.co/kgs/g3L2jU> (accessed 28 March 2018).
52 <https://www.telegraph.co.uk/films/mary-magdalene/contender-for-oscars/> (accessed 28 March 2018).
53 Ibid.

7 Human–Divine Interactions on Screen

MIRACLES

The year is 1923. The scene is close-up footage, played in reverse, of water pouring in to a model, whose walls of water were actually jelly over which water was sprayed, while the figures of the slaves walking on sand were superimposed on the scene. The parting of the Red Sea is happening before the awed eyes of cinema audiences. Probably the miracle on the largest scale, in both Biblical and cinematic terms, providing a dramatic highlight in films narrating the tale of the exodus, DeMille's version of *The Ten Commandments* from 1923 in many ways set the tone for future depictions. His pre-CGI effects were lauded at the time by awestruck viewers and continue to stand up well when viewed with modern eyes. The remake of the movie from 1956 was even more impressive, causing James Thurber to muse ironically, 'It makes you realize what God could have done if he'd had the money.'[1] Again DeMille used reverse shots for the parting of the water, but in this case utilised a life-sized trough rather than a model, and superimposed a storm-cloud-laden sky above. In this case, the walls of water were sideways footage of the backwash created when the water was poured into the trough. Together the elements combined to create one of the greatest effects ever seen until the creation of CGI. As Ilana Pardes puts it:

> DeMille is at his best ... in his innovative reinterpretation of miracle stories ... If God can perform miracles, so can Hollywood. By means of special effects, staffs turn into snakes, the Nile becomes red, a pillar of fire leads the

people, and the sea parts as Moses lifts his rod. DeMille's special effects provide a glimpse not so much of the 'Truth of God' (to use his terms) but rather the 'Truth' of the people. Miracles are meant for the people.[2]

Miracles are one means by which gods and humans make contact in both the Graeco-Roman and Judaeo-Christian traditions. From the earliest representation, divinities have been depicted in their own environment, whether that be Olympus or some amorphous conception of 'heaven' or 'the sky'. Homer, for example, includes scenes of the gods at council or other activities in their divine palace. For mankind, however, it is with relation to themselves that a divinity has most importance, and it is godly interaction with mortals that is most influential. In the case of the Graeco-Roman gods, the involvement of the gods in human affairs is the premise that, as Lloyd Llewellyn-Jones stresses, 'forms the basis for the filmic use of the gods, as the storylines cut between heaven and earth, showing the gods viewing, deliberating on, or interfering in, the lives of the on-screen heroes'.[3] With regard to the Judaeo-Christian divinity, it is his interaction with, and influence over, mortals that gives the story relevance for mankind in general, and film viewers in particular. This is the case even when the movie casts doubt on the very existence of the deity; the very fact that recipients of revelation themselves believe their vision to be sent from God centres the production on a person's relationship with the deity, in whose existence he has absolute faith. With the Jesus biopics, the entire focus is on a divine being, albeit with human elements, interacting with the mortal world.

A cinematic depiction of a miracle is an opportunity to witness the connection between divine and human in spectacular form. This is true both of the characters in the movie and of the audience watching, all of whom recognise the power and glory of the creators (in the case of *The Ten Commandments*, God and DeMille respectively). Not every cinematic attempt at 'the greatest miracle of them all' has succeeded; less impressive partings took place in *Moses the Lawgiver* (1974) and in *Moses* (1995), the latter with Ben Kingsley in the eponymous role, and which employed digital technology to create the effects of this episode for the first time. So common was the trope that it was even parodied in *Bruce Almighty* (2003), where Bruce parts his soup in similar fashion, complete with wind effects.

Nevertheless, miracles are an obviously attractive method for film makers to show divine revelation and affect the audience with a sense of awe. Not only, thanks to the wonders of cinematic techniques, can these be created on screen, but they also have a powerful visual impact, appealing to film makers and audience alike, particularly in the context of epic films. In the words of Michael Wood, such films need 'the big scenes (the orgy, the ceremonial entry into the city, the great battle, the individual combat, and where possible, a miracle or two)'.[4]

This emphasis on 'big scenes' highlights an essential element of a miracle, namely that it is an event through which God can reveal himself not to an individual or small group, but to the world on a wider scale, usually for the purposes of salvation. R. F. Holland postulated three different understandings of miracles: a contingency concept whereby miracles are acts of God in the world, but do not disrupt the natural order; a 'violation' concept, in which the natural order is suspended; and a third idea, which does not concern itself with nature, and in which a miracle is defined by its ability to make God manifest in the world.[5]

It should be noted that in the pagan world, there is no real concept of miracles in the way that Judaism and Christianity understand them. The words used to describe such events are *thauma* and *miraculum*, in Greek and Latin respectively, both of which have the connotation of 'wonder' or 'marvel', but without necessarily including the influence of the divine, or any element of faith. In fact, there is even a negative connotation to the term *miraculum*, since it also means 'trickery', both actual and metaphorical.[6] What seemed like miracles to some were regarded as either magic or fake conjuring by others; most famously, Lucian of Samosata ridiculed both magicians and miracle workers, regarding both with equal contempt.[7] Thus the Greeks and Romans included miracles as more examples of the gods' working in the world, as a natural – or more accurately supernatural – phenomenon, hardly distinguishable from the gods' usual interactions within nature, which they controlled anyway.

Nevertheless, the pagan gods did interact in the mortal Graeco-Roman world, and could send illness, death and misfortune to individuals in order to mete out justice for some misdeed or lack of respect. Similarly, in both Judaism and Christianity there existed a fundamental belief in God's intervention in daily life; in particular from the time that the Bible became accessible to ordinary people, as a result of printing and translations into the vernacular, sickness and misfortune are described as the wages of sin.[8] Such events, whether on a major or localised scale, were regarded not as random, but rather as divine punishment for wrongdoing.

God's interaction in the world took place on universal, national and individual levels, most commonly through nature. Not for nothing are extreme events of nature, such as earthquakes and tsunamis, described as 'acts of God', a phrase that indicates the random nature of the attack and distances them from human responsibility, freeing people from liability for damage.[9] Just as deities can use natural means for retribution, so they may manipulate nature for the purposes of enlightenment or even salvation, in the form of miracles. Although miracles are usually attributed to intentional divine activity, the nature of that activity is not clear or unanimously agreed upon, even within individual religions. Some believe that the term 'miracle' can only be applied to events that could never have a natural explanation, while others dispute this. Beliefs are divided between those that think that God directly manipulates the natural order, and those who believe that nature has been predetermined by God to cause the phenomena.[10]

The question of the true nature of miracles is rarely addressed seriously on screen. Sometimes things are left implied, as in *David and Bathsheba* (1951). When David touches the Ark in penitence, rain begins to fall, bringing the drought, caused by divine retribution, to an end, but with no commentary, since the screenwriter, Philip Dunne, said he 'left it to the audience to decide if the blessed rain came as the result of divine intervention or simply of a low-pressure system moving in from the Mediterranean'.[11] According to this approach, the only 'miraculous' element is the fortuitous timing; Moses himself, played by Burt Lancaster in Gianfranco De Bosio's *Moses the Lawgiver*, declares that, 'A miracle is simply the right thing happening at the right time.'[12]

Such a demythologising approach was taken more recently by Ridley Scott in *Exodus: Gods and Kings* (2014), which took a rationalistic approach to the traditional miracles of the exodus, as he explained in an interview with Peter Chattaway in October 2014:

> 'You can't just do a giant parting, with walls of water trembling while people ride between them', says Scott, who remembers scoffing at biblical epics from his boyhood like 1956's *The Ten Commandments*. 'I didn't believe it then, when I was just a kid sitting in the third row. I remember that feeling, and thought that I'd better come up with a more scientific or natural explanation.'
>
> Scott's solution came from a deep dive into the history of Egypt circa 3000 B.C. After reading that a massive underwater earthquake off the coast of Italy caused a tsunami, he thought about how water recedes as a prelude to such disasters. 'I thought that logically, [the parting] should be a drainage. And that when [the water] returns, it comes back with a vengeance.'[13]

As a result of this approach, perhaps drawing on some traditional Jewish commentaries[14] and Biblical scholars,[15] Scott depicted the ten plagues as evolving naturally; in place of Moses' turning the Nile into blood, crocodiles attack in a killing spree from which the victims' blood flows into the river, polluting it. The other plagues quickly follow, again naturally as one leads to another. Unfortunately, the desire for rationalism did not find favour in the eyes of spectators and critics, who rightly pointed out that rationalism does not necessarily make for spectacular cinematography.[16]

It should not be assumed that a huge scale is necessary for such a spectacular effect; not every miracle is on a national scale like those of the book of Exodus. Some are carried out on an individual level, as in Elisha's revival of the son of the Shunammite woman, or Jesus' healing of the sick. Other Old Testament movies feature such miracles, on occasion directed against other deities, such as in *Head of a Tyrant* (1960), where the statue of the Assyrian idol crumbles away in a burst of divinely sent lightning.[17] Many miracles particularly focus on the Ark of the Covenant, a tradition continued even beyond such epics by later movies such as *Raiders of the Lost Ark* (1981). As well as the miraculous rain in *David and Bathsheba* mentioned above, there is a scene at the end of *Solomon and Sheba* (1959), after Sheba has been stoned by the crowd, in which Solomon carries her into the temple. There the Ark of the Covenant glows with heavenly radiance as the Voice of God speaks, and Sheba's wounds are miraculously healed, fading from her skin before the eyes of the audience. In all scenarios, however, the purpose of a miracle is to provide salvation for the faithful, although there may also be a subsidiary aim of exhibiting God's presence and power in the world.[18]

That God is the power behind the miracle is of crucial importance in both Judaism and Christianity, for it is this that distinguishes miracles from magic, which is carried out by a human agent rather than a divine one. For the pagan world this division, if it existed at all, was far less stark; magic, curses, spells and so on all called upon supernatural powers, which in a polytheistic world are more or less indistinguishable from divine forces.[19]

With regard to Judaism, it is clearly accepted in the Bible, the Talmud and all other ancient and medieval Jewish writings that miracles can and do occur. Since prior to the rise of modern science the concept of laws of nature did not exist, however, miracles were regarded not as suspensions of nature, but as extraordinary events in which God intervened in the world for a particular reason. Precisely because it deviated so much from the normal course of events, a miracle was a sign of divine involvement; the Biblical term נס ('nes') literally means a flag or sign. Because of this understanding, the question arose in medieval Jewish philosophy of how God, who is perfect and without physical aspect, can be said to become manifest in the particular events of the world. It also led to a certain ambivalence regarding miracles; [20] since it was regarded as arrogance to ask for a personal manifestation of divine providence, praying for miracles was far from encouraged. In fact, there is a tendency among the medieval philosophers to explain even the Biblical miracles in natural terms, reflecting the tensions sensed with regard to this issue. It is also the case that, as Kenneth Seeskin puts it, 'Judaism worships a God who does not act in a capricious fashion, and to cite miracles as proof of religious doctrines is to run the risk that the people will be seduced by charlatans.'[21]

In the case of Christianity, the differentiation between trickery and true divine intervention is even more crucial; the ability to perform miracles is one of the things that proves Jesus' divinity and distinguishes him from mankind, despite his human form. Miracles are central to the Gospels, and also proliferate in tales of saints and holy figures, places and objects, where they demonstrate God's continued presence in and interaction with the human world.[22] Miracles are of course an important element in the Jesus narrative, although there is a range of approaches to their presentation, with some movies understanding Jesus' miracles literally and showing them on screen, seeing them as an opportunity for dramatic cinematic impact. Others mention or describe the wonders, but stop short of actually portraying them.[23] Still others play down the miraculous element, de-emphasising the miracles of Jesus that violate natural law.[24] Nevertheless, miracles show him to be the Son of God, with supernatural powers. As early as 1903, Ferdinand Zecca and Lucien Nonquet presented the world with dramatic miracles in their *The Life and Passion of Jesus Christ*, complete with a closing shot of Jesus in Heaven, at God's right hand. In *The Greatest Story Ever Told* (1965) the miracles, apart from the raising of Lazarus, are rather low-key, and far from central. Pasolini's miracles in *The Gospel According to St. Matthew* (*Il vangelo secondo Matteo*) (1964) use few theatrics, but create a powerful impact:

> The miracles of the loaves and fishes and the walking on the water are treated in a low key. Christ tells his disciples to depart in their boat, 'and I will follow you'. No triumphant music, no waving of hands and shouts of incredulity, no sensational camera angles – just a long shot of a solitary figure walking on the water.[25]

Rather more spectacular are the miracles in Zeffirelli's *Jesus of Nazareth* (1977), in which Jesus performs a number of wonders, most spectacularly the raising of Lazarus, to the awe and joy of those witnessing this, and accompanied by the Hallelujah Chorus from

Handel's *The Messiah*. Sykes and Krish's *The Jesus Film* (1979) also shows dramatic miraculous performances on screen including raising the dead, casting out demons, and the loaves and the fishes, each of which causes excited happiness in those witnessing them; but these have little sense of power – more pleasing conjuring trick than God's revelation. In contrast, in *Jesus* (1999), the miracles are the primary cause of faith, while the British animated film *The Miracle Maker* (1999), as its title and the younger target audience reflect, makes the wondrous feats central, with the illness, death and resurrection of Tamar providing a major plot element.

Jesus' miracles are of course signs not only of God's power, but also of Jesus' status as Son of God, indicating his divinity. Other films concerned with Christianity expand this idea, using the performance of miracles to demonstrate divine favour, proving that the chosen recipient is of holy status. In the Catholic Church, this idea is taken even further; in order for canonisation to take place, the prospective saint must have performed a miracle.[26] Thus, miracles are a feature of both biopics of saints' lives and modern-day 'saintly' depictions. The eponymous saint in *Francis of Assisi* (1961) performs a number of miracles, and experiences miraculous events, including receiving the stigmata, a common sign of Christian sainthood. Other examples situate their holy figures in the modern world; Frankie in *Stigmata* (1999) experiences such a phenomenon, with the character being employed in this case to cast criticism on the Catholic Church and hold up the secular figure's true goodness and sanctity in contrast to the hypocrisy and corruption of the priests.[27] Another seemingly unlikely holy figure is the fraudulent Christian faith healer of *Leap of Faith* (1992), in which a man named Jonas Nightingale cons the people in a small town in America through his fake healings and cures, but, in the end, actually restores the ability to walk to a crippled man, although his disability is depicted as possibly psychosomatic, leaving the possibility open that it is not miraculous at all, but allowing those who wish to believe, to do so. Another fake healer features in *Joshua* (2002), a drama that shows a possible second coming of Jesus, in the form of a strange man named Joshua, to a small town in the United States. Over the course of the movie, amongst other feats, Joshua restores sight to a blind woman, showing up the false healer in the process, and then resurrects a man.[28] In all of these cases, the miracles serve the same purpose: to reflect God's having chosen the recipients of the miracles and those who perform them, marking them out as worthy and noble, and carrying out his work, namely glorifying his name in the world.

THEOPHANIES AND EPIPHANIES

While miracles usually involve the discernible presence of a deity on a national scale, on occasion gods may communicate directly or indirectly with individuals, in a revelation that is described as an epiphany, literally a 'manifestation from above', or theophany, 'manifestation of god'. Some miracles do indeed fall into this category – the burning bush is a prime example – but the main aim of these events is communication with the chosen mortal, rather than national salvation. In the ancient world, mystery religions and cults served as vehicles for divine revelation and inspiration, while Greek drama too was intended to produce a state of catharsis or liberation that was also a form of epiphany. Yet unsurprisingly, given the classical gods' anthropomorphic nature, divine revelation most commonly occurs within the classical tradition in the form of the gods appearing personally to individual humans. This convention has been enthusiastically adopted by film makers. In Harryhausen's *Jason and the Argonauts* (1963), for example, Hermes appears in the guise of an old prophet, who then reveals himself to Jason as a god and transports him to Olympus. This revelation takes the form of a screen dissolve, and then the figure is bathed in bright and dazzling light as it grows to gigantic proportions and disappears, only to materialise again on Olympus, all the while accompanied by triumphal, crescendoing music. Hermes then produces Jason himself from his clasped fist, and the hero is able to see Zeus and Hera, as well as the home of the gods, in person.

This depiction is strongly reminiscent of the detailed description in the *Homeric Hymn to Demeter*, where the goddess reveals herself to the family who have taken her in at Eleusis:

> So saying, the goddess changed her size and appearance,
> shedding her old age, and she was totally enveloped in beauty.
> And a lovely fragrance wafted from her perfumed robes.
> The radiance of her immortal complexion
> shone forth from the goddess. Her blond hair streamed down her shoulder.
> The well-built palace was filled with light, as if from a flash of lightning.[29]

This verbal picture captures the majesty and awe inspired by the sight of the immortal, the supernatural atmosphere in which light and fragrance play a central role, and the stature and otherworldliness of even anthropomorphic gods. Sometimes the theophany of the god can even be fatal; when Zeus appeared to Semele in his true form, it was more than she could stand and resulted in her being burned to death by the flames of his power.[30]

In Homer's epics as well, it is clear that the gods frequently inter-fere in the human sphere. Such interventions may be direct and phys-ical, for instance removing a favoured hero from the line of fire of an arrow. The most direct contact is of course in the case of sexual relations between divine and human characters. On other occasions, gods intervene in human affairs without actually appearing to the humans involved, as an unseen influence, inspiring mortals with courage or restraining them from bloodshed or passion. Thus Hera influences Agamemnon to spur on the Achaeans. Some gods were patrons of cities, and therefore are portrayed as fighting passionately for 'their' citizens.[31]

One result of the involvement of the gods in the mortal world is to strengthen the importance of, and give universality of meaning to, the actions of the human characters, for an incident in which a deity intervenes must surely be worthy of note.[32] Yet paradoxically this increased value, as shown by the involvement in human affairs of these superior and divine beings, also increases the importance of the mortals upon whom the epic is focused, with the gods themselves becoming subordinated in importance to human beings.[33] This is a crucial point, for as Emily Kearns puts it:

> As long as we focus on . . . what human–divine relations tell us about the human condition, we have a vision that is at once heroic and (especially in the case of the *Iliad*) tragic. If we allow the focus to shift to the Gods themselves – and the poet of the *Iliad* seems sometimes to encourage this, with his fre-quent scene-setting on Olympus – the result is entertaining, intriguing, but ultimately problematic.[34]

Despite the prominent role of the gods in the Homeric poems, and in particular the *Iliad*, it is mankind, whose importance is highlighted by the presence and concern of the gods, in which the poet is most interested.

According to the classical tradition, it is generally heroes who have personal contact with the gods. Sometimes the relationship between hero and god is closer than that between hero and ordinary mortal, since heroes, in some cases the offspring of the gods themselves, are in every case far removed from ordinary mortals. As Kearns puts it, 'The heroes of the epic were men of another age, privileged to hold converse with Gods at a much lesser distance or a much more nearly equal level than is possible for us now.'[35] Indeed, the ordinary Greek or Roman citizen had little expectation of divine contact or epiphanies as experienced by the heroes of mythology, who often receive assis-tance from a god who has come down to the earthly plane for the sole purpose of aiding them. These heroes are very much like the gods, in that they have enlarged abilities and exaggerated emotions and reactions to situations, indicative of their larger-than-life personalities. As Kearns notes, 'Divine limitations and human excellence go together; perhaps the famous dictum of "Longinus", that Homer made his men Gods and his Gods men, is not so far from the mark.'[36] Nevertheless, the heroes are mortal, death is the expected end for them, and their behaviour is emphatically human. They therefore occupy somewhat of a middle ground between 'ordinary man' and god. Despite this aspect, as humans, the difference between their experiences and those of lesser mortals is one of degree, and just as the gods interacted with these supermen, so, albeit less directly, they might influence the life of ordinary people. Thus even Greeks and Romans of the historical period could experience divine epiphanies, albeit less often than, or without such blasé acceptance as, the heroes of mythology.

While in literature there is no problem describing the appearance of a god to a human, presenting such an encounter in film is rather more complex; how is the audience to know that the character, played by an actor, represents an immortal? One solution is to make the theophany supernatural in appearance. Unlike Jason, Perseus in the second Harryhausen movie, *Clash of the Titans* (1981), does not have a direct encounter with the gods, but they do still show themselves to the characters in the film. Thetis for example takes possession of her cult statute, with Maggie Smith's face projected on to the marble of the figure, appearing in this way to the assembled people to deliver her decree. Zeus, meanwhile, is seen in reflection by Perseus in the polished bronze of his shield.

The remake of this movie from 2010 uses special effects to show the fearsome revelation of a god's presence. In response to the Argive soldiers destroying the cult statue of Zeus, Hades sends his Furies, terrifying winged creatures, who lunge at the soldiers at high speed, attacking and killing them. The Furies then swoop into one group, which turns into a cloud of black smoke, at the centre of which Hades emerges. His arrival on Olympus and in Argos is similarly marked by a cloud, on the latter occasion taking the form of a tornado-like column, spinning at high velocity, with glowing fire at its heart, perhaps evocative of the fires of Hell in Christian theology. Once he has materialised, however, he is not, unlike in *Jason and the Argonauts*, huge in stature, but appears to be of regular height, before levitating once more, his black cloak open wide over his outstretched arms, and becoming smoke again as he departs, in a portrayal that owes more to Voldemort in the Harry Potter films than to any of Harryhausen's gods.

Another technique is to convey divine presence through the reaction of the mortal to the theophany. In the same movie, Zeus' contact with both Perseus' mother, Danae, and Perseus himself, is shown on screen. Early in the film, Zeus is shown descending to earth, flying down in the form of an eagle, in order to rape Danae, here the wife rather than the daughter of Acrisius. Since Zeus then takes on the appearance of Acrisius, an alteration inspired by the birth of Hercules in classical myth, this is, however, not a true theophany. Later in the film, though, Zeus reveals himself to Perseus, appearing as an old man in hooded cloak, but then throwing back the hood to show himself. The only indication that this is a deity is Perseus' somewhat startled expression, for there is no hint of the divine about the god. No longer shining with illumination as he is on Olympus, but clad in dark, long-sleeved, homespun-looking garments, he appears totally human; nor is he, once his identity is established, addressed with any respect by Perseus, who is filled with contempt for all gods and wants only to deny his Olympian heritage. At the end of the film, when Perseus has accepted his destiny and made his peace with Zeus, the god visits him again, still in the human form of earlier in the production, but this time appearing with a flash of fire and a brief roaring sound, and bathed in sunlight, reflecting the upbeat mood and positive relationship between the two at this point.

This approach is maintained in *Wrath of the Titans* (2012), two years later, where Zeus appears to Perseus rather more regally dressed but still without any elements of divinity, and is treated with no more respect or awe than a human by his son.[37] The same goes for Hades, no longer the villain in this production, and now in similar dress to that of Zeus. In fact, the only indication of something other than human is when Zeus dies at the end of the movie, turning to stone, and then dissolving into dust. Ares, like Hades in the first film, appears in a whoosh of dust-cloud, and, although he has superhuman strength and fighting ability, again is shown with no supernatural effects and is treated without awe by the mortals.

Theophany is an underlying principle of the Percy Jackson books and movies, in which the boundaries between the divine and mortal are blurred through the liminal figures of the demi-gods, the offspring of the gods' procreating with humans. According to this scenario, gods appear as mortals when in the mortal world, but divine when on Olympus, situated above the Empire State Building in New York. How the theophany appears to the demi-god hero depends therefore on where the event takes place. Most commonly the Olympian is depicted meeting the mortal within the human setting, in which case he or she is shown as indistinguishable from other people, but when viewed on Olympus, as in the end of the *Percy Jackson and the Lightning Thief* (2010), they appear in fully divine form, towering over their semi-mortal offspring. The reaction of the demi-gods is far from one of reverence or awe, however, and the 'Wow' that Percy exclaims on entering is, apparently, at the sight of Olympus rather than the gods themselves.

Immortals (2011) also has the gods interacting with the world of mortals in disguised form, with Zeus appearing as a mentor in the shape of an old man (John Hurt) to Theseus, to whom he gives counsel. The reason for this assuming of human appearance is that 'none of the mortals on Earth should witness us in our immortal form'.[38] This belief is bound up in the idea voiced by Zeus that the gods must not involve themselves in human wars, merely looking down, albeit with anguish, from their marble perch suspended in outer space. This is apparently because of 'the law' which decrees that 'No god shall interfere in the affairs of man until the Titans are released', for, in Zeus' words, 'If we are to expect mankind to have faith in us, then we must have faith in them. We must allow them to use their own free will.'

The question of the nature of faith is the central principle underlying the film. Theseus, like the director Tarsem Singh himself, is an atheist, who sees the light over the course of the movie. Singh himself talked of the centrality of the concept of wrestling with faith to the film, as he explained, talking of Theseus' transformation, and also of the nature of religious faith:

> I thought that's the movie, you take a non-believer who becomes the most ardent believer there is later, which tends to happen from born-agains or alcoholics, the recovering ones, always the hardcore ones. So I said, 'How do you make a movie about that?' Then I just said, 'But why don't they interfere?' That was the reasoning that I took up with. And the reason was that faith, to keep the nature of things, can only work on faith. If you go into direct interference, you influence that particular problem, ... right from Heisenberg's principle, to the ending scene of *2001*.[39]

In other words, according to this philosophy, divinities cannot interfere in the world, for in order for faith to operate, proof of the existence of deities can never be possible. As Singh argues, 'faith is just by definition belief without proof', and he says of Theseus:

> Once he gets proofs, it tips, the balance is turned. He doesn't have any faith. He's just got definite proof. Now he knows what it's like ... if you're kind of unsure, that's dangerous. Better know! So Theseus actually sees the gods. So when he sees the gods, he's just got definite proof. So he's not, like, a character of faith at all. He is the way I think everybody should be, a non-believer.[40]

While *Immortals* can hardly be accused of deep and consistent theological underpinnings, this conception of the gods as effectively unable to intervene in the world is reminiscent of deism and prevents true theophany from occurring in the normal course of events. After Poseidon upsets the natural order by intervening in the world, however, this changes; first Ares and Athena, and then Zeus himself, appear in their divine form to Theseus, the former to save Theseus, and the latter to punish the younger gods for their interference. Towards the end of the film, the Titans are indeed released and the gods appear, doing battle alongside the humans. In all of these theophanies, the gods appear in swirls of their golden cloaks and land with powerful force, shaking the ground. They are in their divine clothing, and therefore recognisable as gods, but, unusually for cinematic depictions, only because of their exotic dress and accoutrements, rather than any supernatural effects or enlarged size; in every respect, when showing themselves to the mortals, despite their divinity, they seem human in form and appearance.

The pagan world is not the only one to encompass theophany. In the Jewish tradition, a theophany is still regarded as a true and visible vision of God, but while theophanies of pagan anthropomorphic gods are relatively easy to portray on screen, the revelation of the non-anthropomorphic God of the Old Testament as theophany is, unsurprisingly, relatively rare. In those movies in which he is played as taking on human form – as in George Burns' *Oh, God* and its sequels (1977, 19780, 1984), and Morgan Freeman's *Bruce Almighty* and *Evan Almighty* (2007) – he does appear to his chosen mortals, but his physical appearance is undistinguishable from that of humans. In such movies, when God does reveal himself, the reaction of humans is one of disbelief, both at the fact of God appearing to them and at His appearance. This is itself a response to the anthropomorphism, so far removed from Judaeo-Christian tradition, and the character's amazement is played up for comic effect, emphasising the incongruity of both the appearance of the deity and his theophany to an ordinary individual. These individuals' scepticism turns to acceptance when God 'proves' himself to them, through an exhibition of his powers[41] or his intimate knowledge of their private lives. In *Heaven Can Wait* (1978), this joke is played up even more in a metatheatrical manner, for God, played by Whoopi Goldberg, appears as she does to the lead character, Marly, because she 'loves Whoopi', neatly sidestepping the issue of anthropomorphism and the use of the female gender, and also exploiting the idea, verbalised too by George Burns' God, that the deity must appear to humans in a form that is comprehensible to them.

The use of the child figure Malak to portray God in *Exodus: Gods and Kings* is an attempt to keep this recognisable aspect of God, while also conveying his otherness, in his petulance and unmodulated cruelty, and in the disparity between his youth and his cold and mature personality, so that he seems to have a chilling unearthliness, rather Puck-like in his lack of Christian morality.[42] All of this creates a strong impact on the viewer, as well as on Moses himself, who is portrayed as deeply affected by his sight of God, which sends him into a delirious coma. Throughout the film, he alone experiences theophany, and the truth of his visions is doubted by others. Tzipporah tells him, 'You were hit on the head. Anything you saw ... or think you saw afterwards ... was an effect of that', and the proof that the vision was 'all in his head' was the very fact that God appeared to him as a child; Tzipporah believes that it is a delusion, 'Because God isn't a boy!' As a result, the filmgoer is also left with the option of believing that the theophanies are a product of Moses' imagination rather than the truth, a more palatable option for a secular twenty-first-century audience.

Both in the Bible and on screen, there are other ways in which God reveals himself, according to circumstance. Thus for instance, God appears to Moses as a theophany in the burning bush.[43] This episode was immortalised in film in DeMille's *The Ten Commandments*, where the revelation of God occurs in non-human shape, in the form of fire, both at the burning bush and at the divine inscribing of the Ten Commandments. The former in particular, as the first occasion on which Moses experiences theophany, is crucial for projecting the sense of divine presence, and as Burnette-Bletsch stresses, 'Much of this scene's potential power rests on the reactions of fear and awe displayed by the actor portraying Moses himself.'[44] In the case of DeMille's 1956 production, Moses himself is in a state of awe before even experiencing the first theophany, as he climbs towards the supernatural glow he already assumes is divine, and then kneels and prostrates himself reverently in total acceptance that this is indeed a holy encounter. It is only Moses himself who actually hears God speak, in the traditional, heavily magnified, Voice of God motif, which is in fact, as so often, his own, sonically modified voice. Nevertheless – or perhaps because of the fact that God and Moses speak in the same voice, a point emphatically reinforced when Moses thunders at the sinning crowd after the episode of the golden calf – faith and reverence are displayed by all who view the visible phenomena, recognising them as the manifestation of God, in sharp contrast to the wild, orgiastic celebrations around the golden calf, which clearly therefore has no sacredness at all.

The burning bush is not the only occasion on which divine revelation occurs in the Old Testament. Other cases are found, usually signified by marked and unusual natural phenomena. In the wilderness the children of Israel are led by God in the form of a pillar of cloud or of fire, by day and night respectively.[45] The giving of the Ten Commandments at Mount Sinai is also a theophany, God's voice in this case being accompanied by thunder and lightning, huge flames, smoke and trumpet sounds.[46] Among the prophets, both Isiah and Ezekiel experience theophanies as they receive their commissions. Isaiah's vision is of God as a king on his throne, although the prophet sees only his robe, and the seraphim standing before it crying out the word 'Holy!'[47] Ezekiel's revelation is more elaborate, seeing an amazing chariot surrounded by a large cloud, and dazzling light and fire, from which four cherubim appear. Above the cherubim is the throne of God, in which he sits, interestingly in this case, in human form albeit shining and fiery.[48] In both the prophets' theophanies, God is depicted as in the heavenly kingdom, and therefore reveals himself in his full glory, unlike the earlier revelations in which he comes down to the earthly realm, in which case his appearance is seen through extremes of nature.

Somewhere between these two types is a third variation, described in the Psalms, traditionally ascribed to King David. In one of these, David experiences a theophany when he is saved from his enemies by God, who, riding on a cherub in a great wind and surrounded by clouds, among which his brightness shines out, hurls thunder and lightning and rescues David.[49] This vision combines the supernatural heavenly aspects – the light, power, cherub – with the natural extremes of the storm and the physicality of God riding a creature, reflecting the unique nature of this theophany, in which the physical, mortal world and the divine revelation meet. Finally, in stark contrast to these grand and majestic visions of power, God appears to Elijah not in the wind, earthquake or fire he sends, but as a 'still, small voice', in this very personal and intimate revelation and lesson to the prophet.[50]

In keeping with these Biblical passages, some films, particularly the older Biblical epics, portray theophanies without actually showing an anthropomorphic shape. In *Peter and Paul* (1981) Paul's revelation on the road to Damascus is depicted as winds out of which appears a huge ball of light, which results in Paul's becoming blind for some days. Along with this sight, he also, as he later explains, hears the voice of God, who says he is Jesus, and tells him what to do. A similar portrayal, somewhat more technologically advanced, takes place in *St. Paul* (2000), where Paul is seen going in and out of focus, the picture fading and becoming distorted, before he sees a huge fiery vision, and then falls to the ground, howling in agony. Other depictions of revelation are rather more tame, with only the voice of God being heard by the recipient. Thus in *Francis of Assisi*, Francis, in mid-battle, hears an echoing voice, accompanied by heavenly choral music, telling him 'Francis. Put away the sword. Turn back. You will be told what to do.' The effect on him is instantaneous, and he lowers his sword, looking bewildered, and turns around and leaves.

In cases of such personal, non-anthropomorphic revelation, the reaction of the recipient of the revelation is critical, as Rhonda Burnette-Bletsch elaborates:

> Most movies based on the text of Hebrew scripture favor non-corporeal representations of the deity signified by picturesque rays of sunlight breaking through clouds, raging storms or distant thunder, special effects, disembodied voices, and (most importantly) character reactions to these phenomena. A preferred manner of signifying theophany in epic films is by focusing on the uplifted, radiant face of the human recipient as she/he attends to the divine voice, which may or may not be audible to movie-going audiences. Where cinematography and special effects end, it is up to actors to make the audience believe that God has been made manifest onscreen.[51]

Other productions take a middle ground between anthropomorphising God and showing revelation through divine phenomena. The 1966 epic *The Bible: In the Beginning . . .* uses John Hurst's Voice of God for most of the production, with characters such as Adam, Eve and Noah hearing the Voice (which is also that of the narrator of text, in this case the King James version of the Bible), and reacting to it, while looking up at the sky from whence it presumably emanates. On one occasion, however, God is shown as a more anthropomorphic revelation, albeit with Christian overtones. In the episode of the three angels visiting Abraham, all three, moving with majestic slowness, are played by Peter O'Toole, his hooded, bearded face suggesting cinematic portrayals of Jesus, and finally fading to ghostly nothingness, the tripartite group perhaps suggestive of the Holy Trinity. Abraham receives them with reverent awe; he immediately prostrates himself before them, demonstrating instant awareness of the nature of his unusual guests.

This episode is also employed to demonstrate anthropomorphic theophany in the very reverential *The Bible* (2013). This miniseries has the Lord revealing himself to Abraham through a (somewhat more moderated) Voice of God in the first instance, and then appearing physically in the episode of the angels coming to visit Abraham in order to proclaim the upcoming pregnancy of Sarah and the destruction of Sodom. In place of the three angels described in the Bible, it is clear that Abraham is visited here by two angels, with the third figure being God himself. All three wear hooded cloaks, the two angels in red, but the third figure in a brown cloak, the hood of which remains up at all times, and with his face not shown, standing in shadow or with his back to the camera. From the back view and profile, however, the shoulder-length, wavy hair again conjures up images of Jesus on film, continuing the impression of divinity in human form, especially as he appears to be omnipresent (or at least duo-present) since he is both with Abraham and inside the tent with Sarah at the same time. More than anything, however, it is Abraham's awestruck reaction and the reverent expression on his face that really underline the true nature of the third guest. In contrast, Moses, despite being the only prophet in the Hebrew Bible to speak to God face to face, does not have such a theophany, seeing the deity only through the burning bush, as lava-like fire surrounding the tree. God's Voice, accompanied by the sounds of wind and faint choral strains, is higher-pitched and gentler than earlier, traditional renditions, more newscaster than fire and brimstone, but again, Moses' expression is one of awe and pure faith, with no questioning of the declaration that this is the God of Abraham, Isaac and Jacob.

One of the notable elements of *The Bible* miniseries is its use of the angels as a tool for the epiphany. An angel is an obvious medium for conveying the message of God, playing on the etymology of the word, the Greek root of which means 'messenger'. In fact, the character of Malak, which means 'angel' in Hebrew, in *Exodus: Gods and Kings* was said by Ridley Scott to be merely an angel, but he is clearly more than this, despite Scott's attempt to claim otherwise.[52] In this production, the angels recur on multiple occasions after the Abrahamic scene, but always clad in similar ways, with red cloaks worn over armour, giving them an appearance vaguely reminiscent of Roman soldiers. These are based on Christian angelology, in which some angels are the 'Powers', who are warrior angels opposing evil spirits and casting out wickedness. These angels are usually depicted as soldiers wearing full armour and helmet, and with shields and weapons on occasion.[53] In the miniseries, this iconography is appropriate in the section on the destruction of Sodom, but less so on others, such as when an angel appears to the mother of Samson to tell her of her upcoming pregnancy and set out the conditions under which her child must live. On each occasion, the angel is recognised as more than mortal and a representative of God by those to whom he appears, and who bow down or gaze upon the messenger with reverence. The one exception to this is the people of Sodom, who are presumably too wicked to appreciate such sanctity, their blindness to the holy reality proof that they are corrupt and deserving of death.

Similarly, Pasolini's *The Gospel According to St. Matthew (Il vangelo secondo Matteo)* uses an angelic figure to convey theophany, featuring Rossana di Rocco, clad in long white robe, and with dark hair blowing Botticelli-like round her face. Gazing out from the screen with its 'uncompromising monochrome images',[54] di Rocco's Angel is stern, pure and remote, but also comes with reassuring news for the troubled Joseph: that Mary is still a virgin, and God himself has made her pregnant with his Son. Joseph accepts this message without question, a testament to the Angel's power and his recognition of this.

Following the narrative of the Bible itself, the prediction of pregnancy is also conveyed by an angel in *Samson and Delilah* (1996). Samson's mother, Mara, is rather symbolically petting a lost kid when she looks up and sees a hooded, cloaked figure with a staff standing at a distance along with the herd, with the blazing ball of the sun low down behind him, casting a dazzling light whose rays are visible to his right. Clearly recognising this as a supernatural revelation, she turns, to flee in terror, but he appears behind her, the top left-hand side of his face, framed by a white turban, partially visible in close-up behind the branches of a tree. She cringes in dread, but he tells her not to fear and speaks his prophecy, intoning it in a deep, resonant but calm voice, visions of the future appearing before the cowering Mara, before the angel himself dissolves into nothingness and dust blows across the place where he had been standing. Awed and elated, Mara rushes to tell her husband Manoah all, describing the meeting as 'an apparition ... it was like a miracle'. Manoah, however, is disbelieving, reflecting the impact of epiphany on the recipient who has actually experienced it, a factor exploited by the nature of film, with its access to special effects not easily reproduced in less visual media.

Christianity of course has an anthropomorphised version of a non-anthropomorphic God, enabling theophany to take place in in the shape of Jesus. In the Christian religion, the Epiphany refers to the discovery and recognition of Jesus as the Son of God; Western Christians celebrate the Feast of Epiphany on 6 January, in commemoration of the arrival of the Magi, who were the first to recognise the infant Jesus' divinity, in the Revelation of the Incarnation of the infant Christ. In the Eastern church the festival, held on 19 January, marks the baptism of Jesus by John the Baptist, but both mark the same idea: the revelation of Jesus as Christ.[55] A variation of the idea is the Christophany, which is an appearance of Christ in non-physical manifestations, and which typically refers to visions of Christ after his ascension, the most famous example of which is Paul's revelation experienced on the road to Damascus.[56]

Most common in film, however, is the theophany of Jesus himself as he reveals himself to individuals. Before the crucifixion, Jesus is regarded as mortal (albeit often holy and elevated in nature), so it is after the Resurrection that such appearances may be classified as theophanies. These are marked both by special effects that indicate Jesus' specialness and by the reactions of those receiving the epiphanies. As early as DeMille's 1927 *The King of Kings* Jesus' appearances after the Resurrection, first to Mary and then to Mary Magdalene and the apostles, use special effects to convey the supernatural nature of the occurrence. Thus the former meeting is one of the few scenes in colour, while the latter has Jesus surrounded by bright white light, the rays of which surround him like a halo. One or both of these scenes are repeated in myriad movies, including the 55-minute feature *I Beheld His Glory* from 1953, the 1954 *Day of Triumph* and as recently as the miniseries of 2013, *The Bible*.

Almost all of the portrayals of the Resurrection costume the figure of Jesus in a dazzling, white, long-sleeved robe, and many surround him with white light and use a background accompaniment of choral music. In *The Greatest Story Ever Told*, Jesus appears before his rapt disciples, to the accompaniment of the 'Hallelujah' chorus from Handel's *Messiah*, in the sky, framed by clouds, and arms spread wide, as he speaks his instructions, before dissolving into the sky itself. More than three decades later, *Mary, Mother of Jesus* (1999) shows Jesus revealing himself to Mary Magdalene from a roof, against the background of the sky, as he spreads his arms and Mary falls to her knees in awe. *The King of Kings* by contrast has Jesus delivering the same words unseen, but heard by the disciples on the shores of the Sea of Galilee. The apostles then depart silently in different directions, and a hugely elongated shadow of Jesus moves into the screen, falling across the stretched-out fishing nets to create the form of a cross, providing the viewers themselves with a feeling of personal epiphany. Perhaps the least supernatural Resurrection epiphany is that of *Jesus of Nazareth*, which, in keeping with the attempts to set the production in a realistic and historical context, has no lights, music or fanfare, and shows Jesus not in a shining white robe, but in homespun brown as he sits on the floor, surrounded by his disciples, passing on his words of inspiration and comfort. The tone of most of these theophanic scenes, however, is one of quiet conclusion, providing a sense of peace after the traumatic scenes of the Calvary, and aiming to provide a sense of the comfort and inspiration experienced by believers at revelation from their deity.

PROPHECY

A number of movies, both Biblical and mythological, use prophecy as a tool to demonstrate divine inspiration, enabling the god to speak to the chosen mortal, often with special effects highlighting the supernatural communication. Martin Winkler highlights one such typical scene in Carlo Ludovico Bragaglia's *Gli amori di Ercole* (1960), where 'Hercules visits a grotto in which an unspecified but elaborately dressed prophetess resides. She is photographed from a low angle, appearing in subdued light and surrounded by clouds of smoke mysteriously swirling behind her.'[57] This atmosphere is closely bound up with the nature of prophecy, as Martti Nissinen elaborates:

> Prophecy is human transmission of allegedly divine messages. As a method of revealing the divine will to humans, prophecy is to be seen as another, yet distinctive branch of the consultation of the divine that is generally called 'divination'. Among the forms of divination, prophecy clearly belongs to the noninductive kind. That is to say, prophets – like dreamers and unlike astrologers or haruspices – do not employ methods based on systematic observations and their scholarly interpretations, but act as direct mouthpieces of gods whose messages they communicate.[58]

On many occasions, the truth and accuracy of prophetic visions are taken as a given. Perhaps the most famous of mythological prophets is the unhappy Cassandra, daughter of King Priam, doomed always to see true visions but to be believed by no one. As a princess of Troy, Cassandra's prediction of the city's fall is given a role in some cinematic depictions of the Trojan War. She features in a number of productions, albeit few centrally,[59] and her role is always that of the true, but disregarded, prophet.

Sometimes priestesses, while not conventional prophetesses, are also vehicles for prophecy; in *The Legend of Hercules* (2014), for example, the priestess of Hera is also the mouthpiece for the goddess to communicate with Alcmene, who has come to the priestess to pray to Hera for deliverance. Taking possession of the body of her priestess, whose eyes roll in an unconscious trance, Hera responds, speaking in an echoing, electrically modified voice. Later, after Alcmene's suicide, Hercules himself is addressed by the priestess, acting as the voice of wisdom and truth, who urges him to accept his destiny. This priestess is a young woman, acted by 24-year-old Mariah Gale, who plays the role with an earnestness and supernatural eeriness that are one of the highlights of this less than gripping production.

Rather different is Pasolini's treatment of the Pythia at Delphi in his *Oedipus Rex* (1967), in which Oedipus goes to consult the god, and receives a cruelly mocking response listing his fate. This Pythia is an African priestess, in traditional tribal garb, her face hidden by her clay, doll-shaped headdress, with straw for hair that falls over the priestess' face, concealing it as she declaims and cackles insanely. This depiction is described by Winkler as follows:

> A grotesque, callous, and cruel Pythia informs Oedipus of his fate. . . . The priestess's words, her strange dress and appearance, and the setting all empha- size the devastating power of the god over a helpless and barely comprehend- ing human. The Pythia's prophecy condemns Oedipus as someone polluted even before he actually commits any wrong – a particularly annihilating aspect of the divine.[60]

An interesting depiction of prophecy is that seen in the made-for-television miniseries *Hercules* (2005). At the start of this movie Tiresias the prophet is blinded during a religious rite dedicated to Hera, and receives his gift of prophecy from Zeus as compensation for this savage act. This whole production centres on the war between Zeus and Hera – or more accurately between the followers of Zeus and Hera, since, despite the presence of mythological creatures such as nymphs and satyrs, the gods themselves are never seen. Because of this, it is unclear whether it is the gods themselves to blame for the tragic events, or corrupt humans. When Hercules and his sidekick Linus go to the Delphic Oracle to find out how to atone for Hercules' killing his children, the oracle turns out to be Tiresias himself, much to Linus' surprise. In answer to his startled query, Tiresias replies: 'Like nature, Linus, I am many-sided. One thing is always many things, but balance is all, Hercules', to which the hero responds disgustedly, demanding that he not receive 'riddles' and calling Tiresias scornfully a 'man-woman'. Shortly after this, Tiresias leaves Delphi and sets up a shrine in Tiryns, since his visions tell him that great events are to unfold there. It is clear throughout that Tiresias' prophecies are real foretellings; on every occasion they come true. Yet Hercules' attitude towards these prophecies, and the gods themselves, is complex. In an impassioned speech, he declares:

> I am tired of others telling me what the Gods want. I will be my own oracle, speak to them myself. Gods and men, hear the oracle of Hercules. I

pray to Zeus and Hera, Apollo and Artemis, Ares and Athena, to Poseidon, Aphrodite, Pluto, Demeter and all the other Gods and Goddesses! I pray to them one and all and all as one and to all Gods, I make sacrifice, not a sacrifice of blood, but of reverence to their nobility, their love, their honour, their courage, their kindness, their justice. But to their pettiness, their wantonness, their cruelty, their savagery, their vanity, their injustice, I make no sacrifice. I pay no reverence. I deny all that is ungodly in them!

I will worship the beauty they have bestowed, my fellow beings, the animals, the mountains and seas and green Earth, the sky, and the light of the sun and the moon and the stars that keep us from the darkness. I will worship and try to emulate all that is great in the Gods, nothing more. If that is not good enough for them, so be it. When my time comes, they can judge me worthy or not. But if they are truly great and truly just, then they can ask no more of any man than what I offer them.

Such an attitude reflects an underlying, if somewhat confused, belief in this production that religion and human interpretations of deities are dangerous and corrupting influences, and yet the gods themselves, while they may be remote, are not cruel or reprehensible, and the prophecies granted to Tiresias are genuine and true.

A similar attitude may be seen in Tarsem Singh's *Immortals*, where Phaedra, the 'virgin Sibyl' prophetess, is an oracle who has true visions, which she regards as a curse and which stop after she sleeps with Theseus, losing her virgin status. Despite the veracity of her prophecies, Theseus remains an atheist, until he experiences his own theophany; this scepticism is a mark of Singh's attitude towards religion.[61] Nevertheless, this disbelief is not shared by the viewer, who witnesses the oracle's vision along with her, as seen in her mind, when her foot touches the semi-conscious Theseus. The whirling, dizzying style of the apparition creates the impression of possession by a greater force, while the Sibylline and her fellow priestesses wear long red robes, with high, lampshade-style headdresses that cover their faces burka-style, distinctively marking them out as holy, although only one of them actually receives prophecy.

Other prophets are, however, treated negatively in some films. One example is that of the Spartan ephors in *300* (2006). Historically, the ephors were five citizens elected by the Spartan Assembly, responsible for the enforcing of law. The duty was for a period of one year and could only be undertaken once by an individual, thus ensuring an annual change of personnel. In general, rather than influencing the Spartan citizenship, the ephors reflected popular opinion.[62] Their power was great and their responsibilities included legislative, judicial, financial and executive duties,[63] but their role was not primarily religious. In *300*, however, they are described as prophets of the gods, with an oracle they consult on all matters, but they are presented as vile monsters, disfigured, sexually deviant and lecherous, prone to slavering over and licking the semi-conscious and sexy priestess.[64] It also emerges that they are corrupt, refusing Leonidas permission to go to war on the grounds that they must honour a sacred religious festival to prevent Sparta's fall, but in actuality because they have been bribed by Xerxes with gold in order to prevent Sparta from participating in the war.

Such cases are unusual, and prophets are generally treated with respect. This is equally true of Biblical prophets, although false prophets may be mocked, as in *Monty Python's Life of Brian* (1979), in which Brian finds himself on the Street of the Prophets, amongst a line-up of wildly raving fortune tellers and proclaimers of doom. In straight adaptations, however, prophets are often dignified and severe characters, delivering their messages in stately manner.[65] Thus the Canadian-American actor Raymond Hart Massey, 'known for his commanding, stage-trained voice',[66] took the role of Nathan in *David and Bathsheba*, also with a staff, but in sombre brown and with a purple cloak. Samuel, meanwhile, is a somewhat less powerful but more venerable figure, with the usual staff as mark of his office, but with white hair and long white beard. The same features occur in *Sins of Jezebel* (1953), in which John Hoyt played a white-bearded, majestic Elijah. Similarly, William Devlin, as Nathan the prophet in *Solomon and Sheba*, dressed in traditional Biblical-style robes and headdress and carrying a staff, delivers his lines with a Shakespearean intonation, as he declaims God's word with stern authority. Even in *The Story of Ruth* (1960), the 'holy man', Jehoam, played by Eduard Franz, who had taken the role of King Ahab in *Sins of Jezebel* and Jethro in DeMille's *The Ten Commandments*, sports a white beard and carries the obligatory cane as he majestically delivers voiceovers and enigmatic prophecies. More than two decades later, in Rossellini's *Il messia* (1975), the prophet Samuel bears the same hallmarks, being depicted with a long white beard and holding the usual staff as he talks with the elders of Israel.

In all of these depictions, the interpretation is broadly the same. The prophet is the Voice of God, a powerful and upright figure, whose task is to pass on the divine message. In both Judaism and Christianity, any mortal can experience revelation, although certain individuals are chosen to be prophets or have direct communication with God. The basis for this selection is generally a virtuous personality – God speaks to Noah, for example, because he was righteous in his generation – but the prophets are not in any way superhuman, a fact that allows for the hope of revelation and divine contact to be extended to ordinary people.

Because of this, the righteousness of the prophet is not to be questioned by the audience, although it may be by the protagonists. Adele Reinhartz disagrees, maintaining that

> For all of the focus on the commandments and their divine origin, Old Testament films subtly criticize those who keep to them too strictly. In *David and Bathsheba*, the prophet Nathan is portrayed as a narrow-minded legalist who cares more for the letter of the law than the spirit of love.[67]

Since the focus of this film, however, is on David's own understanding that love does not justify his actions, and his salvation is prerequisite on his comprehension of his sin, this does not really seem to be the case, and in the less religiously antagonistic atmosphere of the era in which the film was produced, it seems unlikely to have been the intended portrayal. It seems far more credible that the aim was to convey the prophet as the messenger of God, passing on divine predictions that inevitably hold truth.

The characterisation of the stern prophet comes directly from the Old Testament, where he was a person selected by God to be a channel to pass on his words to others. At the dawn of history, according to Biblical tradition, God chose certain individuals – Noah, Abraham and his descendants – and spoke to them directly, putting words or images into their heads; the exception to this was Moses, who, the Bible states and Rabbinic teaching emphasises, conversed with God, face to face.[68] Just as the classical hero's exalted status was indicated by divine patronage, so the prophet's being chosen for his task also reflected his having found favour in God's eyes. In many cases in this tradition, the prophet himself was reluctant to take on the task; Moses and Jeremiah both protested fervently, and Jonah attempted to evade the task by fleeing the country. The Hebrew prophets in general, in fact, suffered greatly as a result of the divine inspiration. To quote Karen Armstrong,

> The prophets of Israel experienced their God as a physical pain that wrenched their every limb and filled them with rage and elation. The reality that they called God was often experienced by monotheists in a state of extremity: we shall read of mountain tops, darkness, desolation, crucifixion and terror. The Western experience of God seemed particularly traumatic. What was the reason for this inherent strain? Other monotheists spoke of light and transfiguration. They used very daring imagery to express the complexity of the reality they experienced, which went far beyond the orthodox theology.[69]

Such an experience inevitably makes for a sometimes severe depiction of the prophet, though perhaps none is as harsh as that in one of the more recent depictions of the reception of prophecy, namely that of Darren Aronofsky's *Noah* (2014). God, called throughout 'The Creator', is never seen or heard in the film, his message being conveyed entirely through the character of Noah and his prophetic visions. These are in the form of dreams, which are viewed by the audience, and which cause Noah great distress. Yet he himself is not even certain at first of the prophetic nature of the visions; when his wife asks 'Did he speak to you?', his answer is only, 'I think so.'

God himself is, in fact, notably absent from this version of the story. As mentioned above,[70] he is referred to in the creation only as having made man and woman. Nor is this very minimal role in creation, necessarily the truth, for it is voiced by Noah, while the running text at the beginning of the movie does not mention God at all, leaving open the possibility that this is merely human belief as opposed to truth. Nowhere in this movie is any 'Voice of God' ever heard; rather we see Noah's dreams, and hear the words of Methuselah and Noah, explaining their beliefs. It even seems that Noah may have hallucinated God's will after drinking a potion given to him by Methuselah, increasing the possibility that these 'prophecies' are the thoughts of a madman, rather than genuine revelations. Although Noah is strongly affected by his visions, in a manner that is perhaps closer to the tortured emotions of the Old Testament prophets, the element of doubt as to their veracity turns him from passionate prophet into religious fanatic, with whom little sympathy is felt.

DIVINATION

'I humbly ask that auguries be taken that Rome might know that the gods favour my actions', demands Julius Caesar at the beginning of the fourth episode of the HBO-BBC's *Rome* (2005–7), Season 1. But it is immediately clear there is a danger that the augury will not support him. 'You've entered the City under arms. I must warn you that seldom augurs well', warns the priest. From Caesar's reply, 'The gods know my intentions are peaceful. The people must know it also', and the agreement of the priest to the augury ('So be it. Auguries will be taken on the first clean morning. Let the birds fly where they may'), it is already clear that there is more than pure religious devotion behind this ritual. This suspicion is confirmed in a later exchange between the two men, as Caesar bribes the priest to find favourable omens:

Caesar: Tell me, how is Caecilia ?
Chief Augur: She's healthy, I thank you.

Caesar: Good. I recall I forgot her last birthday. . . . Perhaps she would forgive my rudeness were I to send her a gift. . . . Perhaps she would accept some money. 100,000 sesterce, say ?

Chief Augur: Oh, that's very kind of you. I'm afraid my wife is a woman of expensive tastes . . . .

Caesar: 200,000.

Chief Augur: That is a very generous, and I may say, appropriate gift. She would be under great obligation to you.

Caesar: To think well of me would be her only obligation.

Chief Augur: She's always thought well of you. It is not unethical she continue to do so.

Caesar: We understand each other. *(aside)* Make a note of it. 200 to the chief augur.

The scene of the augury itself is then shown in detail, and it is clear that the auguries are explicitly manipulated to provide the required outcome, and give a positive omen for Caesar's occupation of the city. Finally, Caesar's satisfied smile, smacking of a job well done, indicates the success of his bribe.[71]

Divination was an omnipresent element of the ancient world, enabling people to receive otherwise hidden information from the gods, and divine approval of actions through commonly accepted techniques and signs. These signs included augury, the observation of natural conditions and phenomena, throwing pebbles or dice, examination of sacrificial entrails, and hydromancy, as well as prophecies received at oracular shrines. Different kinds of omens were interpreted by a range of figures, both professional and non-professional.[72] There was no doubt in the minds of the ancient Greeks, Israelites or early Christians that divination was genuine, and that, in the words of Cicero, there was no people in the world *quae non significari futura et a quibusdam intellegi praedicique posse censeat* ('who do not believe that future things are shown by signs, and that they are able to be understood and foretold by certain people').[73]

The excerpt from *Rome* above demonstrates the attitude of the production team towards the question of ancient religion in general and divination in particular. Both Jonathan Stamp, the consultant historian for the series, and Bruno Heller, the director, stress that one of their aims in making the series was to make the audience understand just how different ancient Rome was from the modern world, which they felt had been 'totally impregnated with and repressed by Judeo-Christian morality'.[74] In order really to understand Roman society, they felt that the viewers had to be removed from their unconsciously absorbed Christian morality, which was very foreign to the pagan mindset. This was opposed to other productions which they felt, in Stamp's words, took a 'pastiche approach' and 'overlaid a modern morality on top' of ancient Rome; Stamp and Heller tried to show it as utterly alien with regard to religious customs.[75] The scene of corruption with regard to religious ritual in the form of divination was surely intended to highlight what those making the series understood as a lack of connection between religion and morality in the ancient world, and its political exploitation by the elite.

The point is reinforced by the scene immediately following, featuring the lower-class character Vorenus and his wife, after a disastrous event to celebrate Vorenus' new business and obtain the god Janus' favour, which ended in the breaking of the bust of Janus and a family fight. Niobe, Vorenus' wife, tries to console him, saying, 'We'll go to the priests of Janus tomorrow first thing, and have the day absolved. It's costly, but . . .', but Vorenus is not prepared to do this. 'An omen is an omen. And this is as bad as they come. No point throwing money at it.' Earlier in the episode, another act of divination had already taken place, when Niobe consults a fortune teller who receives enlightenment through the examination of the entrails of an animal. Again this lends an exotic feel, as well as highlighting the contrast between the simple and unsophisticated beliefs of the lower ranks, and the cynical manipulation by the upper classes.

Doctor Who (2005–) used the sets from HBO-BBC's *Rome* in the episode 'The Fires of Pompeii' (2008), which also featured divination in the form of two cults, the female Sibylline sisters and the male augurs. Both groups are shown to have true knowledge of the future, but this is given a scientific explanation, due to the influence of alien forces, rather than one from any religious truth. Nevertheless, the conceit works on the principle of divination being a common feature of the ancient world; it was in fact an omnipresent element, enabling people to receive otherwise hidden information from the deities. Even Judaism, in which sacrifices, in contrast to many in the pagan world, did not involve prophecy or revelation by the deity, had a means by which divine purpose could be revealed, namely through consultation of the *urim v'hatumim*, elements of the breastplate worn by the High Priest, attached to the apron known as the *ephod*.[76] In general though, other forms of supernatural predictions were discouraged, with consultation of those that use divination, soothsayers, enchanters, sorcerers, charmer, mediums and necromancers being explicitly forbidden by the Old Testament.[77]

The very range of terms listed here, however, gives some indication of the prevalence of such customs in the ancient Near East, which in turn allows for the trope of the ancient soothsayer to be exploited on screen to convey exoticism. Occasionally such a mechanism is actually utilised to indicate veracity to the audience, in a somewhat metatheatrical nuance, as the modern viewers are aware of the truth that the characters themselves are not. Thus *I, Claudius* (1976) features a scene in which a *haruspex* interprets the depositing of a wolf-cub by an eagle into the young Claudius' lap as a sign that Claudius will one day rule as Rome's protector. His family laugh this off in disbelief, but the audience of course know that this is a true prediction. Similarly, a vision of the Sibyl appears in the first episode in order to declare that Claudius will survive to become emperor, and in the last to explain future events. This apparition is really more of a literary device to prepare for the discovery of Claudius' secret writings as revealed on modern screens than true prophecy, but it does play on the convention of the divination as a symbol of antiquity, and, in this case at least, is shown to be genuine.

PRAYER

Miracles, epiphanies and prophecies are not experiences with which the average cinema goer is conversant on a personal basis. Prayer, however, is familiar to all, whether they themselves pray or not; the prayers recited and taught by Jesus in the various biopics provide the watcher with a sense of identity and recognition. Although at its most basic prayer may be defined as, in John of Chrysostom's words, 'conversation with God',[78] prayers may take a wide range of forms. They may be written, oral, sung, thought, or expressed through wordless emotion, part of ritual and canonised, or spontaneous. Prayers may be accompanied by ritualised physical movements or actions, performed in specified postures or places, and at specific times.

Because of its wider implications and contexts, the very act of praying in both Biblical and mythological films conveys particular messages to the audience. On many occasions, it is an appeal to the divinity for help or even salvation. Thus mythological characters go to the temples of gods, or stand before their statues, in order to ask for divine blessings or to request the gods' help. Jason in Harryhausen's *Jason and the Argonauts* goes to the temple of Hermes, Hercules in the 2005 miniseries goes to Delphi, and even Disney's Hercules in the 1997 film goes to the temple of Zeus in order to pray to the god, his divine father. In this case Hercules is even depicted kneeling with clasped hands and bowed head, and starting his petition 'Oh mighty Zeus, please hear me and answer my prayer', in a portrayal that is a hundred per cent Christian.

In actual fact, ancient prayer, although it was a common feature, was not in this form at all. In Homeric epic, heroes are seen frequently praying; the way they pray is, as far as is known, very similar to that employed by Greeks of later periods. Kearns neatly summarises the process:

> They pray with some special request in mind, they remind the Gods of their past benefits and promise gifts for the future if their prayer is granted. Very often they perform animal sacrifice, whether to bolster up their request or to make good a promise, or even as a pious preliminary to eating. The centrality of animal sacrifice to Greek religious practice is abundantly clear from other sources, and in the epic it is indicated from an Olympian perspective by the keenness of the Gods to receive sacrifice, wherever it may be performed and – other things being equal – their regard for those who offer it.[79]

In general, the role of prayer in Greek religion is to focus the ritual, in order to ensure that the gods understand what is needed and why it should be granted. Prayers involve invocation of the god, justification of why the prayer should be answered, and a formal request for what is required. Such prayers are not meek; the word 'to pray', *euchesthai*, also means in Homeric Greek 'to boast', indicating the confidence with which the petitioner approached the deity, believing that he or she is worthy of the gods' benevolence. Similarly, they were uttered, aloud, in standing position and with upraised hands.[80] Roman prayers were also declaimed, often with the head covered by the *toga praetexta*, and ideally directed towards the east.[81] Romans extended their hands towards a god or temple, or touched the altar, when uttering prayers.[82]

When pagan prayer is so depicted on screen, it immediately strikes the viewer, steeped in the Judaeo-Christian tradition, as foreign, and indeed it is a tool through which the otherness of the ancient world may be emphasised. In the HBO-BBC production *Rome*, characters are shown praying to various gods, according to their individual needs; Vorenus, for example, is seen on his knees before a small shrine, his wife and daughter standing beside him, the hands of all three uplifted and eyes shut in reverent devotion. This manner of prayer may seem glamorously foreign to the modern viewer. Such worship often takes place at the household shrines that appear on a regular basis in the various homes, complete with lighted candles that highlight the figurines of the gods and the ancestral masks. In fact, everyday rituals and prayers are seen throughout the production. Mira Seo emphasises the quantity of religious rituals, and in particular the prominence of personal devotions, in religious practice portrayed in the series, and points out that this is despite the fact that academic opinion holds that 'the notion of personal "faith" or "belief" is essentially a notion inappropriately applied to Greek and Roman religion from Christian ideology'.[83] Since the creators of the series were fanatical about researching ancient Rome and meticulous in their production, such an alteration cannot be random carelessness and must be deliberate. Seo considers this issue, concluding that the 'gendered religious behavior and its concomitant spatial segregation of the genders' is as 'a way to compensate for the surprisingly "free" nature of Roman male–female interaction portrayed in the series'.[84] This is undoubtedly true, but I would argue that the specific depiction of how humans in the series turn to the gods also highlights both their similarity to, and difference from, modern society. Bruno Heller and Jonathan Stamp stress a major difference between the two, emphasising that Roman religion was 'about functionality', not morality.[85] Discussing the issue, Heller states:

> People were in constant conversation with the gods . . . Switching allegiances from one god to the other or trying to find out what god is applicable to the situation makes a difference to people's behavior and morality when they don't have that overarching superego telling them what's right and wrong. It makes for, in many ways, a freer and more liberated society, but on the other hand a far more brutal and cruel one.[86]

While this is true, it is also the case that Roman religion was very concerned with the use of precise language, and Roman prayers were formulaic and archaically stylised. Pragmatic in nature and contractual in form, their usual aim was supplication for a particular purpose, and, like the prayers of ancient Greece, accompanied sacrifice. Such pragmatism with regard to the gods – deities in which, contrary to modern secularism, they clearly believe – seems amusing and startling to modern eyes. Titus Pullo, while in prison at one point, prays earnestly, eyes raised to the roof:

> Forculus, if you be the right god for the business here, I call on you to help me. If you will open this door, then I will kill for you a fine white lamb, or, failing that, if I couldn't get a good one at a decent price, then six pigeons. This, Forculus, I vow to you.[87]

Similarly, scenes such as the elaborate public sacrifice marking Caesar's triumph, and even more, the graphic and bloody *taurobolium* (bull sacrifice) scene (see Figure 7.1) and Servilia's cursing of Atia, all depict the religion of the Romans as something exotic and bizarre, adding to the appeal of the series.

Despite this emphasis on the exotically different, the attitudes towards prayer and ritual may strike chords. In many cases, those

Figure 7.1 Atia soaked in the blood of the sacrificed bull in the *taurobolium* scene in *Rome* (2005–7), Season 1. HBO-BBC.

practising the ancient religion on screen in this production exhibit the sincerity and piety shown by those practising the monotheistic religions with which the audience is familiar. The reaction of panic at the accidental breaking of the statue of the god Janus mentioned above recalls modern superstitions, while the deliberate smashing of another in the second season as an act of sacrilege conjures up images of similar deeds by religious fanatics sometimes seen in recent years. Even lack of respect for the gods, as reflected in Mark Antony's bored and restless fidgeting through a religious ceremony of induction, strikes a chord in modern audiences. Such imagery conveys the impression that despite the seemingly outlandish nature of Roman religion, people's attitudes towards the gods were in many ways as varied as those found in the twenty-first century, and their reactions towards what they regarded as divine are likewise unchanged.

It is not only in films in the pagan context that prayer is seen; it plays an important role in Biblical film, as Adele Reinhartz explains:

In the epics, the victory of faith is assured by prayer. The lives of the female protagonists of *The Story of Ruth, David and Bathsheba*, and *Solomon and Sheba*, for example, are all threatened because they are sentenced to death by stoning for idolatry (Ruth, Sheba) or adultery (Bathsheba). Ruth is saved by

Naomi's prayer, Sheba by Solomon's, and Bathsheba by David's, which also saves all of Israel when God responds by ending the drought.[88]

Prayer is indeed fundamental to Judaism. From the time of the destruction of the temple in Jerusalem in 70 CE, and the consequent removal of the ability to sacrifice, Judaism moved from a temple-/ priest-based religion to one centred on the teachings and rulings of the rabbis. Rabbinic Judaism decreed that prayer could, and did, provide a substitute for, as opposed to supplement to, sacrifice.[89] Just how radical a notion this was at the time is hard for modern minds to comprehend, but it was this perhaps more than any other change that allowed Judaism to survive not only the destruction of the temple, but also two thousand years of exile. One of the reasons the rabbis were able to draw such a conclusion was Judaism's unusual stress on prayer even in the Bible and pre-exilic days, and its wide variety of forms. To quote René Lebrun:

> In Judaism there is a fundamental conviction that it is both possible and desirable for humans to address God and that God can and will respond. The God of the Hebrew Bible is characterized as 'You who will listen to prayer' (Ps. 65.2 [= 65.3 Hebrew]). Words of prayer can be articulated by an individual or by a community; spontaneously or according to set formula; in the elevated language of poetry or in ordinary prose style; set to music and sung or simply spoken; formulated in the second person to address God directly or in the third person to speak about God.[90]

Prayer in Judaism was and is used for a wider range of uses than in pagan religions; people prayed not only in order to request things from God, but also to praise Him and to thank Him for benevolence. It fills a central role in modern Judaism, as it has for at least two millennia, if not longer. It is mandated three times a day for men, and ideally communally, is accompanied by ritualised movements, and is undertaken seated or standing, but almost never kneeling. Unlike the pagan religions, Judaism is still practised today, a fact that influences cinematic depictions of Jewish communications with God.

The same is true of Christianity, the religion with which most Western viewers were, at least until recently, familiar. Growing out of Judaism, early Christian prayer shared many characteristics with that of the earlier religion, but it soon developed independent features. Most notably, the Lord's Prayer evolved as a focal point of religious practice, to be said three times a day.[91] This prayer was not adopted to the exclusion of those that could be offered both privately or communally; there were others, sometimes composed spontaneously, but in other cases with formal structures and offered at set times. Hymns also evolved far more centrally than in Judaism, with singing becoming 'a common way of conveying basic Christian teachings' in the post-Easter Christian movement.[92] Another change was the adoption of the kneeling posture, until then only found in the ancient world in cases of desperate need.[93] All of these elements evolved in the first centuries of Christianity and remain constant to the present day, and their purpose was to provide a channel of communication between man and deity.

On screen, the act of prayer is an indication to the audience of the worthiness of the supplicant; the act of praying indicates piety and ensures God's grace and positive response. In Biblical movies, whether based on the Old or the New Testament, such appeals to the divine often mimic the gestures or positions, or even words, of modern prayer. Thus King David in *David and Bathsheba* prays on his knees, hands clasped, begging for Bathsheba's life to be spared and her sins forgiven. He does so in Biblical-sounding 'archaic' language influenced by Psalm 51 in particular, but using phrases and expressions from a range of verses.[94] The Queen of Sheba in *Solomon and Sheba* also comes into the temple, prostrating herself on the steps and praying for Solomon to be saved, again using Biblical phrasing:

> Lord God, hear the prayer of thy servant. Mine was not the strength to save my lord Solomon from himself. But thine is the power. Let not thy wrath descend upon him. Look into his heart and pity him. But if it be thy will to punish him, visit it upon me in his stead.[95]

In *The Robe* (1953), Marcellus grips the wall and prays in an adaptation of Psalm 22 and indeed of Jesus' words on the cross, asking in anguish, 'Father in Heaven … Why hast thou abandoned him?' Mel Gibson's *The Passion of the Christ* (2004) has Jesus praying in words reminiscent of the psalms, particularly 16 and 31: 'Shelter me, O Lord. I trust in You. In You I take refuge.' Samson in both the 1949 movie and the 1984 version (both entitled *Samson and Delilah*) stands, hands braced against the pillars of the Philistine temple, and prays, blind eyes closed. In the earlier film, whereas slightly earlier, his prayer to God has been in modern language, addressing him as 'you', here at the climax, it becomes 'thee' as he cries, 'I pray thee, strengthen me, Oh God. Strengthen me only this once.' By contrast, the 1984 version has him requesting 'Oh God, give me strength, just once more', with his head thrown back and his arms at shoulder height, evoking images of Jesus on the cross. The 1996 miniseries, again with the same title, uses similar language, depicting him saying 'Now, O God of Israel, grant me that for which I was born. Grant me the strength again just once. O God, forgive Samson, God of Israel.'

Even in older epic movies, women seem to pray in less Biblical language. Lygia in *Quo Vadis* (1953) prays kneeling before a cross on the wall, but her prayers are spoken wishes more than formal ritual. Other movies also present prayer less formally, as a personal turning to God; two film versions of the book of Esther (*Queen Esther* (1999) and *One Night with the King* (2006)), show Esther seated and pouring out her heart to God in desperate pleading.[96]

Lygia's earnest and sincere prayer is contrasted sharply by juxtaposing it with the scene of pagan ritual and prayer that follows it, in which the priestess, her arms cast wide open and to heaven in a triumphant pose that is strikingly at odds with the humble Christian petition of Lydia, proclaims, 'Gods of Rome, mighty, eternal, beneath whose auspices Rome rules the world. Hear us, we worship you. Venus, Goddess of Love; Mars, God of War; Juno, goddess of heaven; Jupiter father of the gods', before finishing, in a clear moment of ridicule, 'and Nero, his divine son'.[97] This final flourish is intended to indicate the shallowness and lack of truth in the pagan religion, contrasted to Christianity.

NOTES

1 Fraser (1988: vii).
2 Pardes (1996: 25–6).
3 See Llewellyn-Jones (2007: 426).
4 Wood (1975: 175).
5 Holland (1967). See also Sanders (2002: 7–10, 103–23).
6 Garland (2011: 75).
7 See in particular Lucian, *Alexander the False Prophet*.
8 Loimer and Guamieri (1996).
9 Kennedy (2006).
10 Basinger (2011).
11 Richards (2008: 102).
12 Elley (1984: 35).
13 <http://www.patheos.com/blogs/filmchat/2014/10/exodus-gods-and-kings-no-parting-of-the-red-sea-also-christian-bale-says-moses-was-likely-schizophrenic.html> (accessed 1 May 2018).
14 Maimonides was sceptical of miracles, except in very rare cases. See Drazin (2000: 187–96). The Hertz translation of the Chumash, following this lead, writes on the plagues: 'The first nine plagues, though often spoken of as wonders, are not fantastic miracles without any basis in natural phenomena. . . . Between June and August, the Nile usually turns a dull red, owing to the presence of vegetable matter. Generally after this time, the slime of the river breeds a vast number of frogs; and the air is filled with swarms of tormenting insects. We can, therefore, understand

that an exceptional defilement of the Nile would vastly increase the frogs which swarm in its waters; that the huge heaps of decaying frogs would inevitably breed great swarms of flies, which, in turn, would spread the disease-germs that attacked the animals and flocks in the pest ridden region of the Nile' (Hertz 1960: 188).

15 Particularly Hort (1957).

16 In the words of Joe Neumaier in the *New York Daily News* (1 December 2014), 'Scott's staging of the Red Sea scene is technically cool but dramatically a drip. The water recedes instead of rises. The effects are naturally greater than in 1956, but emotionally underwhelming.' <http://beta.nydailynews.com/entertainment/movies/exodus-gods-kings-earns-star-article-1.2040665> (accessed 2 May 2018). Similarly, another reviewer writes, 'These all get trampled by Scott's goofy, literalist rationalism, which tries to invent a scientific explanation for everything – the Red Sea parts because of a tidal wave, the Plague Of Boils is caused by disease spread during the Plague Of Flies – while preserving a sense of Sunday school spectacle, and ends up working as neither. (Scott and his screenwriters more or less give up when it comes to the Plague On The First Born.) At least DeMille knew how to put on a show' (Ignatiy Vishnevetsky, 'Christian Bale leads a slog through the Old Testament in Ridley Scott's *Exodus*', Av Film (11 November 2014), <https://film.avclub.com/christian-bale-leads-a-slog-through-the-old-testament-i-1798182172> (accessed 2 May 2018).

17 Elley (1984: 31).

18 The ten plagues clearly have this purpose, but the greater purpose was to persuade Pharaoh to release the Israelites in order to bring about their salvation from slavery.

19 Garland (2011).

20 See e.g. Maimonides, *Guide for the Perplexed* 2.22.

21 Seeskin (2011: 254).

22 See Blackburn (2011); Ward (2011).

23 Reinhartz (2007: 104).

24 Humphries-Brooks (2006: 72).

25 <https://www.rogerebert.com/reviews/great-movie-gospel-according-to-st-matthew-1964> (accessed 3 May 2018).

26 See Sanders (2002: 7–10).

27 Ibid. 111–13.

28 Ibid. 103–4.

29 *Homeric Hymn to Demeter* 275–80 (trans. Gregory Nagy). <http://www.stoa.org/diotima/anthology/demeter.shtml> (accessed 12 April 2018).

30 Diodorus Siculus, 4. 2. 1; Ovid, *Metamorphoses* 3.273–315.

31 Kearns (2006: 61).

32 Llewellyn-Jones (2007: 435).

33 Kearns (2006: 72).

34 Ibid. 73.

35 Ibid. 64.
36 Ibid.
37 Hephaestus also appears, played by a long-haired, eccentric-looking Bill
    Nighy, but it is made clear that he has lost his divinity by this stage, and
    thus it is unsurprising that he displays no physical signs of godliness.
38 *Immortals* at 00:16:34 minutes.
39 <https://www.cinemablend.com/new/Immortals-Director-Tarsem-
    Singh-Talks-About-Ill-Fated-Horses-His-Films-27865.html> (accessed
    29 April 2018).
40 Ibid.
41 In the case of *Bruce Almighty*, for example, he magically extends at
    great speed the drawer containing Bruce's files, sending him flying across
    the room.
42 See Collins (2016: 35).
43 Exodus 3:2–4:17.
44 Burnette-Bletsch (2016: 305).
45 Exodus 13:21.
46 Exodus 19:16–25.
47 Isaiah 6.
48 Ezekiel 10.
49 Psalms 18.
50 1 Kings 19:11–13.
51 Burnette-Bletsch (2016: 301).
52 See ibid. 306: 'Malak remains the face of God in this film – speaking for
    the Israelite deity in the first person, claiming responsibility for choosing
    Moses (Christian Bale), inflicting the plagues, and giving the law. Other
    than a single line in which Moses says that he is "tired of talking with
    a messenger", nothing else in this picture would indicate that he is
    anything other than God. The name Malak (which means "messenger")
    appears only in the credits and is never spoken in the film. In fact, when
    Moses asks the boy's name, he twice responds "I am" (Exod. 3:13–14).'
53 Michalak (2012).
54 Elley (1984: 45).
55 For the history of the Feast of Epiphany, see Bradshaw and Johnson
    (2011).
56 Acts 9:3–9.
57 Winkler (2009: 83).
58 Nissinen (2017: 1).
59 Giorgio Ferroni's *La guerra di Troia* (1962), Marc Allegret's *The Face
    That Launched a Thousand Ships* (1953), Mario Camerini's *Ulysses*
    (1954), Franco Rossi's television *L'Odissea* (1968), Michael Cacoyannis'
    The Trojan Women (1971), Enzo G. Castellari's *Hector the Mighty*
    (1975), Woody Allen's *Mighty Aphrodite* (1995), Chuck Russell's *The
    Scorpion King* (2002), John Kent Harrison's *Helen of Troy* (2003) and
    Disney's animated television series *Hercules*.

60 Winkler (2009: 78).

61 See pp. 158 and 189.

62 Jones (1967: 30).

63 For a detailed description of the ephors' role and duties, see Rahe (2015: 17–24).

64 This has occasioned considerable internet discussion. See e.g. <https://forum.rpg.net/archive/index.php/t-317214.html>; <https://aelarsen.wordpress.com/tag/frank-miller/> (both accessed 29 April 2018).

65 Although Jesus is often portrayed as a prophet, because the figure is also regarded as a deity, I include these depictions under theophanies rather than prophecies.

66 <https://en.wikipedia.org/wiki/Raymond_Massey> (accessed 29 April 2018).

67 Reinhartz (2016a: 782–3).

68 Numbers 12:6–8; Exodus 23:11; Deuteronomy 34:10.

69 Armstrong (1993: 11).

70 See pp. 55–6.

71 On this episode, see also Seo (2008: 169–70).

72 See Johnston (2008: 3).

73 Cicero, *De Divinatio* 1.2.

74 Roblin (2015: 150–1).

75 In the interviews on the bonus DVD accompanying the show. DVD *Rome*, Season 1, Warner Brothers 2005, with Kevin McKidd, Ray Stevenson, Polly Walker, Ciaran Hinds . . . HBO Video, 2006.

76 See Van Dam (1997); Houtman (1990).

77 Deuteronomy 18:10–11.

78 *In Genesim (Homiliae)* 30.5. Quoted by Hammerling (2008: 3).

79 Kearns (2006: 64).

80 On these points, see Johnston (2008: 362–3) (entry on Greek prayer by Christopher Faraone).

81 Vitruvius, *De Architectura* 4.5.

82 See e.g. Horace, *Odes* 3.23; Virgil, *Aeneid* 4.219.

83 Seo (2008: 168).

84 Ibid. 176.

85 <https://www.youtube.com/watch?v=myAOjN8oYoo> (accessed 7 May 2018).

86 <http://www.beliefnet.com/entertainment/tv/the-pagans-of-rome.aspx> (accessed 7 May 2018).

87 *Rome*, Season 1, Episode 1, 'The Stolen Eagle', 0:28.

88 Reinhartz (2016b: 187).

89 See Spinner (2003); Bokser (1981).

90 Johnston (2004: 357) (entry by Lebrun).

91 McGowan (2014: 189).

92 Johnston (2004: 368) (entry by Derek Kreuger).

93 McGowan (2014: 187).

94 'O God. Thou God of my early youth hear my prayer. Let thine eyes which alone see clearly fall upon thy worthless servant. In all things have I failed thee. My life is a waste. My crimes are many and terrible. To my sons, I have bequeathed the evil that is in my blood. I have led my people into misery and want. I have used thee with ingratitude and betrayed thy trust. I have been a faithless shepherd. I am dust in the sight of thine eyes. I am less than the meanest creature crawling on the earth. And, yet, O God I am also thy creation. Take not thy Holy Spirit from me. Thy spirit which abode with me in the wilderness. I ask nothing for myself, O God. By my sins I have put myself beyond the compass of thy forgiveness. But lift thine hand from thy people who suffer for my crimes. Forgive them the sin that is not theirs but mine. Let the land thou gavest their fathers flow once more with thine abundance. And let Bathsheba live to praise thy name and testify to thy mercy. Show her the loving kindness of thy heart. Cleanse her from sin and let thy punishment fall on thy servant who has earned it. Look not on the sinner who comes before thee but on the boy he was who loved thee and who would have died for thee. Make my heart as his. Let the boy live again in his innocence. Grant him thy mercy and take this David's life.' David and Bathsheba 1:41–1:45.

95 *Solomon and Sheba*, 1:32.

96 In the most recent version, *The Book of Esther* (2013), Esther is shown early in the film lighting the Sabbath candles and reciting an English translation of the accompanying blessing, with her eyes shut, but her later prayers before facing the king are not shown.

97 Reinhartz (2016b: 187).

8 Blurring the Boundaries: Apotheoses and Deicides

January 2018: 'JESUS HAS RISEN', ran the small headline in red block capitals, immediately above the real major news in a font four times as big: 'Mel Gibson Is Seriously Moving Forward with a Passion of the Christ Sequel'.[1] After the controversial big box-office success of *The Passion of the Christ* (2004), the story is not yet over; where the earlier movie focused on the killing of Christ, the new one is scheduled to highlight his Resurrection, the proof of his apotheosis and divinity. Despite the supposed eternal essence of a god, the idea that the boundaries between human and divine can become blurred continues to fascinate. This can happen either in the form of mortals becoming gods, or in that of gods, despite their supposed immortality, actually dying. Both of these have been seen on screen, with the killing of deities a relatively recent phenomenon, an examination of which, together with the attitude towards apotheosis, sheds light on some aspects of contemporary thought concerning the roles of man and god in the modern world.

APOTHEOSIS: ZEROS TO HEROES TO GODS

Graeco-Roman Apotheoses

With regard to apotheosis, the mythological figure from the ancient world who experienced this was Hercules, and the various screen depictions of the hero deal with this in different ways. Disney's 1997 movie, for example, has Hercules earning his immortality, but then rejecting it. The means by which Hercules won his transformation to divinity was his courage and willingness to sacrifice himself, risking his life by diving into the river of death to save his girlfriend, Meg. His rejection of the ultimate goal for which he has striven all his life is motivated by something even greater than the desire for glory and eternal fame, in the Disney world view, namely love, as he gives up immortality in order to live with her on Earth.

The decision to remain mortal is rooted in the characterisation utilised by Disney. Hercules, while retaining his amazing physical strength, is notably awkward and clumsy as a teenager, and remains so with regard to affairs of the heart as an adult. Where many other adaptations show Hercules as a Superman figure, with boundless abilities, Disney has chosen to make him more of a Peter Parker Spider-Man character than a Clark Kent. What defines him as much as his physical strength, however, is his innate virtue and integrity. He is a stereotype of the innocent farm-boy motif of American film, as represented by figures such as Luke Skywalker and, again, Clark Kent, with his pure innocence and values, and his journey of self-discovery as his innate heroism emerges.[2] Another parallel has been highlighted by Mark I. Pinsky, who points out, 'Hercules can be summed up in one sentence: A child is born divine, lives on earth through young adulthood, inspires the love of a fallen woman, dies, lives again and returns to earth.'[3] This Jesus figure is not sent to the world to save mankind, nor is his journey really one of salvation for anyone other than himself, but he is presented as a role model, and the decision to remain as a human is in keeping with this agenda, whereby the hero becomes a figure who can inspire the young audience and whom they can emulate.[4]

Other screen versions of the Hercules myth generally avoid the issue of apotheosis at all. *Hercules* (2005), despite its fantasy elements of nymphs, satyrs, centaurs and monsters, like Petersen's *Troy* from the previous year, removes the actual gods from the action, and attempts to put a rationalising spin on the tale. Although the focus of this *Hercules* is on the effect that religion has on mankind, the movie does not imply that the gods – in contrast to the various mythical creatures, who do appear on screen – actually exist. In place of mythological divine interventions, psychological and physical explanations are provided for the events of the film. Thus, in this version Hercules' divine parentage is rejected entirely, his birth being the outcome of his mother being raped by a Cretan soldier on the night that her husband returned home. Hercules is persecuted not by Hera, but by his own mother, Alcmene, who is a priestess of Hera, with

Amphitryon championing Zeus, whom he believes to be Hercules' real father. Even Hercules' famous superhuman strength is assigned to his determination and exercise regime, while in the final scene of the movie he is married to his beloved, Deinara, with no mention of death, let alone apotheosis.

Neither of the two 2014 Hercules movies (*Hercules* and *The Legend of Hercules*) feature the hero becoming a god either, although in the latter he is the son of Zeus, as a result of Alcmene's prayers to Hera, when she can no longer tolerate her husband's thirst for power and warmongering. As a result of this petition, Hera allows Zeus to impregnate Alcmene with Hercules, the man who will be 'the saviour of her people', and a demi-god. Such phrasing could have paved the way for Hercules' eventual apotheosis, either as a Jesus-like figure or in the traditional mythological mode. Yet neither of these options occurs, and the movie ends with the birth of the baby son of Hercules and his wife, Hebe, in this version a human princess and his true love, and with Hercules himself standing on the ramparts of his city, watching protectively over his kingdom, but in no way divine. The second of the productions from this year makes Hercules even more human, with no superhuman abilities, and much emphasis placed on the idea of spin; at the beginning of the film, after an impressive montage of Hercules (Dwayne 'The Rock' Johnson) wrestling a lion and fighting with a giant boar, the film cuts to a scene by a campfire, where it is revealed that these feats were merely stories, exaggerated by Hercules' nephew Iolaus to intimidate their enemies. Hercules is not the son of Zeus, Hera does not figure, and the gods are merely creations of religious superstition. Based on Steve Moore's comic book *Hercules: The Thracian Wars*, this Hercules is a 'con man . . . a soldier of fortune with no noticeable godliness'.[5] As such, he is not divine, nor does he become so, in this movie.

Although Hercules is the only ancient hero to achieve apotheosis, other screen heroes in recent years have earned that privilege. *Immortals* (2011) is, in part at least, the story of Theseus' journey from non-believer to believer to, ultimately, apotheosis itself. Reflecting modern questions of atheism and agnosticism, it is apparent that according to the internal logic of this movie, the gods do exist, but their role in the world is unclear to mortals. Unlike in the Percy Jackson films (2010, 2013), these gods are remote and in fact are forbidden by law to intervene in human affairs, as Zeus himself states:

> I obey the law. No god shall interfere in the affairs of man unless the Titans are released. If we are to expect mankind to have faith in us, then we must

have faith in them. We must allow them to use their own free will. If any of you come to the aid of man or otherwise influence the affairs of mankind as a god ... the punishment will be death.

This attitude means that they do not intervene to help even those who believe in and worship them, and terrible suffering occurs in this world, as Hyperion, the evil villain of the piece, declares:

I, too, cried to the heavens for help. But instead of mercy, I was met with silence. And the wretched sight of my family ... suffering like animals until their deaths. Your gods will no longer mock me. I will release the Titans.

Such theological difficulties lead logical people to believe that there are no gods. Theseus himself is at first an atheist, who tells his mother, 'Mother, your gods are children's stories. My spear is not', and later explaining his faithlessness, in a similar way to that of Hyperion, since his mother was 'a woman of faith and her gods were absent when she needed them the most'. Theseus' atheism is somewhat ironic since it flourishes in spite of the fact that he enjoys the friendship and protection of an old man who is revealed to be none other than Zeus himself. This guidance is despite Zeus' own decree forbidding such interaction, a problem he resolves by reasoning he has influenced Theseus for years, 'as one of them. Never as a god. Only as his friend.'

Theseus is faced with the proof of the gods' existence, due to Ares' and Athena's intervention to save his life. After this occurs, however, Zeus tells Theseus that he will receive no more help from the gods and he must justify the faith Zeus has in him alone. In other words, the gods do exist, but this does not affect man's role and responsibilities. Even their power does not really affect the world, according to this theology, for it is used against the Titans rather than against humans. At the end of the film, the mortally wounded Theseus is also transported to Olympus, as reward for his sacrificing his own life, and given a place among the gods, apparently in response to Athena's plea to her father not to forsake mankind. Yet the meaning of this apotheosis in unclear. The end of the movie states:

'All men's souls are immortal. But the souls of the righteous are immortal and divine. Once a faithless man, Theseus gave his life to save mankind and earned a place amongst the gods.'

Theseus himself possesses no godlike abilities, yet he is superior to the gods through his own moral character, and it is this which gives him immortality. The immortals in this version then are not the gods at all, but righteous humans, leaving the place of the gods marginalised and uncertain.

This is perhaps unsurprising bearing in mind the views of the director, Tarsem Singh, who describes himself as an atheist and a blasphemer since the age of nine, although his mother is devoutly religious. Stating that neither the Greeks nor the gods attracted him to the project, he explains that his mother once turned to him when he was 'crapping on religious stuff' and said, 'How do you think you are as successful as are if it wasn't for praying?' This provoked him to consider the scenario of the existence of a god, and the salvation of a human, because of the belief of another.

> 'You know what, the worst thing that could happen is a guy like me dies and there is a god up there and he goes, 'You fuck! I was dying to screw you up but because of this woman' ... and I just thought that would be really interesting'.[6]

Tarsem's aim, then is to explore the effect of changing belief on personality. In Henry Cavill's words:

> Theseus' reasons of existence change throughout; he goes from atheist to martyr, ultimately. At the beginning it's merely to protect his mother and himself; that's the only reason why he fights or exists. And then it adapts for revenge. And then beyond that for things that are greater than he is.[7]

Whether the things that are 'greater than he is' are gods, however, in any traditional sense, remains unclear. Theseus meanwhile becomes a Jesus figure, sacrificing himself to save others, as 'he goes from atheist to martyr'.

Similarly, in *Clash of the Titans* (2010) and its sequel *Wrath of the Titans* (2012), the question of apotheosis appears, but is rejected. In these films, the hero himself is the son of Zeus, but, resentful at the death of his family, Perseus at first does not believe in his divine origins; later, when convinced of his true paternity, he wants no help from the gods, refusing to pray to Zeus for aid when injured, as he declares, 'if I do this, I do it as a man'. He turns down his divine father's offer of divinity on two separate occasions, determined to live as a human, although over the course of the film mutual filial-paternal love and respect develop between Perseus and Zeus.

This rejection of divinity is not a modern invention; in the ancient world too, humans occasionally refused deification, as in the case of Odysseus, who spurned both Circe's and Calypso's offers of immortality. Immortality itself, however, is of course the reward of all heroes, in that their name lives on beyond them, in the cases of the Greek heroes for thousands of years, and thus even when deification is offered and ostensibly rejected, it has actually on some level taken place.

In a more tangible sense, the process of deification is generally something greater than everlasting fame, however. Apart from myth-ological heroes, the other ancient beings thought to undergo deifica-tion were the Roman emperors. After the death of Julius Caesar, the Roman Senate voted to give him divine honours,[8] thereby effectively adding him to the Roman pantheon as a god. This was an act with-out precedent in Roman history, but which would have an effect on Roman politics and religion thereafter. While actual apotheosis of an emperor does not take place on screen, the idea of deification is something that is exploited to demonstrate the extreme corruption and even madness of the Roman leader, particularly in the cases of Caligula and Nero. In *Quo Vadis* (1953), for example, Peter Ustinov's Nero is convinced of his own divinity, but is subtly mocked for this by his own subjects, who pretend to fawn on him, making it clear that his ridiculous ideas are nothing more than lunacy. Thus on one occasion, he cries, 'Do I live for the people or do the people live for me?', to which Petronius answers, 'You are the sun in their sky! Does the sun have privacy?' Nero, however, considers himself in a worse position than the sun, since 'The sun has the night!' whereas 'These people expect me to shine daily – hourly!'

Such preposterous exaggeration makes a mockery of the very idea of a human being transformed into a deity, but a more sinister side is seen in the BBC series *I, Claudius* (1976), where Caligula proclaims his own deification, declaring that he has become Zeus, a claim accepted by the Senate. He then goes on to pronounce that his sister, Drusilla, is also his wife, Hera. When Drusilla informs him of her pregnancy, fearing that his child will become greater than himself, he, in perhaps the most horrifying scene of the entire series, attempts to recreate the birth of Athena, cutting his unborn child from inside his sister and eating it. Apparently the shot of Caligula cutting the baby from Drusilla's womb had to be re-edited several times due to its provocative and extreme nature, the final edit taking place on the day of the episode's premiere by order of Bill Slater, then head of Serials Department. After this broadcast and its repeat two days later, the scene was edited once again, however, removing the shot of the baby, with the episode ending only with Claudius' horrified look in response to the act that he sees, but which the audience do not.[9]

Apotheosis for Believers: Jesus and the Resurrection

The very extreme nature of the *I, Claudius* episode again serves to highlight the disbelief in, and rejection of, the idea of human apotheosis in modern society. This is principally because it is regarded as untrue and contrasted with the genuine apotheosis accepted by the Western world, in the form of Christianity, with which it is, albeit sometimes unconsciously, contrasted. The transformation of Jesus from his human form to the Son of God, as he dies to save the world, sacrificing himself to cleanse the sins of others, is the central and fundamental core belief of Christianity; yet it does not invariably feature in the Jesus biopics. As Pamela Grace explains:

> Some Jesus films end with the crucifixion, either implying that Jesus was a mortal being or eliminating the need to take a position on the resurrection. At the opposite end of the spectrum, some films delight in the spectacle of the savior emerging from his tomb and/or ascending to heaven.[10]

Other films take a middle ground, hinting at the Resurrection or having Jesus talk of it, but not showing events after the crucifixion. Even films that do emphasise the Resurrection do not show a transformation of Jesus on screen, but focus on Jesus' resurrected appearance to his followers. In Reinhartz's words:

> At the most, we see an image of the resurrected Jesus, as in Gibson's *The Passion of the Christ*, which shows us a perfectly whole and healthy Jesus, exactly as he must have been before his ordeal, with the exception of the nail holes in his hands and feet.[11]

At this stage, then, Jesus does not appear different or divine as such, but is clean, healed and with an aura of peace and contentment around him, often indicated by being bathed in light, with accompanying musical track, and speaking in a calm, measured tone. The most apotheosis-like version is that of *The Greatest Story Ever Told* (1965), which concludes with Max von Sydow's Jesus declaring over a backdrop of clouds, 'And Lo! I am with you. Unto the end of the world', before appearing as he rises up against the painted ceiling depicting the heavens in the dome of the Byzantine church from which he had appeared at the beginning of the movie, the whole scene accompanied by the triumphant 'Hallelujah' chorus of Handel's *Messiah* (see Figure 8.1).

Other biopics are less forthright about depicting the Resurrection, but the motif of apotheosis, with Christian overtones, can be found in other movies set in the ancient world. In movies featuring early Christianity, believers receive a glorified life after death that parallels that of Jesus himself and is akin to deification. The final scene of *The Robe* (1953), for example, shows Marcellus and Diana, condemned to death but walking forward to their execution side by side, heads

Figure 8.1 Jesus (Max von Sydow) against the painted ceiling of the Byzantine
church in the final shot of *The Greatest Story Ever Told* (1965).
George Stevens Productions.

held high; they smile at each other and clouds form behind them to
create the impression of ascension into the heavens, while a chorus
sings a triumphal 'Hallelujah' accompanying their march,

Even movies not explicitly about Christianity utilise the apotheosis idea; in these films, the hero undergoes a form of deification
that is not actual apotheosis but exploits images and ideas of such
an occurrence, to provide a hopeful ending for otherwise tragic
characters. Spartacus is one such figure, even being crucified at the
end of the film, but he is visited, while on the cross, by Virinia,
holding his newborn son, providing the hero with an afterlife that
makes him akin to a deified being. In the words of Stephenson
Humphries-Brooks:

> Spartacus after death on the cross was to have been burned and his ashes
> scattered in secret to ensure that his memory would disappear. Instead, he
> attains apotheosis and immortality by fathering a freeborn heir who will
> know and carry on the story. The filmic language fosters an iconography
> unmistakably parallel to Jesus and in some ways more complete.[12]

Similarly, Maximus in *Gladiator* (2000) is in many ways transformed
and becomes a kind of god when he wins popularity from the crowd
and becomes a gladiator celebrity, and thereby sets himself on the
path to his final redemption. The final stage is a different kind of
transformation into grace, however, as he finds 'eternal happiness in
death, reunited with his wife and child in a heavenly version of his
idyllic Spanish estate'.[13]

DEICIDES

Killing the Olympians

Clearly, the idea of humans achieving immortality is a common theme on screen, but recently there has been a trend in the reverse direction, namely for gods to lose their divinity. As Vincent Tomasso points out, this is not a situation without precedent in the ancient world. Nevertheless, the sources in which the idea is found are ones of which adaptors within modern popular culture are generally unaware. As such, what Tomasso calls the 'twilight motif' is something that can be regarded as a recent modern twist, rather than an influence from the classical world.[14] Tomasso differentiates between two alternative perspectives on the twilight motif, one by which the gods lose their immortality due to human progress – in Tomasso's words, 'the Greek gods vanish when humanity has progressed beyond them' – and another in which 'the gods die violently on screen'.[15] I would suggest that there is overlap between the two groups delineated by Tomasso, both of which stem from an underlying belief in the superiority of mankind to these deities.

Tomasso places in his first category, in which humans have 'outgrown' the gods, the two Harryhausen movies (*Jason and the Argonauts* (1963) and *Clash of the Titans* (1981)) and the *Star Trek* (1966–9) episode 'Who Mourns for Adonais?' (1967).[16] In the earlier of the films, *Jason and the Argonauts*, Hera tells Zeus that he is the god of many men, but that this is only so as long as people have belief in the gods; 'when those men no longer believe in you, then you will return to nothing'. *Clash of the Titans* also indicates that the gods' time may be ending, as discussed above.[17] A similar idea, as already discussed, can be seen in 'Who Mourns for Adonais?', where the gods left the Earth and returned to their home planet when humans no longer worshipped them, after which they 'spread themselves upon the wind ... thinner, and thinner, until only the wind remained'.

In all of these productions, the gods existed at some point, but their relevance has now faded, causing them in turn to disappear. The argument can be taken further and extended, for the implication is that people not only do not need these gods, but are actually superior to them, a motif that can be seen in other movies as well. In the remake of *Jason and the Argonauts* (2000), Zeus and Hera are portrayed as a beautiful couple in sky, lounging on the clouds, squabbling and bickering with each other. This Zeus is vengeful, jealous and lascivious, attempts to makes Jason's life an impossible struggle, and tries unsuccessfully to seduce Medea. The fact that he does not succeed in either aim is down to the innate qualities possessed by the two humans, and also because of the true love that has developed between them. These gods are actually stated to be inferior to mortals in their behaviour and morality, with Hera declaring to Zeus, 'They put us to shame.'

Nowhere is it stated that such an attitude leads to the gods' demise, but it does underpin the ideas in the earlier version of the tale upon which this miniseries was based. More explicitly, in the recent Percy Jackson movies, the gods are presented as a dysfunctional family, from whom very few moral lessons may be learned; they are described by Luke in the first movie as 'all . . . the same. Selfish'.

One of the reasons Luke feels this way about the gods is the fact that the divine parents have abandoned their semi-divine off-spring. It emerges, however, that they are forbidden by fate and by the decrees of Zeus (it is unclear what the relationship between these two is) to have any physical contact with them, as Poseidon, Percy's father, tells his son towards the end of *Percy Jackson and the Lightning Thief* (2010). He explains that when he was with the infant Percy and his mother, he 'became less concerned with [his] responsibilities' and was 'becoming human'. When Percy queries whether this was a bad thing, he is told that 'Zeus thought so', and that this was the reason for the ban on parent–child contact, but it is clear that this abandonment was far from easy thing for Poseidon. In the end, the gods are depicted as rather sad creatures, unable to love fully, and in a way handicapped in comparison to the humans, who can do so, as epitomised by Percy's relationship with his mother. According to this idea, it is the ability to conduct a loving relationship that separates god from mortal, and in the end even has the potential to destroy immortality, although this does not actually take place in this series.

Other recent productions do create scenarios of the gods dying or being killed, however, sometimes violently and on screen. The impact of an immortal being struck down is very powerful, completely over-turning and challenging ideas fundamental to traditional Western society. In *Hercules: The Legendary Journeys* (1994, 1995–9) and *Xena: Warrior Princess* (1995–2001) the gods are condemned, not only for their lack of morality, but also because they represent the old and patriarchal order. As Tomasso writes:

> The Olympians do not want the status quo to change, a change that is rep-resented by the values of the female protagonist Xena and of the humanist Hercules. Classical antiquity, as represented by the Greek gods, is a stifling

and disabling force of the past, whose constituents seek to prevent change at all costs.[18]

While both *Hercules: The Legendary Journeys* and *Xena* attack the Greek gods, they do not entirely condemn the Judaeo-Christian religions. Xena 'helps enact the movement from worship of the Greek gods to worship of the Judeo-Christian god', as does Kirk in 'Who Mourns for Adonais?' when he tells Apollo that humans have no need for a plurality of gods, but 'find the One quite adequate'.[19] A different approach can be seen in *Immortals*, however, where religion in general is the target, a product of the modern secular society, in which deities of all kinds are viewed with suspicion. Ironically, bearing in mind the title of the movie, in *Immortals* the gods can be, and are, killed; by the end of the film, most of the gods have met their demise, and only Poseidon and Zeus, carrying the body of Athena, return to Olympus, having crushed the Titans. It appears that mankind is actually responsible for this state of affairs, for it is the faith and prayers of mortals that ensure the gods' immortality. Thus these deities need man even more than man needs them. As a result of human non-belief, the Greek gods have gradually become weaker, with the exception of Hades, who, unlike the other gods, does not need men's faith and worship, but only their fear. Even in this case, the principle of human emotions and relationship with the gods having the power to sustain them remains, however, and is clearly influenced by Tarsem Singh's own philosophies, leading to the possible implication that the superhuman beings are more a product of human imagination than real entities.

Deicide in Christianity: Killing Jesus on Screen

The most common deity to suffer death is, of course, Jesus, whose death is shown on screen, with responsibility for the deed being cast upon either the Jews or the Romans or both. Unsurprisingly, in DeMille's 1927 *The King of Kings*, with its evangelical agenda, the Jews are portrayed as responsible. The original version made this so clear that it led to protests by Bnei Brith and other organisations, causing DeMille to alter some elements, emphasising the Roman subjugation of the Jews, who had no freedom, and centring the blame more on Caiaphas, the High Priest. Since Caiaphas himself was, however, a classic caricature of the evil and greedy Jew, complete with a tall headdress that looks vaguely horned, the charge of deicide is barely weakened in this movie.[20]

By contrast, George Stevens' *The Greatest Story Ever Told* went to extremes not to present the Jews as Christ-killers. While a negative presentation of the long-dead and often villainised ancient Romans is unproblematic, the same cannot be said for the depiction of the Jews. The Church has a long history of holding the Jews responsible for Jesus' death, which formed a central element of anti-Semitic rhetoric.[21] Stevens, who had been one of the liberating soldiers at Dachau, not only presents the Jews as victims, employing strong Holocaust imagery, but also lays the blame for Jesus' conviction and execution on individual characters, who are motivated by personal interests and greed, rather than on the people as a whole. There is not even complete support for the denunciation of Jesus in the Sanhedrin in this version, as the members are split between his supporters and his opponents, with internal politics rather than questions of religion or blasphemy the central issue. Similarly, the people themselves are less than enthusiastic about crucifying Jesus, with cries of 'release him' penetrating as loudly as those demanding crucifixion. Even the arch villain Judas is rehabilitated in *The Greatest Story Ever Told*, as, when Jesus is arrested, he seems bewildered and declares that Jesus is the 'purest, kindest man' that he has ever met.[22]

Franco Zeffirelli's *Jesus of Nazareth* (1977) goes even further. The 1960s and 1970s saw a change in the attitude of Catholicism towards Judaism, as anti-Semitism became less acceptable, and the *Nostra Aetate* declaration of the Second Vatican Council in 1965 by Pope Paul VI repudiated the ancient charge against the Jews of deicide. Zeffirelli declared that this edict was his 'deepest motivation' for making the programme, leading him to want to remove the stigma of deicide from the Jews. As he explained:

> I don't only wish to re-evoke the story of Christ, but also the tragedy of the blaming of the Jewish people, which should no longer exist. I want to clarify the reasons that were behind your ancestors' decisions and – within my film – help all to understand them.[23]

To make this clear, Zeffirelli's Jesus and his compatriots are very Jewish indeed, set in a clear historical and cultural context,[24] and the Romans are demonised as brutal oppressors of the Jews. Zeffirelli thus attempted 'to show how, in the face of Roman arrogance . . . the people's sense of humiliation was . . . proportionate to the insults and scorn they received',[25] a factor which led to Jewish unrest in Judaea. This in turn caused Pontius Pilate to be wary of Jesus, and, fearful of the threat that he posed, it was Pilate who pronounced the sentence of crucifixion on him.

So far had the pendulum swung in the direction of freeing the Jews from blame that a film critic, Dwight Macdonald, was astounded when a chance remark he made in 1967 that placed responsibility for Jesus' death on the Jews caused him to be attacked for anti-Semitism. Describing the incident two years later he explained:

> When I made my gaffe two years ago, I took it for granted, as a WASP by upbringing, that the biblical account of the trial and crucifixion of Jesus was correct. Since then, I've learned, by the chancy methods that journalists learn things, that a good case can be made out that the Gospel writers, for prop-agandist reasons, played down the part of the Romans in the tragedy and played up that of the Jews. So I'm willing to agree that the matter is obscure and that the hundred or so readers who wrote in objecting to my remarks may have been right about the historical fact. But I'm not willing to admit . . . that my error – if it was such – was evidence of racial prejudice.

Tellingly, he continued:

> We live in a time when the pendulum of social justice has swung back too far, when certain racial groups are sacrosanct, so that when one states, depending on the New Testament, that certain Jews two thousand years ago wanted Jesus killed, one is accused of denouncing all Jews today as 'Christ killers'.[26]

Clearly outraged, Macdonald's comments reflect both a latent belief in the dogma of Jewish deicide, and an acknowledgement that anti-Semitism in the form of a general charge of the murder of Jesus against the Jewish people was unacceptable. It might have been expected that almost four decades later, this old charge would have been laid to rest, and the stigma of deicide removed from the Jewish people. Mel Gibson's *The Passion of the Christ*, however, spoken entirely in Latin and Aramaic, despite its stated aim of showing shared responsibility by all sinners – Gibson includes himself as first among them and in the film, the hand that holds the nail that pierces Jesus is his own – blatantly directs the blame towards the Jews. The matter was exacerbated by Gibson's marketing the movie as 'the only authentic film about the Passion', deepening the blatant anti-Semitism of the film, and packaging it as 'the truth'.[27]

Pamela Grace outlines 'the multiple ways in which *The Passion* creates an overall sense of guilt and blame, and then directs the blame toward the Jews'.[28] Apart from the notorious cry of the people, 'His blood be on us and on our children', from which Gibson agreed to remove the subtitle but not the audio track, the movie shows Pontius Pilate desperately trying to avoid crucifying Jesus, while the Jews viciously bay for his blood. As Grace explains, the major means of focusing blame on the Jews was:

primarily through images, particularly images unaccompanied by words, that the film associates the Jews with violence and evil. As the familiar biblical passion story unfolds, a series of extra-biblical images appear on screen, constituting an ongoing, usually silent, embellishment of the central story. This secondary material consists of images such as Satan drifting across the frame in the company of the priests as they watch the scourging and then appearing a second time – now as a grotesque parody of a Madonna and child – holding a monstrous baby who smiles at the brutality.[29]

KILLING AND BECOMING GODS: SOME CONCLUDING THOUGHTS

These apotheoses on film demonstrate differing attitudes towards the gods with regards to paganism and Christianity. Mythological and historical deifications are rejected, with mankind actually being touted as superior to the gods in the case of Hercules, Perseus and Theseus, and the concept of apotheosis mocked in the case of the Roman emperors. A similar message emerges when these gods are killed on screen. Despite their presumed immortality, these deities are really ephemeral and of finite existence. Their death symbolically indicates both the superiority of humans, who continue to exist, and even rule the world, in a way the divinities do not, and the passing of their age and power, giving way to either secularism or Christianity.

This concept of supersession (applied here not to Christianity replacing Judaism, but to its superseding the paganism of the ancient world) is also reflected in the deification and apotheosis of Jesus, which are, naturally, regarded and portrayed completely differently from those of the Greek gods. Since Jesus' elevation and Resurrection are facts accepted without doubt by believers, they are treated with reverence on screen. Even when portrayed for a secular audience, the meaning and underlying assumptions are clear; one faith is genuine and the other is not. While Zeus and his children may be killed off, Jesus still must never die, and indeed, those who might be regarded as responsible for his crucifixion may still be portrayed as deserving of censure.

NOTES

1 <https://www.vanityfair.com/hollywood/2018/01/mel-gibson-passion-of-the-christ-sequel-jim-caviezel> (accessed 23 August 2018).
2 See Byrne and McQuillan (1999: 154).
3 Pinsky (2004: 178).
4 See Maurice (forthcoming).

5 <https://filmschoolrejects.com/hercules-review-no-gods-reasonable-am ounts-of-glory-5759d3372bf8/> (accessed 8 May 2018).

6 <https://www.empireonline.com/movies/features/immortals-set/> (acce ssed 3 June 2018).

7 <http://www.joblo.com/horror-movies/news/set-visit-immortals-part-2- the-cast-and-the-director> (accessed 3 June 2018).

8 Plutarch, *Caesar* 67:4; Suetonius, *Divus Julius* 88.

9 <http://www.bbc.co.uk/blogs/genome/entries/2d039235-8a57-4265-a6 07-7f534af7950f> (accessed 9 May 2018).

10 Grace (2009: 72).

11 See Reinhartz (2007: 111).

12 Humphries-Brooks (2006: 106).

13 Albu (2008: 199).

14 Tomasso (2015: 147–60).

15 Ibid. 149.

16 See pp. 79–80.

17 See p. 84.

18 Tomasso (2015: 152–3).

19 Ibid.

20 See Maurice (2016: 299).

21 See Wistrich (1991).

22 Ibid. 304.

23 Zeffirelli (1984: 11–12).

24 Maurice (2016: 307–8).

25 Zeffirelli (1984: 30).

26 Macdonald (1969: 428), also quoted by Reinhartz (2007: 275).

27 For an outline of the anti-Semitic elements from a non-academic Catholic source, see <https://www.ncronline.org/news/media/decade-later-pas sion-still-raises-questions-anti-semitism> (accessed 10 May 2018).

28 Grace (2009: 143).

29 Ibid. 146.

Postscript: Some Closing Observations

Over the past century, which is approximately the period that the medium of film has been in existence, the world has changed radically. One of the biggest alterations in Western society is with regard to religion. In the first half of the twentieth century, most people in Britain and the United States would have described themselves as Christian,[1] with 91 per cent of Americans identified as Christian (either Protestant or Catholic) in 1948. Over the past seventy years, however, mainstream Christianity has been on the decline; although America is still the country with the largest number of self-identified Christians, with 70 per cent of the population identifying in this way, a far greater proportion of Christians are now non-denominational, with Protestantism declining from 69 per cent of these in 1948 to 38 per cent in 2017. More significantly, those identifying as having no religion has increased from 2 per cent to 20 per cent in the same period.[2]

In the first half of the twentieth century, culminating in the golden age of the epic movie, with its Biblical blockbusters and sword and sandal movies depicting brave Christians against evil Romans, God, religion and Christianity were treated with the respect that society as a whole felt in connection with these subjects. God was represented by a powerful, authoritative voice and revealed through marvellous miracles, the best that technology could create, with no effort being spared to demonstrate his wonder to the contemporary world.

As secularism grew, the attraction and the selling power of Biblical movies decreased, and on the rare occasions when they did appear it was on television, in *Moses the Lawgiver* (1974) and more notably *Jesus of Nazareth* (1977). In place of Old Testament epics, Jesus biopics and ancient movies of early Christianity, God appears much more commonly in comedy, where the faults of an imperfect world, at odds with the idea of its creation by a perfect deity, are shown up in humorous fashion, by actors such as George Burns (the *Oh, God* movies) and George Plimpton (*Religion, Inc./ A Fool and his Money*). On other occasions, he becomes a symbolic figure of power, more universal, generic 'good guy', let down by failing mortals, but kindly and forgiving of their foibles, a benevolent Christian vicar figure, such as portrayed by Morgan Freeman.

The pagan gods appeared more frequently in this period, in television series such as *Hercules: The Legendary Journeys* (1994, 1995–9) and *Xena: Warrior Princess* (1995–2001), and in movies such as Harryhausen's two fantasy-style epics *Jason and the Argonauts* (1963) and *Clash of the Titans* (1981),[3] and are portrayed either as pseudo-Judaeo-Christian deities, with Zeus taking on the role of the Biblical God, or as divinities who have faded away and lost their relevance with the passing of the classical era. They are, nonetheless, treated with respect; these gods are perhaps criticised obliquely or explicitly, particularly Zeus and Hera for their lack of marital harmony, but they are not killed or censured, and are depicted as powerful deities, worshipped and revered by their followers.

Since the beginning of the second millennium the situation has become far more extreme. The number of those no longer defining themselves as having a religion has doubled in the United States, while a recent survey found that in 2017, 53 per cent of all British adults had no religious affiliation, and only 8 per cent of those who did were either Anglican or Catholic.[4] At the same time, religious issues have come to the fore. Muslim immigration in Europe and the USA has altered the make-up and perception of both Islam and religion in general, despite the fact that the number of Muslims is often wildly exaggerated in the media, and they number today in England 5.02 per cent of the population, and in the United States only 1.1 per cent. At the same time, the growth of Christian fundamentalism in the USA, which has increased in popularity at the expense of mainstream Protestantism, has widened the gap between secular and religious still further. Since Hollywood in general, and film makers in particular, tend to be liberal in their outlook, such ideas have spilled over into film, where they appear as tensions and a negative attitude towards all religion, especially under a right-wing Republican government, feared by many in the film industry as likely to curb civil rights. It is no coincidence that the recent television adaptation (and expansion) of Margaret Atwood's *The Handmaid's Tale* (2017–18), which depicts a totalitarian regime brought about and ruled by perverted fundamentalist ideas of Christianity, has not only been produced at this time, but has also attracted a huge following of those fearful that it presages all too well things about to happen in current society. Christianity has also not been helped by the uncovering of scandals within the Catholic Church. Such negative publicity has had an impact on how practitioners of the religion are regarded by the wider society, including on screen, where nuns, for example, have been transformed from 'beautiful and serene to weird and nasty'.[5] Similarly, novels such as those by Dan Brown have done a great deal to increase suspicion of the religion.[6]

Against this background, not only Christianity but other religions and, by extension, deities have been portrayed with growing negativity and suspicion on screen since the late 1990s, with gods being regarded as false or evil, or even being killed, and priests and believers portrayed often as at best misguided, and at worst fanatically closed-minded and dangerous. As seen on screen, the contemporary attitude towards organised religion in general and towards the Judaeo-Christian faiths in particular is overwhelmingly negative. Despite this approach, it is notable that some things are still untouchable; there has not yet been a movie in which Jesus is not depicted as the son of God, or a good and holy man. While Christ may die on the cross, he cannot yet be attacked and his reputation destroyed on screen.

Even more strikingly, the lack of belief in God, and the distrust of organised religion (which in itself is hardly new, and is beautifully highlighted by *Monty Python's Life of Brian* (1979)), has not led to a lack of interest in making films on these themes. Rather than a cessation of movies about God, or gods, there has been an outpouring of such productions, both about Greek mythology and on Biblical themes, and their depictions reveal an almost traumatised relationship with the divine. As much as they deny his existence, many of the recent movies seem to be angry with God. In this world of postmodern secularism on the one hand, and religious extremism on the other, man's contemporary questioning of belief and religion can be seen writ large on the medium of the big screen. In the sophisticated world of twenty-first-century Hollywood, where CGI allows miracles to be created on a daily basis, it seems that cinema continues to demonstrate a deep fascination with the idea of divinity, even as it rather uncomfortably denounces its very existence.

NOTES

1 On the strong commitment to the beliefs of Christianity, and the association of this religion with morality in the English mind, see Forster (1972).
2 These statistics are from the Gallup polls: <http://news.gallup.com/poll/1690/religion.aspx> (accessed 30 May 2018).
3 On the change in epic movies and their so-called return with *Gladiator*, see Elliott (2014: 1–16).
4 <https://www.theguardian.com/world/2017/sep/04/half-uk-population-has-no-religion-british-social-attitudes-survey> (accessed 30 May 2018).
5 Dans (2009: 343). A notable exception is the popular BBC production *Call the Midwife* (2012–), which won the award for religious programme of the year in 2016, <https://inews.co.uk/culture/television/call-the-midwife/> (accessed 30 May 2018); but it is also striking that this depiction is regarded as counter-cultural: <http://postconsumereports.blogspot.com/2012/10/is-call-midwife-most-countercultural.html> (accessed 30 May 2018).
6 Dan Brown, *Angels and Demons* (2000), *The Da Vinci Code* (2003), *Origin* (2017).

Filmography

FEATURE FILMS

300 (2006). Directed by Zack Snyder. Warner Bros. Pictures.

Acid House (1998). Directed by Paul McGuigan. FilmFour Distributors.

The Adventures of Baron Munchausen (1988). Directed by Terry Gilliam. Prominent Features/Laura-Film *The Adventures of Hercules* (1985). Directed by Luigi Cozzi. United Artists/Metro-Goldwyn-Mayer.

Almost An Angel (1990). Directed by John Cornell. Paramount Pictures.

Athena, the Goddess of War (2015). Directed by Patrick Desmarattes. Maiden Comics Studios.

Bedazzled (1967). Directed by Stanley Donen. Twentieth Century Fox.

Ben-Hur (1959). Directed by William Wyler. Metro-Goldwyn-Mayer.

Ben-Hur (2016). Directed by Timur Bekmambetov. Paramount Pictures/ Metro-Goldwyn-Mayer.

The Bible: In the Beginning . . . (1966). Directed by John Huston. Twentieth Century Fox.

Blasphemy, the Movie (2001). Written and directed by John Mendoza. Mendoza Entertainment.

The Book of Esther (2013). Directed by David A. R. White. Pure Flix Entertainment.

Boxcar Bertha (1972). Directed by Martin Scorsese. American International Pictures.

The Brand New Testament (2015). Directed by Jaco Van Dormael. Terra Incognita Films/Le Pacte.

Bruce Almighty (2003). Directed by Tom Shadyac. Universal Pictures.

Christus (1916). Directed by Giulio Antamoro. Società Italiana Cines.

Clash of the Titans (1981). Directed by Desmond Davis. Charles H. Schneer Productions.

Clash of the Titans (2010). Directed by Louis Leterrier. Warner Bros. Pictures.

Color of the Cross (2006). Directed by Jean-Claude La Marre. Twentieth Century Fox.

David and Bathsheba (1951). Directed by Henry King. Twentieth Century Fox.

Day of Triumph (1954). Directed by John T. Coyle and Irving Pichel. Century Films.

Dogma (1999). Written and directed by Kevin Smith. Lions Gate Films.

Dr No (1962). Directed by Terence Young. United Artists.

ECupid (2001). Directed by J. C. Calciano. Cinema 175.

Evan Almighty (2007). Directed by Tom Shadyac. Universal Pictures.

Exodus: Gods and Kings (2014). Directed by Ridley Scott. Chernin Entertainment/Scott Free Productions/Babieka/Volcano Films..

Fantasia (1940). Directed by Joe Grant and Dick Huemer. Walt Disney Pictures.

Fatal Attraction (1987). Directed by Adrian Lyne. Paramount Pictures.

Four Rooms (1995). Directed by Allison Anders, Alexandre Rockwell, Robert Rodriguez and Quentin Tarantino. Miramax.

Francis of Assisi (1961). Directed by Michael Curtiz. Twentieth Century Fox.

From the Manger to the Cross (1912). Directed by Sidney Olcott. Kalem Company.

The Girl with the Dragon Tattoo (2011). Directed by David Fincher. Columbia Pictures.

Gladiator (2000). Directed by Ridley Scott. DreamWorks/Universal Pictures.

Gli amori di Ercole (1960). Directed by Carlo Ludovico Bragaglia. Contact Organisation/Grandi Schermi Italiani/Paris Interproduction.

The Goddess of Spring (1934). Directed by Wilfred Jackson. Walt Disney Productions.

Gods Behaving Badly (2013). Directed by Marc Turtletaub. Big Beach Films.

The Gospel According to St. Matthew (*Il vangelo secondo Matteo*) (1964). Directed by Pier Paolo Pasolini. Arco Film/Lux Compagnie Cinématographique de France.

The Greatest Story Ever Told (1965). Directed by George Stevens. George Stevens Productions.

The Green Pastures (1936). Directed by Marc Connelly and William Keighley. Warner Bros. Pictures.

Hail Mary (*Je vous salue, Marie*) (1985). Directed by Jean-Luc Godard. Sara Films.

Head of a Tyrant (1960). Directed by Fernando Cerchio. Universal Pictures.

Heaven Can Wait (1978). Directed by Warren Beatty and Buck Henry. Paramount Pictures.

The Help (2011). Directed by Tate Taylor. Dreamworks.

Hera Purple: Devil Goddess (2001). Directed by Kil Chae Jeong. Pathfinder Pictures.

Hercules (1983). Directed by Luigi Cozzi. Cannon Italia SrL/Golan-Globus.

Hercules (1997). Directed by John Musker and Ron Clements. Walt Disney Pictures.

Hercules (2014). Directed by Brett Ratner. Paramount Pictures/Metro-Goldwyn-Mayer/Flynn Picture Company.

Hercules and Xena – The Animated Movie: The Battle for Mount Olympus (1997). Directed by Lynne Naylor. Renaissance Pictures/Universal Cartoon Studios.

Hercules: The Brave and the Bold (2013). Written by David A. Malone and Tim Holmes. Directed by David A. Malone. 3 Kings Productions.

Hercules in Hollywood (2005). Directed by John Michael Ferrari and Pepper Jay. EagleEye Pictures/Pepper Jay Productions/Talk of the Town Productions.

Hercules in New York (1970). Directed by Arthur A. Seidelman. RAF Industries.

Here Comes Mr Jordan (1941). Directed by Alexander Hall. Columbia Pictures.

Hidden Figures (2016). Directed by Theodore Melfi. Twentieth Century Fox.

Horns (2013). Directed by Alexandre Aja. Dimension Films/RADIUS-TWC.

The Hunger Games (2012). Directed by Gary Ross. Lionsgate Films.

I Beheld His Glory (1953). Directed by John T. Coyle. Cathedral Films.

Il messia (1975). Directed by Roberto Rossellini. Orizzonte 2000/Procinex/France 3 (FR 3)/Teléfilm.

Immortals (2011). Directed by Tarsem Singh. Relativity Media.

Jason and the Argonauts (1963). Directed by Don Chaffey. Columbia Pictures.

Jesus Christ Superstar (1973). Directed by Norman Jewison. Universal Pictures.

The Jesus Film (1979). Directed by Peter Sykes and John Krish. Warner Bros. Pictures.

Joshua (2002). Directed by Jon Purdy. Paramount Studios.

Juno (2007). Directed by Jason Reitman. Fox Searchlight Pictures.

The Killers (1946). Directed by Robert Siodmak. Universal Pictures.

The King of Kings (1927). Directed by Cecil B. DeMille. DeMille Pictures Corporation..

King of Kings (1961). Directed by Nicholas Ray. Metro-Goldwyn-Mayer/Samuel Bronston Productions.

La Belle et la Bête (1946). Directed by Jean Cocteau. DisCina.

La Mariée était en noir (1968). Directed by François Truffaut. United Artists.

Last Days in the Desert (2016). Directed by Rodrigo García. Broad Green Pictures.

The Last Temptation of Christ (1988). Directed by Martin Scorsese. Universal Pictures/Cineplex Odeon Films.

Leap of Faith (1992). Directed by Richard Pearce. Paramount Pictures.

Legend (1985). Directed by Ridley Scott. Universal Pictures/Twentieth Century Fox.

The Legend of Hercules (2014). Directed by Renny Harlin. Summit Entertainment/Millennium Films.

The Life and Passion of Jesus Christ (1903). Directed by Lucien Nonguet and Ferdinand Zecca. Pathé Frères.

A Life Less Ordinary (1997). Directed by Danny Boyle. Channel Four Films/Twentieth Century Fox.

A Little Bit of Heaven (2011). Directed by Nicole Kassell. Millennium Entertainment/The Weinstein Company.

Little Hercules in 3-D (2009). Directed by Mohamed Khashoggi. Innovate Entertainment.

The Little Mermaid (1989). Directed by John Musker and Ron Clements. Walt Disney Pictures.

Little Nicky (2000). Directed by Steven Brill. New Line Cinema.

Mannequin (1987). Directed by Michael Gottlieb. Gladden Entertainment.

Mary Magdalene (2018). Directed by Garth Davis. Focus Features.

Mary Mother of Christ (2014). Directed by Alister Grierson. Aloe Entertainment/Brightlight Pictures.

A Matter of Life and Death/Stairway to Heaven (1946). Directed by Michael Powell and Emeric Pressburger. Eagle-Lion Films.

The Messiah (2007). Directed by Nader Talebzadeh. Abdollah Sa'eedi.

The Milky Way (1969). Directed by Luis Buñuel. Greenwich Film Production/Fraia Film.

The Miracle Maker (1999). Directed by Stanislav Sokolov and Derek W. Hayes. Icon Entertainment International.

Mister Frost (1990). Directed by Philip Setbon. AAA Productions/Hugo Films/Overseas Multi Media.

Monty Python's Life of Brian (1979). Directed by Terry Jones. HandMade Films.

Moses (1976). Directed by Gianfranco De Bosio. ITC/RAI.

The Nativity Story (2006). Directed by Catherine Hardwicke. Temple Hill Entertainment/New Line Cinema.

Night Life of the Gods (1935). Directed by Lowell Sherman. Universal Pictures.

Noah (2014). Directed by Darren Aronofsky. Paramount Pictures.

Oedipus Rex (1967). Directed by Pier Paolo Pasolini. Arco Film.

Oh, God (1977). Directed by Carl Reiner. Warner Bros. Pictures.

Oh, God, Book II (1980). Directed by Gilbert Cates. Warner Bros. Pictures.

Oh, God! You Devil (1984). Directed by Paul Bogart. Warner Bros. Pictures.

The Omen (1976). Directed by Richard Donner. Twentieth Century Fox.

The Omen (2006). Directed by John Moore. Twentieth Century Fox.

One Night with the King (2006). Directed by Michael O. Sajbel. Gener8Xion Entertainment.

One Touch of Venus (1948). Directed by William A. Seiter. Universal Pictures.

The Passion of the Christ (2004). Directed by Mel Gibson. Icon Productions.

Percy Jackson and the Lightning Thief (2010). Directed by Chris Columbus. Fox 2000 Pictures.

Percy Jackson and the Sea of Monsters (2013). Directed by Thor Freudenthal. Fox 2000 Pictures.

Poseidon (2006). Directed by Wolfgang Petersen. Warner Bros. Pictures.

The Poseidon Adventure (1972). Directed by Ronald Neame. Twentieth Century Fox.

Prince of Egypt (1997). Directed by Brenda Chapman, Steve Hickner and Simon Wells. DreamWorks Pictures.

Prometheus (1998). Directed by Tony Harrison. Arts Council of England/Film Four/Holmes Associates.

Prometheus: Retribution (2014). Directed by Bob Woolsey. VFS Entertainment Business Management.

Quo Vadis (1953). Directed by Mervyn LeRoy. Metro-Goldwyn-Mayer.

Raiders of the Lost Ark (1981). Directed by Steven Spielberg. Lucasfilm Ltd.

The Redeemer (1959). Directed by Joseph Breen and Fernando Palacios. Cruzada del Rosario en Familia/Family Theater Inc./Varios.

Religion, Inc./A Fool and his Money (1989). Directed by Daniel Adams. Blossom Pictures/Chronicle Films.

Risen (2016). Directed by Kevin Reynolds. Columbia Pictures.

The Robe (1953). Directed by Henry Koster. Twentieth Century Fox.

Rosemary's Baby (1968). Directed by Roman Polanski. Paramount Pictures.

Saint Mary (2000). Directed by Shahriar Bahrani. Sima Film/WN Media.

Samson and Delilah (1949). Directed by Cecil B. DeMille. Paramount Pictures.

The Shack (2017). Directed by Stuart Hazeldine. Summit Entertainment.

Sins of Jezebel (1953). Directed by Reginald Le Borg. Lippert Pictures.

Solomon and Sheba (1959). Directed by King Vidor. United Artists.

Son of God (2014). Directed by Christopher Spencer. Metro-Goldwyn-Mayer.

Son of Man (2006). Directed by Mark Dornford-May. Lorber Films.

The Song of Bernadette (1943). Directed by Henry King. Twentieth Century Fox.

Spartacus (1960). Directed by Stanley Kubrick. Bryna Productions/Universal Pictures.

Sponge Bob Square Pants Movie (2004). Directed by Stephen Hillenburg. Nickelodeon.

Stigmata (1999). Directed by Rupert Wainwright. Metro-Goldwyn-Mayer.

The Story of Ruth (1960). Directed by Henry Koster. Twentieth Century Fox.

The Ten Commandments (1923). Directed by Cecil B. DeMille. Paramount Pictures.

The Ten Commandments (1956). Directed by Cecil B. DeMille. Paramount Pictures.

Tenacious D in The Pick of Destiny (2006). Liam Lynch. Red Hour films/ New Line Cinema.

Time Bandits (1981). Directed by Terry Gilliam. HandMade Films/Janus Films.

Toast with the Gods (1995). Directed by Eric Magun and Latino Pellegrini. DED Films.

Le Tonnerre de Jupiter (1903). Directed by Georges Méliès. Georges Méliès/ Star-Film.

Troy (2004). Directed by Wolfgang Petersen. Warner Bros./Helena Productions.

Vamping Venus (1928). Directed by Edward F. Cline. First National Pictures.

The Witches of Eastwick (1987). Directed by George Miller. Warner Bros. Pictures.

Wonder Woman (2017). Directed by Patty Jenkins. Warner Bros. Pictures.

Wrath of the Titans (2012). Directed by Jonathan Liebesman. Warner Bros.

The Young Messiah (2016). Directed by Cyrus Nowrasteh. Focus Features.

TELEVISION MOVIES, MINISERIES AND SERIES

The Avengers (1962–4). Created by Sydney Newman, ITV/ABC/Thames

The Bible (2013). Created by Mark Burnett and Roma Downey. LightWorkers Media.

Botticelli's Venus: The Making of an Icon (2016). Directed by Maurice O'Brien. BBC.

Call the Midwife (2012–). Created by Heidi Thomas. Neal Street Productions/BBC.

A Child Called Jesus (1987). Directed by Franco Rossi. Reteitalia.

Class of the Titans (2006–8). Created by Chris Bartleman and Michael Lahay. Studio B Productions and Nelvana Limited.

The Collector (2004–6). Created by Jon Cooksey and Ali Marie Matheson. Chum Television.

Doctor Who (2005–). Created by Sydney Newman. BBC.

For the Love of Zeus (2015–18). Created by Sharlene Humm. BackLot Studios Production Company.

The Furchester Hotel (2014–17). Created by Belinda Ward. CBeebies/ Sesame Workshop.

Gli amici di Gesù: Maria Maddalena (2000). Directed by Raffaele Mertes and Elisabetta Marchetti. Epsilon TV Production/Lux Vide.

A God Named Pablo (2010–15). Created by Caleb Claxton and Jeff Hirbour. American Famous Productions.

God, the Devil and Bob (2000). Created by Matthew Carlson. NBC/Adult Swim.

Goddess of Love (1988). Directed by Jim Drake. NBC.

Gory Greek Gods (2004). Created by Arif Nurmohamed. BBC.

The Handmaid's Tale (2017–18). Created by Bruce Miller. Daniel Wilson Productions, Inc./The Littlefield Company/White Oak Pictures/MGM Television.

Hercules (1998–9). Directed by Phil Weinstein. Walt Disney Television.

Hercules (2005). Directed by Roger Young. Hallmark Entertainment/ Lionsgate.

Hercules: The Legendary Journeys (TV movies, 1994; TV series, 1995–9). Created by Christian Williams. Universal Pictures.

I, Claudius (1976). Directed by Herbert Wise. BBC.

Jason and the Argonauts (2000). Directed by Nick Willing. Hallmark Entertainment/Panfilm.

Jason and the Heroes of Mount Olympus (2001–2). Created by Florence Sandis. Saban International.

Jesus (1999). Directed by Roger Young. Antena 3 Televisión/ARD/Beta Film.

Jesus of Nazareth (1977). Directed by Franco Zeffirelli. ITC (Incorporated Television Company)/RAI Radiotelevisione Italiana.

L'Odissea (1968). Created by Mario Bava and Franco Rossi. RAI.

Man Seeking Woman (2015). Created by Simon Rich. Broadway Video/ Allagash Industries/FXP.

Maria, Daughter of Her Son (2000). Directed by Fabrizio Costa. Canale 5/ Titanus.

Mary, Mother of Jesus (1999). Directed by Kevin Connor. HCC Happy Crew Company/The Shriver Family Film Company/Hallmark Entertainment / NBC.

Mary of Nazareth (2012). Directed by Giacomo Campiotti. Lux Vide/ Tellux Film.

Monty Python's Flying Circus (1969–74). Created by Graham Chapman, John Cleese, Eric Idle, Terry Jones, Michael Palin and Terry Gilliam. BBC.

Moses (1995). Directed by Roger Young. Antena 3 Televisión/Beta Film/ British Sky Broadcasting.

Moses the Lawgiver (1974). Directed by Gianfranco De Bosio. ITC/RAI.

The Muppet Show (1976–81). Created by Jim Henson. The Jim Henson Company/Associated Television/ITC Entertainment.

The Muppets' Wizard of Oz (2005). Directed by Kirk R. Thatcher. Jim Henson Company/Fox Television Studios.

Mythic Warriors: Guardians of the Legend (1998–2000). Directed by Jim Craig. Nelvana and Marathon Media.

MythQuest (2001). Directed by Stefan Scaini, Manfred Guthe, Nicholas Kendall, Rob W. King and Paul Schneider. Minds Eye.

The Nativity (1978). Directed by Bernard L. Kowalski. 20th Century Fox Television.

The Odyssey (1997). Directed by Andrei Konchalovsky. American Zoetrope/ Beta Film/Hallmark Entertainment.

Olympus (2015). Created by Nick Willing. Reunion Pictures/ Tremadoc Productions.

Olympus 7-0000 (ABC Stage 67) (1966). Directed by Stanley Prager. ABC.

The Omen (1995). Directed by Jack Sholder. Twentieth Century Fox Television.

Once Upon a Time (2011–18). Created by Edward Kitsis and Adam Horowitz. ABC.

Peter and Paul (1981). Directed by Robert Day. Universal Pictures.

The Poseidon Adventure (2005). Directed by John Putch. Larry Levenson Productions.

Queen Esther (1999). Directed by Raffaele Mertes. Five Mile River Films/ Lux Vide/Beta Film/Quinta.

Rome (2005–7). Created by Bruno Heller, William J. MacDonald and John Milius. HBO-BBC.

Rosemary's Baby (2014). Directed by Agnieszka Holland. NBC.

Sabrina, Teenage Witch (1996–2000). Created by Nell Scovell. Hartbreak Films/Viacom Productions/Finishing the Hat Productions.

Samson and Delilah (1984). Directed by Lee Philips. ABC.

Samson and Delilah (1996). Directed by Nicolas Roeg. Beta Film/Lube Productions/Lux Vide/Turner Pictures.

Saturday Night Live (1975–). Created by Lorne Michaels. NBC.

Sesame Street (1969–). Created by Joan Ganz Cooney and Lloyd Morrisett. PBS.

The Simpsons (1989–). Created by Matt Groening. Gracie Films/20th Century Fox Television/Klasky Csupo/Film Roman/Fox Television Animation.

South Park (1997–). Created by Trey Parker and Matt Stone. Celluloid Studios/Braniff Productions/Parker-Stone Productions/South Park Studios/Comedy Partners.

Sponge Bob Square Pants (1999–). Created by Stephen Hillenburg. United Plankton Pictures/Nickelodeon Animation Studios/Rough Draft Studios.

St. Paul (2000). Directed by Roger Young. Ceska Televize/KirchMedia/ LuxVide/Quinta Communications/ RAI Radiotelevisione Italiana.

Star Trek (1966–9). Created by Gene Roddenberry. Desilu Productions/ Norway Corporation/ Paramount Television.

Supernatural (2005–). Created by Eric Kripke. Warner Bros. Television.

Titans of Newark (2012). Directed by Michael J. Marino. Chapman University.

Troy: Fall of a City (2018). Created by David Farr. BBC.

Up Pompeii! (1969–70). Created by Talbot Rothwell and Sid Colin. BBC/ ITV.

Valentine (2008–9). Created by Kevin Murphy. Media Rights Capital/Five & Dime Productions/Valentine's Day.

Wishbone (1995–8). Created by Rick Duffield. Big Feats! Entertainment.

Xena: Warrior Princess (1995–2001). Created by John Schulian and Robert
   G. Tapert. Renaissance Pictures/MCA Television.
Young Hercules (1998–9). Created by Andrew Dettmann, Rob Tapert and
   Daniel Truly. MCA Television.

Bibliography

Abele, Elizabeth (2013). *Home Front Heroes: The Rise of a New Hollywood Archetype, 1988–1999*. Jefferson, NC: McFarland.

Albu, Emily (2008). 'Gladiator at the Millennium', *Arethusa* 41.1: 185–204.

Armstrong, Karen (1993). *A History of God: The 4,000-Year Quest of Judaism, Christianity, and Islam*. New York: Ballantine Books.

Babington, Bruce and Peter William Evans (1993). *Biblical Epics: Sacred Narrative in the Hollywood Cinema*. Manchester: Manchester University Press.

Bakker, Freek L. (2009). *The Challenge of the Silver Screen: An Analysis of the Cinematic Portraits*. Leiden: Brill.

Barber, Charles (1997). 'The Truth in Painting: Iconoclasm and Identity in Early-Medieval Art', *Speculum* 72.4: 1019–36.

Baring, Anne and Jules Cashford (1993). *The Myth of the Goddess: Evolution of an Image*. London: Arkana/Penguin.

Basinger, David (2011). 'What is a Miracle?', in Graham H. Twelftree (ed.), *The Cambridge Companion to Miracles*. Cambridge: Cambridge University Press, 19–35.

Benko, Stephen (1993). *The Virgin Goddess: Studies in the Pagan and Christian Roots of Mariology*. Leiden: Brill.

Bietoletti, Silvestra (2009). *Neoclassicism and Romanticism* (trans. Angela Arnone). New York and London: Sterling.

Bigham, Steven (1995). *Image of God the Father in Orthodox Theology and Iconography*. Huntsville, AL: Oakwood.

Blackburn, Barry L. (2011). 'The Miracles of Jesus', in Graham H. Twelftree (ed.), *The Cambridge Companion to Miracles*. Cambridge: Cambridge University Press, 113–30.

Blundell, Sue and Margaret Williamson (1998). *The Sacred and the Feminine in Ancient Greece*. London and New York: Routledge.

Blunt, Anthony (1985). *Artistic Theory in Italy, 1450–1600*. Oxford: Oxford University Press.

Bober, Phyllis and Ruth Rubinstein (2010). *Renaissance Artists and Antique Sculpture: A Handbook of Sources*, 2nd edn. Turnhout: Harvey Miller.

Bokser, Baruch (1981). 'Ma'al and Blessings over Food: Rabbinic

Transformation of Cultic Terminology and Alternative Modes of Piety', *Journal of Biblical Literature* 100.4, 557–74.

Bolen, Jean Shinoda (2014). *Artemis: The Indomitable Spirit in Everywoman.* San Francisco: Conari Press.

Boss, Sarah Jane (2007). *Mary: The Complete Resource.* London: Continuum.

Bowra, C. M. (1988). *The Greek Experience.* New York: New American Library.

Bradshaw, Paul F. and Maxwell E. Johnson (2011). *The Origins of Feasts, Fasts and Seasons in Early Christianity.* London and Coleville, MN: Liturgical Press.

Brandon, S. G. F. (1975). 'Christ in Verbal and Depicted Imagery', in Jacob Neusner (ed.), *Christianity, Judaism and other Greco-Roman Cults: Studies for Morton Smith at Sixty. Part Two: Early Christianity.* Leiden: Brill, 164–72.

Brenner, Carla McKinney and Julie Warnement (1996). *The Inquiring Eye: Classical Mythology in European Art.* Washington, DC: National Gallery of Art.

Brown, S. C. (1982). *The Intelligible Universe.* New York: Macmillan.

Brumble, David (1998). 'Let Us Make Gods in Our Image: Greek Myth in Medieval and Renaissance Literature', in Roger D. Woodard (ed.), *The Cambridge Companion to Greek Mythology.* Cambridge: Cambridge University Press, 407–24.

Burkert, Walter (1985). *Greek Religion* (trans. John Raffan). Cambridge, MA: Harvard University Press.

Burnette-Bletsch, Rhonda (2016). 'God at the Movies', in Rhonda Burnette-Bletsch (ed.), *The Bible in Motion: A Handbook of the Bible and Its Reception in Film, Part 1.* Berlin and Boston: De Gruyter, 299–326.

Butler, Ivan (1969). *Religion in the Cinema.* New York: A.S. Barnes.

Byrne, Eleanor and Martin McQuillan (1999). *Deconstructing Disney.* London and Sterling, VA: Pluto Press.

Calame, Claude (1999). *The Poetics of Eros in Ancient Greece* (trans. Janet Lloyd). Princeton: Princeton University Press.

Collins, Matthew A. (2016). 'Depicting the Divine: The Ambiguity of Exodus 3 in *Exodus: Gods and Kings*', in David Tollerton (ed.), *Biblical Reception, 4. A New Hollywood Moses: On the Spectacle and Reception of Exodus: Gods and Kings.* London: Bloomsbury, 9–39.

Crist, Judith (21 February 1965). 'A Story Too Great To Be Told?', *New York Herald Tribune*, 271.

Cyrino, Monica (2010). *Aphrodite.* London and New York: Routledge.

Cyrino, Monica (2018). 'Russell Crowe and Maximal Projections in Noah (2014)', in Antony Augoustakis and Stacie Raucci (eds), *Epic Heroes on Screen.* Edinburgh: Edinburgh University Press, 93–110.

Cyrino, Monica and Meredith Safran (eds) (2015). *Classical Myth on Screen.* New York: Palgrave Macmillan.

Dans, Peter E. (2009). *Christians in the Movies: A Century of Saints and Sinners*. Plymouth: Sheed and Ward.

Davies, Brian (2004). 'Anselm and the Ontological Argument', in Brian Davies and Brian Leftow (eds), *The Cambridge Companion to Anselm*. Cambridge: Cambridge University Press, 157–78.

Deacy, Susan (2008). *Athena*. London and New York: Routledge.

Dowden, Ken (2006). *Zeus*. London and New York: Routledge.

Drazin, Israel (2000). *Maimonides: Reason Above All*. Jerusalem and New York: Gefen.

Duggan, W. J. (1979). 'Anthropomorphism', in Paul Kevin Meagher, Thomas C. O'Brien and Consuelo Maria Aherne (eds), *Encyclopedic Dictionary of Religion*. Washington, DC: Corpus, 195–6.

Durley, Michael P. (2000). *Mary in Film: An Analysis of Cinematic Presentations of the Virgin Mary from 1897–1999: A Theological Appraisal of a Socio-Cultural Reality* (unpublished thesis). Dayton: The International Marian Research Institute.

Dyer, Richard (1979). *Stars*. London: BFI.

Ebertshäuser, Caroline, Herb Haag, Joe H. Kirchberger and Dorothee Sölle (1998). *Mary: Art, Culture, and Religion through the Ages*. New York: Crossroad.

Elley, Derek (1984). *The Epic Film: Myth and History*. London: Routledge.

Elliott, Andrew B. R. (2014). *The Return of the Epic Film: Genre, Aesthetics and History in the 21st Century*. Edinburgh: Edinburgh University Press.

Erhardt, Michelle A. and Amy M. Morris (2012). *Mary Magdalene: Iconographic Studies from the Middle Ages to the Baroque*. Leiden and Boston: Brill.

Evans, Andrew and Glenn D. Wilson (1999). *Fame: The Psychology of Stardom*. London: Vision.

Every, George (1970). *Christian Mythology*. Worthing: Littlehampton Book Services.

Federow, Stuart (2012). *Judaism and Christianity: A Contrast*. Bloomington: iUniverse.

Ferguson, George (1977). *Signs and Symbols in Christian Art*. Oxford: Oxford University Press.

Feuerbach, Ludwig (1841). *The Essence of Christianity* (trans. Marian Evans), 3rd edn. London: Kegan Paul, Trench, Trübner.

Fine, Lawrence (1984). *Safed Spirituality: Rules of Mystical Piety, the Beginning of Wisdom*. Mahwah, NJ: Oaulist Press.

Finkelberg, Margalit (ed.) (2011). *The Homer Encyclopedia*, 3 vols. Malden, MA, and Oxford: Wiley-Blackwell.

Fischer-Hansen, Tobias and Birte Poulsen (2009). *From Artemis to Diana: The Goddess of Man and Beast*. Copenhagen: Museum Tusculanum Press.

Forster, Peter G. (1972). 'Secularization in the English Context: Some Conceptual and Empirical Problems', *Sociological Review* 20: 153–68.

Fowler, Robert (2006). *The Cambridge Companion to Homer*. Cambridge: Cambridge University Press.

Fraser, George MacDonald (1988). *The Hollywood History of the World*. London: Penguin.

Fyfe, Aileen (2004). *Science and Salvation: Evangelical Popular Science Publishing in Victorian Britain*. Chicago: University of Chicago Press.

Garland, Robert (2011). 'Miracles in the Greek and Roman World', in Graham H. Twelftree (ed.), *The Cambridge Companion to Miracles*. Cambridge: Cambridge University Press, 75–94.

Grace, Pamela (2009). *The Religious Film: Christianity and the Hagiopic*. Malden, MA, and Oxford: Wiley-Blackwell.

Graf, Fritz (1993). *Greek Mythology: An Introduction* (trans. Thomas Marier). Baltimore: Johns Hopkins University Press.

Griffith-Jones, Robin (2008). *Mary Magdalene: The Woman Whom Jesus Loved*. Norwich: Canterbury Press.

Guthrie, Stewart Elliot (1997). 'Anthropomorphism: A Definition and a Theory', in Robert W. Mitchell, Nicholas S. Thompson and H. Lyn Miles (eds), *Anthropomorphism, Anecdotes, and Animals*. Albany: State University of New York Press, 50–8.

Gwynne, Paul (1995). 'A Renaissance Image of Jupiter Stator', *Journal of the Warburg and Courtauld Institutes* 58: 249–52.

Hallet, Christopher (2005). *The Roman Nude: Heroic Portrait Statuary*. Oxford: Oxford University Press.

Hallpike, C. R. (1969). 'Social Hair', *Man* (n.s.) 4.2: 256–64.

Hammerling, Roy (2008). *A History of Prayer: The First to the Fifteenth Century*. Leiden: Brill.

Hansen, Kathryn Strong (2015). 'The Metamorphosis of Katniss Everdeen: *The Hunger Games*, Myth, and Femininity', *Children's Literature Association Quarterly* 40.2: 161–78.

Hansen, William (2004). *Classical Mythology: A Guide to the Mythical World of the Greeks and Romans*. Oxford: Oxford University Press.

Harris, Stephen and Gloria Platzner (2007). *Classical Mythology: Images and Insights*, 5th edn. New York: McGraw-Hill.

Harryhausen, Ray and Tony Dalton (2003). *Ray Harryhausen: An Animated Life*. London: Aurum Press.

Harryhausen, Ray and Tony Dalton (2005). *The Art of Ray Harryhausen*. London: Aurum Press.

Hedley, Douglas and Chris Ryan (2013). 'Nineteenth-Century Philosophy of Religion: Introduction', in Graham Oppy and N. N. Trakakis (eds), *The History of Western Philosophy of Religion. Vol. 4: Nineteenth-Century Philosophy of Religion*. London and New York: Routledge, 1–20.

Henrichs, Albert (2010). 'What is a Greek God?', in Jan Bremmer and Andrew Erskine (eds), *The Gods of Ancient Greece: Identities and Transformations*. Edinburgh: Edinburgh University Press, 19–40.

Hertz, J. H. (1960). *The Pentateuch and Haftorahs*. London: Oxford University Press.

Hinson, E. G. (1996). *The Early Church: Origins to the Dawn of the Middle Ages*. Nashville, TN: Abingdon Press.

Holland, R. F. (1967). 'The Miraculous', in D. Z. Phillips (ed.), *Religion and Understanding*. Oxford: Blackwell, 155–70.

Hort, Greta (1957). 'The Plagues of Egypt', *Zeitschrift für die Alttestamentliche Wissenschaft* 69: 84–103.

Houtman, C. (1990). 'The Urim and Thummim: A New Suggestion', *Vetus Testamentum* 40.2: 229–32.

Hughes, Howard (2011). *Cinema Italiano: The Complete Guide from Classics to Cult*. London and New York: I. B. Tauris.

Humphries-Brooks, Stephenson (2006). *Cinematic Savior*. Westport, CT: Praeger.

James, Paula (2011). *Ovid's Myth of Pygmalion on Screen: In Pursuit of the Perfect Woman*. London and New York: Continuum.

Jevons, Frank B. (1913). 'Anthropomorphism', in James Hastings (ed.), *Encyclopedia of Religion and Ethics*. New York: Charles Scribner's Sons, 573–74.

Johnston, Robert K. (2000). *Reframing Theology and Film*. Grand Rapids, MI: Baker Books.

Johnston, Sarah Iles (2004). *Religions of the Ancient World*. Cambridge, MA, and London: Harvard University Press.

Johnston, Sarah Iles (2008). *Ancient Greek Divination*. Malden, MA, and Oxford: Wiley-Blackwell.

Jones, A. H. M. (1967). *Sparta*. Cambridge, MA: Harvard University Press.

Jones, Catherine and Atsushi Tajima (2015). 'The Caucasianization of Jesus: Hollywood Transforming Christianity into a Racially Hierarchical Discourse', *The Journal of Religion and Popular Culture* 27.3: 202–19.

Joost-Gaugier, Christiane L. (2002). *Raphael's Stanza della Segnatura: Meaning and Invention*. Cambridge: Cambridge University Press.

Kearns, Emily (2006). 'The Gods in the Homeric Epics', in Robert Fowler (ed.), *The Cambridge Companion to Homer*. Cambridge: Cambridge University Press, 59–73.

Kelly, Henry Annsgar (2006). *Satan: A Biography*. Cambridge: Cambridge University Press.

Kennedy, Donald (2006). 'Acts of God?', *Science* 311.5759: 303–4.

Kerényi, Carl (1975). *Archetypal Images in Greek Religion: 5. Zeus and Hera: Archetypal Image of Father, Husband, and Wife* (trans. Christopher Holme). Princeton: Princeton University Press.

Kessler, Edward (2007). *What Do Jews Believe? The Customs and Culture of Modern Judaism*. New York: Walker.

Kessler, Herbert L. (2000). *Spiritual Seeing: Picturing God's Invisibility in Medieval Art*. Philadelphia: University of Pennsylvania Press.

Kia-Choong, Kevin Teo (2013). 'Review of Catherine O'Brien, *The Celluloid*

Madonna: From Scripture to Screen', *Journal of Religion and Popular Culture* 25.1: 169–70.

Kindt, Julia (2012). *Rethinking Greek Religion*. Cambridge: Cambridge University Press.

Kinnard, Roy and Tony Crnkovich (2017). *Italian Sword and Sandal Films, 1908–1990*. Jefferson, NC: MacFarland.

Kozlovic, Anton (2008). 'From Holy Harlot to Passionate Penitent: Mary Magdalene in Cecil B. DeMille's *The King of Kings* (1927)', *Journal for the Academic Study of Religion* 21: 345–65.

Kurzman, C., C. Anderson, C. Key, Y. O. Lee, M. Moloney, A. Silver and M. W. V. Ryn (2007). 'Celebrity Status', *Sociological Theory* 25.4: 347–67.

Larson, Jennifer Lynn (2007). *Ancient Greek Cults: A Guide*. New York and London: Routledge.

Larson, Jennifer (2015). *Understanding Greek Religion: A Cognitive Approach*. London: Routledge.

Law, Stephen (2011). *Humanism: A Very Short Introduction*. Oxford: Oxford University Press.

Lee, H. D. P. (trans.) (1965). *Plato, Timaeus*. Baltimore: Penguins.

Leith, Sam (14 May 2010). 'The Return of Swords 'n' Sandals Movies', *The Financial Times*.

Lesher, James H. (1992). *Xenophanes of Colophon: Fragments: A Text and Translation with a Commentary*. Toronto: University of Toronto Press.

Levack, Brian P. (2006). *The Witch-Hunt in Early Modern Europe*, 3rd edn. London and New York: Routledge.

Lindberg, Carter (2008). *Love: A Brief History Through Western Christianity*. Malden, MA, and Oxford: Blackwell.

Lindsay, Richard (2015). *Hollywood Biblical Epics: Camp Spectacle and Queer Style from the Silent Era to the Modern Day*. Denver: Praeger.

Livingston, Sonja (2015). *Queen of the Fall: A Memoir of Girls and Goddesses*. Lincoln: University of Nebraska Press.

Llewellyn-Jones, Lloyd (2007). 'Gods of the Silver Screen', in Daniel Ogden (ed.), *A Companion to Greek Religion*. Malden, MA: Blackwell, 423–38.

Llewellyn-Jones, Lloyd (2009). 'Hollywood's Ancient World', in Andrew Erskine (ed.), *A Companion to Ancient History*. Malden, MA, and Oxford: Wiley-Blackwell, 564–79.

Llewellyn-Jones, Lloyd (2013). 'Ray Harryhausen and Other Gods: Greek Divinity in *Jason And The Argonauts* and *Clash Of The Titans*', in S. Green and P. Goodman (eds), *Animating Antiquity: Harryhausen and the Classical Tradition. New Voices in Classical Reception Studies*, Conference Proceedings 1: 3–20.

Loimer, Hermann and Michael Guamieri (1996). 'Accidents and Acts of God: A History of the Terms', *American Journal of Public Health* 86.1: 101–7.

Lyden, John (2003). *Film as Religion: Myths, Morals, and Rituals*. New York: New York University Press.

Lyden, John (ed.) (2009). *The Routledge Companion to Religion and Film*. Oxford and New York: Routledge.

McCaughey, Martha and Neal King (2001). *Reel Knockouts: Violent Women in the Movies*. Austin: University of Texas Press.

Macdonald, Dwight (1969). *Dwight Macdonald on Movies*. New York: Prentice Hall.

McDonald, Paul (2000). *The Star System: Hollywood's Production of Popular Identities*. London: Wallflower.

McGowan, Andrew B. (2014). *Ancient Christian Worship: Early Church Practices in Social, Historical and Theological Perspective*. Grand Rapids: Baker Academic.

McKinney Brenner, Carla and Julie Warnement (1996). *The Inquiring Eye: Classical Mythology in European Art*. Washington, DC: National Gallery of Art.

Malone, Peter (1989). 'Martin Scorsese's *The Last Temptation of Christ*', *Cinema Papers* 71: 4–7.

Malone, Peter (2012). *Screen Jesus: Portrayals of Christ in Television and Film*. Plymouth: Scarecrow Press.

Marlina, Leni (2015). 'The Discussion on Female Heroes in Respect of Gender Socialisation of Girls: Retelling Myths of Psyche, Artemis and Katniss', *Linguistics and Literature Studies* 3.2: 41–45, <http://www.hrpub.org> (accessed 19 November 2017).

Mathews, Thomas F. (1993). *The Clash of Gods: A Reinterpretation of Early Christian Art*. Princeton: Princeton University Press.

Mathews, Thomas F. and Norman E. Muller (2005). 'Isis and Mary in Early Icons', in Maria Vassilaki (ed.), *Images of the Mother of God: Perceptions of the Theotokos in Byzantium*. Aldershot: Ashgate, 3–11.

Maurice, Lisa (2016). 'Swords, Sandals and Prayer-Shawls: Depicting Jews and Romans on the Silver Screen', in David Schaps, Uri Yiftach and Daniela Dueck (eds), *When the First Western Empire Met the Near East*. Trieste: Edizioni Università di Trieste, 295–324.

Maurice, Lisa (forthcoming). 'Disney's *Hercules* in Context: Mouse-Morality for Mini-Heroes', in Alastair Blanshard and Emma Stafford (eds), *The Modern Hercules*. Vol. 2. Leiden: Brill.

Medved, Harry and Michael Medved (1980). *The Golden Turkey Awards*. London: Angus & Robertson.

Meynell, Hugo (1977). 'The Intelligibility of the Universe', in S. C. Brown (ed.), *Reason and Religion*. Ithaca: Cornell University Press, 23–43.

Michalak, Aleksander R. (2012). *Angels as Warriors in Late Second Temple Jewish Literature*. Tübingen: Mohr Siebeck.

Miles, Geoffrey (1999). *Classical Mythology in English Literature: A Critical Anthology*. London and New York: Routledge.

Monaghan, Patricia (2004). *The Goddess Path: Myths, Invocations &*
Rituals, 5th edn. St. Paul, MN: Llewellyn, 127–9.

Morford, Mark and Robert J. Lenardon (2003). *Classical Mythology*, 7th
edn. Oxford and New York: Oxford University Press.

Nissinen, Martti (2017). *Ancient Prophecy: Near Eastern, Biblical, and*
Greek Perspectives. Oxford: Oxford University Press.

O'Brien, Catherine (2009). 'The Life of Mary in Film: Marian Film in the
Twenty-First Century', *Marian Studies* 60: 287–96.

O'Brien, Catherine (2011). *The Celluloid Madonna: From Scripture to*
Screen. New York: Columbia University Press.

Ogechukwu, Nwaocha (2012). *The Devil: What Does He Look Like?* Salt
Lake City: Millennial Mind.

Pak-Shiraz, Nacim (2011). *Shi'i Islam in Iranian Cinema: Religion and*
Spirituality in Film. London and New York: I. B. Tauris.

Pardes, Ilana (1996). 'Moses Goes Down to Hollywood: Miracles and Special
Effects', *Semeia* 74: 25–6.

Pinsky, Mark I. (2004). *The Gospel According to Disney: Faith, Trust, and*
Pixie Dust. Louisville, KY: Westminster John Knox Press.

Pirenne-Delforge, Vinciane (2011). 'Introduction', in Amy C. Smith and
Sadie Pickup (eds), *Brill's Companion to Aphrodite*. Leiden: Brill,
3–16.

Pirenne-Delforge, Vinciane and Gabriella Pironti (July 2015). 'Greek
Myth and Religion', in *Oxford Classical Dictionary*, <http://classics.ox
fordre.com/view/10.1093/acrefore/9780199381135.001.0001/acrefore-
9780199381135-e-3011?product=orecla#acrefore-9780199381135-e-
3011> (accessed 30 November 2018).

Platt, Verity (2011). *Facing the Gods: Epiphany and Representation in*
Graeco-Roman Art, Literature and Religion. Cambridge: Cambridge
University Press.

Pringle, Gill (1 December 2006). 'There's Something about Mary', <http://
www.independent.co.uk/artsentertainment/films/features/tthe-nativity
story-theres-something-about-mary-426445.html> (accessed 19 March
2018).

Rahe, Paul Anthony (2015). *The Grand Strategy of Classical Sparta: The*
Persian Challenge. New Haven, CT, and London: Yale University Press.

Ramji, Rubina (2003). 'Representations of Islam in American News and
Film: Becoming the "Other"', in Jolyon P. Mitchell and Sophia Marriage
(eds), *Mediating Religion: Conversations in Media, Religion and Culture*.
London: T&T Clark, 65–72.

Ramji, Rubina (2009). 'Muslim in the Movies', in William Blizek (ed.), *The*
Continuum Companion to Religion and Film. London and New York:
Continuum, 177–87.

Reinhartz, Adele (2007). *Jesus of Hollywood*. Oxford: Oxford University
Press.

Reinhartz, Adele (2010). 'Jesus in Film', in Delbert Burkett (ed.), *The*

Blackwell Companion to Jesus. Malden, MA, and Oxford: Wiley-Blackwell, 519–31.

Reinhartz, Adele (2013). *Bible and Cinema: An Introduction.* London and New York: Routledge.

Reinhartz, Adele (2016a). 'Ambivalence towards Judaism in the Bible Movies', in Rhonda Burnette-Bletsch (ed.), *The Bible in Motion: A Handbook of the Bible and Its Reception in Film, Part 1.* Berlin and Boston: De Gruyter, 782–91.

Reinhartz, Adele (2016b). 'The Bible Epic', in Rhonda Burnette-Bletsch (ed.), *The Bible in Motion: A Handbook of the Bible and Its Reception in Film, Part 1.* Berlin and Boston: De Gruyter, 175–92.

Richards, Jeffrey (2008). *Hollywood's Ancient Worlds.* London: Continuum.

Rippin, Ann (2003). 'Images of Athena and Hera in Nike's "Goddess" Campaign', *Ephemera* 3.3: 185–96.

Roblin, Isabelle (2015). 'I, *Claudius* (1976) vs *Rome* (2005), or Ancient Rome Revisited by Television', *TV/Series* 7: 141–60, <http://tvseries.revues.org/29>5 (accessed 21 August 2018).

Rudolph, Conrad (1993). 'In the Beginning: Theories and Images of Creation in Northern Europe in the Twelfth Century', *Art History* 22.1: 3–55.

Rudolph, Conrad (2004). 'Communal Identity and the Earliest Christian Legislation on Art: Canon 36 of the Synod of Elvira', in Terryl Kinder (ed.), *Perspectives for an Architecture of Solitude: Essays on Cistercians, Art and Architecture in Honour of Peter Fergusson.* Turnhout and Cîteaux: Brepols and Cîteaux Commentarii Cistercienses, 1–7.

Russell, Jeffrey Burton (1981). *Satan: The Early Christian Tradition.* Ithaca and London: Cornell University Press.

Russell, Jeffrey Burton (1984). *Lucifer: The Devil in the Middle Ages.* Ithaca and London: Cornell University Press.

Sacks, Jonathan (2009). *Covenant & Conversation: A Weekly Reading of the Jewish Bible. Vol. 1.* New Milford, CT, London and Jerusalem: Maggid Books.

Sanders, Ed, Chiara Thumiger, Christopher Carey and N. J. Lowe (eds) (2013). *Erôs in Ancient Greece.* Oxford: Oxford University Press.

Sanders, Theresa (2002). *Celluloid Saints: Images of Sanctity in Film.* Macon, GA: Mercer University Press.

Schefold, Karl and Luca Giuliani (1992). *Gods and Heroes in Late Archaic Greek Art.* Cambridge: Cambridge University Press.

Schenck, Kenneth (2005). *A Brief Guide to Philo.* Louisville, KY: Westminster John Knox Press.

Schubart, Rikke (2007). *Super Bitches and Action Babes: The Female Hero in Popular Cinema, 1970–2006.* Jefferson, NC, and London: McFarland.

Seeskin, Kenneth (2011). 'Miracles in Jewish Philosophy', in Graham H. Twelftree (ed.), *The Cambridge Companion to Miracles.* Cambridge: Cambridge University Press, 254–70.

Seo, J. Mira (2008). 'The Gender Gap: Religious Spaces in *Rome*', in Monica

Cyrino (ed.), *Rome Season One: History Makes Television*. Malden, MA, and Oxford: Wiley-Blackwell, 168–78.

Shah, Ali Zulfiqar (2012). *Anthropomorphic Depictions of God: The Concept of God in Judaic, Christian, and Islamic Traditions: Representing the Unrepresentable*. Herndon, VA: International Institute of Islamic Thought.

Shapiro, J. S. (2000). *Oberammergau: The Troubling Story of the World's Most Famous Passion Play*. New York: Pantheon Books.

Singer, Michael (1988). 'Cinema Savior', *Film Comment* 24.5: 44–7.

Smith, Amy C. and Sadie Pickup (eds.) (2011). *Brill's Companion to Aphrodite*. Leiden: Brill.

Smith, W. B. (1980). 'The Theology of the Virginity *In Partu* and its Consequences for the Church's Teaching on Chastity', *Marian Studies* 31: 99–110.

Solomon, Jon (2001). *The Ancient World in Cinema*, 2nd edn. New Haven, CT, and London: Yale University Press.

Spinner, Gregory (2003). *After the Temple, Before the World: Redefining Sacrifice in Ancient Judaism*. Chicago: University of Chicago Press.

Stacey, Jackie (1991). 'Feminine Fascinations: Forms of Identification in Star–Audience Relations', in Christine Gledhill (ed.), *Stardom: Industry of Desire*. London: Routledge, 141–63.

Stafford, Emma (2004). *Life, Myth, and Art in Ancient Greece*. Los Angeles: Getty.

Staley, Jeffrey L. and Richard Walsh (2007). *Jesus, the Gospels, and Cinematic Imagination: A Handbook to Jesus on DVD*. Louisville, KY, and London: Westminster John Knox Press.

Stevenson, Tom (1998). 'The "Problem" with Nude Honorific Statuary and Portraits in Late Republican and Augustan Rome', *Greece and Rome* (2nd ser.) 45.1: 45–69.

Syndicus, Eduard (1962). *Early Christian Art*. London: Burns & Oates.

Tatum, W. Barnes (1997). *The Cinematic Jesus*. Santa Rosa: Polebridge Press.

Tauranac, John (2014). *The Empire State Building: The Making of a Landmark*. Ithaca: Cornell University Press.

Taylor, Joan E. (2018). *What Did Jesus Look Like?* London and New York: Bloomsbury T&T Clark.

Thumiger, Chiara (2013). 'Mad Erôs and Eroticized Madness in Tragedy', in Ed Sanders, Chiara Thumiger, Christopher Carey and N. J. Lowe (eds), *Erôs in Ancient Greece*. Oxford: Oxford University Press, 27–40.

Tomasso, Vincent (2015). 'The Twilight of Olympus: Deicide and the End of the Greek Gods', in Monica S. Cyrino and Meredith E. Safran (eds), *Classical Myth on Screen*. Basingstoke and New York: Palgrave Macmillan, 147–57.

Trzaskoma, Stephen (2013). 'From Gamer to Animator: The Evolving Role of Zeus in Harryhausen's *Jason and the Argonauts* and *Clash of* the Titans', in S. Green and P. Goodman (eds), *Animating Antiquity: Harryhausen and the Classical Tradition. New Voices in Classical Reception Studies*, Conference Proceedings 1: 20–8.

Van Dam, Cornelius (1997). *The Urim and Thummim: A Means of Revelation in Ancient Israel*. Winona Lake, IN: Eisenbrauns.

Van Riel, Gerd (2013). *Plato's Gods*. London: Ashgate.

Veith, Gene Edward (25 March 2000). 'God, the Networks, and Bob: Taking the Name of the Lord thy God in a Cartoon Comedy', *Culture* 15.12, <https://world.wng.org/2000/03/god_the_networks_and_bob> (accessed 13 September 2016).

Vernant, Jean-Pierre (1991). *Mortals and Immortals: Collected Essays*. Princeton: Princeton University Press.

Vine, Angus (2016). 'Myth and Legend', in Andrew Hadfield, Matthew Dimmock and Abigail Shinn (eds), *The Ashgate Research Companion to Popular Culture in Early Modern England*. London: Routledge, 103–18.

Walsh, Richard (2003). *Reading the Gospels in the Dark: Portrayals of Jesus in Film*. Harrisburg, PA: Trinity Press International.

Ward, Benedicta (2011). 'Miracles in the Middle Ages', in Graham H. Twelftree (ed.), *The Cambridge Companion to Miracles*. Cambridge: Cambridge University Press, 149–64.

Warner, Marina (2013) *Alone of All Her Sex: The Myth and the Cult of the Virgin Mary*, 2nd edn. Oxford: Oxford University Press.

Watson, Paul (2012). 'Star Studies: Text, Pleasure, Identity', in Jill Nelmes (ed.), *Introduction to Film Studies*. New York: Routledge, 166–86.

Weisbrot, Robert (1996). *Xena, Warrior Princess: The Official Guide*. New York: Doubleday.

Weisbrot, Robert (1998). *Hercules: The Legendary Journeys. The Official Companion*. New York: Bantam Doubleday Dell.

Weiss, Dov (2017). *Pious Irreverence: Confronting God in Rabbinic Judaism*. Philadelphia: University of Pennsylvania Press.

Wenskus, Otta (2002). '*Star Trek*: Antike Mythen und moderne Energiewesen', in Martin Korenjak and Karlheinz Töchterle (eds), *Pontes II: Antike im Film I*. Innsbruck: Studien Verlag, 130–2.

Williams, Michael (2017). *Film Stardom and the Ancient Past: Idols, Artefacts and Epics*. Basingstoke: Palgrave Macmillan.

Winkler, Martin (2001). *Classical Myth & Culture in the Cinema*. Oxford: Oxford University Press.

Winkler, Martin M. (2009). *Cinema and Classical Texts: Apollo's New Light*. Cambridge: Cambridge University Press.

Wistrich, Robert S. (1991). *Antisemitism: The Longest Hatred*. New York: Pantheon.

Wood, Michael (1975). *America in the Movies; or, 'Santa Maria, It Had Slipped My Mind'*. London: Secker & Warburg.

Woolger, Jennifer Barker and Roger J. Woolger (1987). *The Goddess

Within: A Guide to the Eternal Myths that Shape Women's Lives. New York: Fawcett Columbine.

Wyke, Maria and Pantelis Michelakis (2013). *The Ancient World in Silent Cinema*. Cambridge: Cambridge University Press.

Yorulmaz, Bilal and William L. Blizek (October 2014). 'Islam in Turkish Cinema', *Journal of Religion & Film* 18.2, <http://digitalcommons.unomaha.edu/jrf/vol18/iss2/8> (accessed 16 May 2018).

Zanker, Paul (1995). *The Mask of Socrates: The Image of the Intellectual in Antiquity*. Berkley and Los Angeles: University of California Press.

Zeffirelli, Franco (1984). *Franco Zeffirelli's Jesus; A Spiritual Diary*. New York: Harper & Row.

Zeyl, Donald (Spring 2014). 'Plato's *Timaeus*', in Edward N. Zalta (ed.), *The Stanford Encyclopedia of Philosophy*, <https://plato.stanford.edu/archives/spr2014/entries/plato-timaeus> (accessed 3 February 2018).

Zolotnikova, Olga A. (2013). *Zeus in Early Greek Mythology and Religion: From Prehistoric Time to the Early Archaic Period*. Oxford: Archaeopress.

Index